Chicken Soup for the Soul®

The Story behind the Song

Chicken Soup for the Soul: The Story behind the Song
The Exclusive Personal Stories behind 101 of Your Favorite Songs
Jack Canfield, Mark Victor Hansen, Jo-Ann Geffen. Foreword by Lamont Dozier

Published by Chicken Soup for the Soul Publishing, LLC   www.chickensoup.com

The publisher gratefully acknowledges the many publishers and individuals who
granted Chicken Soup for the Soul permission to reprint the cited material.

*Front and back cover illustration courtesy of iStockphoto.com/ Maliketh and / A-Digit. Interior
illustration courtesy of iStockphoto.com/ dra_schwartz*

Cover and Interior Design & Layout by Pneuma Books, LLC

For more info on Pneuma Books, visit www.pneumabooks.com

Distributed to the booktrade by Simon & Schuster. SAN: 200-2442

Publisher's Cataloging-in-Publication Data
(Prepared by The Donohue Group)

Chicken soup for the soul : the story behind the song : the exclusive personal
  stories behind 101 of your favorite songs / [compiled by] Jack Canfield, Mark
  Victor Hansen, Jo-Ann Geffen ; foreword by Lamont Dozier.

  p. : ill. ; cm.

  ISBN: 978-1-935096-40-5

1. Lyric writing (Popular music)--Literary collections. 2. Lyric writing (Popular music)-
-Anecdotes. 3. Lyric writing (Popular music)--History and criticism. 4. Popular
music--Writing and publishing--History and criticism. I. Canfield, Jack, 1944- II.
Hansen, Mark Victor. III. Geffen, Jo-Ann. IV. Dozier, Lamont.

PN6071.M87 C45 2009
810.8/02/0357   2009935760

PRINTED IN THE UNITED STATES OF AMERICA
on acid∞free paper
18 17 16 15 14 13 12 11 10 09   01 02 03 04 05 06 07 08 09 10

Chicken Soup for the Soul®
The Story behind the Song

The Exclusive Personal Stories behind 101 of Your Favorite Songs

Jack Canfield
Mark Victor Hansen
Jo-Ann Geffen

Foreword by Lamont Dozier

Chicken Soup for the Soul Publishing, LLC
Cos Cob, CT

To my son, Jeremy,
who has always been my reason
to get up in the morning and of late,
has given me tremendous inspiration.

I couldn't have done this without him.

~Jo-Ann Geffen

Table of Contents

Foreword

A songwriter has many reasons why he or she writes a song. Sometimes the idea for the song comes to you in a melody, or sometimes the idea comes to you in a lyric. Many times songwriters collaborate on their songs, which then involves two or more songwriters contributing to the art of the song.

Many times you hear someone speaking and if you're a good listener, you can pick up on a great title or story and run with the idea. I always refer to my ideas as coming to me from my Muses.

I have used the above-mentioned ways throughout my life, and then of course there are those songs that come from personal experiences. And sometimes I believe that those are the best songs that I've written.

Many of my own songs have come out of my memory bank where first impressions and feelings have been stored for years. A simple touch or softly spoken word can trigger my feelings and then a new song begins for me. I can remember special events by songs I've heard in my life. I believe that a song marks history just as much as a political event or birthday celebration. Why is it that we can hear a song and remember exactly where we were at the time we first heard the song and the feelings we were experiencing at the time, or see a face from the past? A song can evoke all of these memories and feelings in each and every one of us and that stays with us all forever.

When Jo-Ann Geffen told me her idea for writing this book, I was instantly excited that the Chicken Soup for the Soul publishers were going to publish a book that would give insight into the songs that have shaped all of our lives in one way or another.

I was thrilled to add my little stories to this impressive group of songs and authors whom Jo-Ann has assembled with such grace. The stories behind the songs are often just as poetic as the songs themselves.

The music industry is one that is filled with so many ups and downs, so much rejection and so much hope. When a songwriter finally decides on joining the melodies and the lyrics together to form a new song, not only does the marriage have to be perfect for the feeling of the song to stick with the listener, but also the art of expressing oneself in this manner takes courage and faith. Each new song and songwriter has at one time felt these feelings and expressed them to someone. The songwriter has exposed a little of their own individual soul each time they write a song, and allowed their emotions and feelings to leak out for public consumption and very possibly rejection. Rejection from a person they really love or from an artist who does not want to sing the song happens all the time. But this "intellectual property," as a song is often referred to, is already alive. It is too late for the songwriter to take back the song as it has happened already.

The one hundred and one songs that are included in this book are written by some of the world's greatest songwriters of contemporary times. I am a fan of each and every song and songwriter you will read about.

Jo-Ann Geffen is the perfect author to be able to convince the songwriters to give their own personal stories about the songs they have written, thus the "story behind the song" is a private insight into each contributor's life experience.

I am honored to be included in this book, and honored that my good friend for so many years, Jo-Ann Geffen has asked me to write this foreword to a book that I know will be special to everyone who reads it.

~Lamont Dozier

Christina Aguilera

"Fighter"

Written by Christina Aguilera and Scott Storch
Recorded by Christina Aguilera

I wrote this for my sophomore album, *Stripped*, and I was very determined for it to reflect who I was. The first record was what the label wanted and created. There was a huge pop explosion at the time and I was part of that wave. I felt stifled. I was thankful that the early success allowed me the freedom to write what I wanted for the next one.

I was 21 and I had a lot on my mind. I had been performing in front of an audience since I was 6, helping to make a living for my family. I grew up in a very chaotic and abusive home where I didn't feel very safe. I started writing music, both melodies and lyrics, when I was 15. In retrospect, I realize I used it as a release, a therapeutic outlet. It was the way I found my voice. I connected with the music and escaped from my home life. In school, I was picked on and alienated because of my passion for music. So I harbored a little personal pain but the seemingly negative things made me smarter and stronger.

I took notice early of the people all around me in the business who were there for the wrong reasons.

I wrote "Fighter" when I was on tour promoting my first CD. I was coming up with titles and ideas and deciding what I wanted to write about. I had to sit down and make sense of my feelings and experiences. I learned a lot from the first record that helped me to develop. I took the good and the bad and considered some of the choices I made and became better because of it.

I called the CD *Stripped* because I wanted to strip away the pieces of myself from the first record that I felt weren't me. I was searching for truth. We can all look at our pasts, childhoods, home lives and it's easy to be a victim or victimize yourself—but I didn't want to do that. I was feeling lots of pent up emotions and they all came to a head in "Fighter."

I wanted my songs to have positive empowering messages, especially to women so they could feel strong and speak for themselves. My father dominated our household and I didn't want to feel weak.

Makes me that much stronger
Makes me work a little bit harder
Makes me that much wiser
So thanks for making me a fighter
Made me learn a little bit faster
Made my skin a little bit thicker
Makes me that much smarter
So thanks for making me a fighter

Sometimes people try to put their negativity on you. I was telling one person in particular, at that time, that he couldn't haunt me.

After all of the fights and the lies
Guess you're wanting to haunt me
But that won't work anymore.

It was very freeing.

I try to write lyrics and music that people can relate to and that help them to find personal strength. I try to communicate universal ideas and thoughts that help them to get through the day or the year a bit better.

"Fighter"

After all you put me through
You'd think I'd despise you
But in the end I wanna thank you
'Cause you made me that much stronger.

Well I thought I knew you
Thinking that you were true
Guess I, I couldn't trust,
Called your bluff, time is up,
'Cause I've had enough.
You were there by my side,
Always down for the ride
But your joy ride just came down in flames
'Cause your greed sold me out in shame, mm hmm.

After all of the stealing and cheating
You probably think that I hold resentment for you
But uh uh, oh no, you're wrong
'Cause if it wasn't for all that you tried to do
I wouldn't know just how capable
I am to pull through.
So I wanna say thank you
'Cause it

Makes me that much stronger
Makes me work a little bit harder
Makes me that much wiser,

So thanks for making me a fighter;
Made me learn a little bit faster
Made my skin a little bit thicker
Makes me that much smarter
So thanks for making me a fighter.

Never saw it coming,
All of your backstabbing
Just so you could cash in on a good thing
Before I'd realized your game.
I heard you're going 'round
Playin' the victim now
But don't even begin feelin' I'm the one to blame
'Cause you dug your own grave.

After all of the fights and the lies
Guess you're wanting to haunt me
But that won't work anymore,
No more, uh uh, it's over.
'Cause if it wasn't for all of your torture
I wouldn't know how to be this way now
And never back down.
So I wanna say thank you
'Cause it

Makes me that much stronger
Makes me work a little bit harder
Makes me that much wiser
So thanks for making me a fighter;
Made me learn a little bit faster
Made my skin a little bit thicker
Makes me that much smarter
So thanks for making me a fighter.

How could this man I thought I knew

Turn out to be so unjust, so cruel?
Could only see the good in you
Pretended not to see the truth
You tried to hide your lies,
Disguise yourself through
Living in denial
But in the end you'll see
You won't stop me.

I am a fighter
(I'm a fighter)
I ain't gonna stop
(I ain't gonna stop)
There is no turning back,
I've had enough.

Makes me that much stronger
Makes me work a little bit harder
Makes me that much wiser
So thanks for making me a fighter;
Made me learn a little bit faster
Made my skin a little bit thicker
Makes me that much smarter
So thanks for making me a fighter.

Thought I would forget
But I, I remember
Yes I remember
I'll remember
Thought I would forget
But I remember
Yes I remember
I'll remember

Makes me that much stronger

Makes me work a little bit harder
Makes me that much wiser
So thanks for making me a fighter;
Made me learn a little bit faster
Made my skin a little bit thicker
Makes me that much smarter
So thanks for making me a fighter.

Lyrics by Christina Aguilera. Music by Christina Aguilera and Scott Storch. © 2002 XTINA MUSIC; CAREERS-BMG MUSIC PUBLISHING INC; TVT MUSIC INC.

Art Alexakis

"Father of Mine"

Written by Art Alexakis
Recorded by Everclear

A good lyric, a good story, and a good melody make a good song. The production is the gravy. This song is universal as it has no social or economic boundaries.

"Father of Mine" is autobiographical. It's about my father splitting from our family and divorce from a kid's point of view. I wrote it after being divorced from the mother of my kid and expressed the disillusionment everyone feels.

I was born in Santa Monica, California in 1962, the youngest of five children in a very dysfunctional family. There was constant fighting. My father was physically abusive to the point where there were fist fights amongst the family. Clearly, he was not a good father or husband. It was a very emotional time. When I was six, my mom left my dad.

Women had no rights then so, although my mom owned a couple of houses, without my dad signing them over—which he wouldn't do, she couldn't get a loan and the houses went into foreclosure. She wanted the five of us to grow up in our house. We ultimately moved to a housing project in Culver City in Los Angeles even though she worked two jobs to support us. We never missed a meal and always had clean clothes, a place to live and plenty of love.

She was from the south, not very well educated, out of her mind a lot, but loved her children fiercely. The main things she gave me were tenacity and a sense of right and wrong. In 1978 she died from her sixth bout with cancer, but she was ready to go. She left me with weirdness and a lot of songs.

My dad had moved to Florida because he couldn't be extradited from there to adhere to the Deadbeat Dad laws. In Florida, he met another woman and supported her kids. I've spoken in front of the Congressional sub-committee on Bill HR 1488 which tried to take the power to effect existing laws from the states to the federal government. It did not pass.

My dad's almost 90 now and still doesn't get it. The last time I spoke with him was when my mom was terminally ill. He said he wanted to see my daughter and I told him that in order to have a relationship, all he had to do was call my mother and be accountable and let her talk, and I'd forgive him. He never made the call.

My role models were a drug addict brother who overdosed and a drug addict brother-in-law who could never control his demons and was abusive to my sister, who finally left him.

The whole idea of being a parent is that we can give our kids less damage than our parents gave us. My oldest daughter is a great human being; my little one is fiery. I love being a parent. It's the best thing in the world. It makes it all make sense to me.

When my first baby was born, Everclear was a brand new band. It was two years before we had a label deal. I was on welfare and started crying one night. I realized I wasn't the main priority anymore. Once I accepted that, I knew that I'd figure it out. I had to.

I love moms. People don't usually get salted in life, they're not as interesting until they're parents. I could be in a line at Wal-Mart and be behind an NRA (National Rifle Association) person with nothing in common except that she's a mom and I'm a dad. There's a universal understanding and bond that allows us to connect and communicate.

"Father of Mine"

Father of mine
Tell me where have you been.
You know I just close my eyes
My whole world disappeared.

Father of mine
Take me back to the day
Yeah, when I was still your golden boy
Back before you went away.

I remember blue skies
Walking the block
I loved it when you held me high,
I loved to hear you talk.

You would take me to the movies,
You would take me to the beach,
Take me to a place inside
That was so hard to reach.

Father of mine
Tell me, where did you go?
You had the world inside your hand
But you did not seem to know.

Father of mine
Tell me, what do you see
When you look back at your wasted life

And you don't see me?

I was ten years old
Doing all that I could
It wasn't easy for me
To be a scared white boy in a black neighborhood.

Sometimes you would send me a birthday card
With a five dollar bill.
Yeah, I never understood you then
And I guess I never will.

Daddy gave me a name
My daddy gave me a name
Then he walked away.
Daddy gave me a name
Then he walked away.
My daddy gave me a name…

Daddy gave me a name
My daddy gave me a name
Then he walked away.
Daddy gave me a name
Then he walked away.
My daddy gave me a name…

Yeah, yeah, oh yeah

Father of mine
Tell me where have you been?
I just close my eyes
And the world disappeared.

Father of mine
Tell me how do you sleep

With the children you abandoned
And the wife I saw you beat?

I will never be safe
I will never be sane
I will always be weird inside
I will always be lame.

Now I'm a grown man
With a child of my own
And I swear that I'm not gonna let her know
All the pain I have known.

Then he walked away.
Daddy gave me a name
Then he walked away.
My daddy gave me a name
Then he walked away.
My daddy gave me a name
Then he walked away.

My daddy gave me a name
Then he walked away
Then he walked away
Then he walked away.

Lyrics and Music by Art Alexakis. © 1997 Evergleam Music/Songs of Universal, Inc/Montalupis Music/

Commongreen Music/Irving Music, Inc.

Paul Anka

"My Way"

Written by Paul Anka
Recorded by Frank Sinatra

I became globalized early in my career. I traveled internationally a great deal as a kid and lived in several countries.

I was sitting outside my house in the countryside in France one day and heard a Claude François record. As a musician, I hear lots of options in songs and that held true with this one.

It was the late '60s and, on my way home to the United States, I stopped in Paris. I was pretty well connected there so I found the publisher of the song and met with him and told him I thought the song was interesting. He asked what I wanted and I said, "The rights." We signed a simple two-page contract that I took back to the States with me. I transformed the record to a piano lead sheet and put it in my drawer to come back to later.

I had a close relationship with Frank Sinatra at the time because we worked together many times when the Rat Pack was at the Sands Hotel and I was the youngest performer in Las Vegas. We spent quite a bit of time together; he was like a mentor to me. Thus, one of my career goals was to write for him even though I knew he hated pop music. He liked Gershwin, Porter. That was his kind of music.

Don Costa was my A&R/producer and part of my life from age 16 on. I introduced Frank to Don, who subsequently became his record producer.

I played the Fontainebleau in Miami and, on one occasion, Frank was doing a detective movie down there. We got together for dinner and he told me that he was tired of the government's Mafia accusations. They were bugging his phones so he had to change his number every other day. He'd go into rooms and there'd be holes in the walls from pulling out the phones and installing new ones. He said he was quitting the business, getting out of the public eye. I couldn't fathom him not being in our lives.

I knew that Don (Costa) was doing one more album with Frank so I pulled out the sheet of the French song and thought about what Frank would say if he were writing it. The song morphed itself. I began typing and it wrote itself in about five hours. I typed everything. I was in the habit of using a typewriter from my days working at a newspaper when I had aspirations to be a journalist. I kept the typewriter next to my piano whenever I wrote.

The first line is metaphorical, referring not only to age but to the fact that he was going to quit:

And now, the end is near
And so I face the final curtain.

I called Don and Frank at Caesar's Palace in Las Vegas to let them know I'd written a song for him and that I wanted to do a piano demo and get it to him. Shortly after that, I was playing the Sahara and had it delivered to him. I got a call that Frank wanted to do it.

They recorded it in Los Angeles at United Recording studio. Sinatra said, "Kid, I want you to hear something." He always called me kid; in fact, he made robes for the Rat Pack and me with our names on them — mine said KID.

Costa got on the phone and put it to the speaker and played the recording. I knew then that this was the turning point in my career and my life. There was something in the mix that Sinatra wasn't happy with, so after the records were pressed, he had them throw out 50,000 records and press the corrected version. This record turned everything around for him, too.

My record company at the time, RCA Victor, was unhappy. They had wanted me to record it but in my mind, I was old enough to write it but not to record it. It was not proper casting and I knew I had to check my ego at the door. You need the right artist to make a song happen. Lots of people have recorded this song, but his is the important version for me.

"My Way"

And now, the end is near
And so I face the final curtain.
My friend, I'll say it clear,
I'll state my case, of which I'm certain.

I've lived a life that's full,
I've traveled each and ev'ry highway
And more, much more than this,
I did it my way.

Regrets, I've had a few
But then again, too few to mention.
I did what I had to do
And saw it through without exemption.

I planned each charted course;
Each careful step along the byway,
But more, much more than this,
I did it my way.

Yes, there were times, I'm sure you knew,
When I bit off more than I could chew.
But through it all, when there was doubt,
I ate it up and spit it out.
I faced it all and I stood tall
And did it my way.

I've loved, I've laughed and cried.
I've had my fill; my share of losing.
And now, as tears subside,
I find it all so amusing.

To think I did all that;
And may I say — not in a shy way,
No, oh no not me,
I did it my way.

For what is a man, what has he got?
If not himself, then he has naught.
To say the things he truly feels,
And not the words of one who kneels.
The record shows I took the blows —
And did it my way!

Paul Anka

"The Longest Day"

Written and Recorded by Paul Anka

When I was about 20 or 21, I was hired as an actor in *The Longest Day* produced by Darryl Zanuck, who was quite a character—and I only mean that in a good way. He hired the cast of 100 stars, John Wayne, Richard Burton, Sean Connery were just a few, and the teen contingent I was a part of—Tommy Sands, Fabian—and put us all on the beaches of Normandy in the movie based on the book by Cornelius Ryan.

On one occasion at lunch, when we'd take our breaks, I asked Mr. Zanuck if I could write the music for the film. He was a great guy, with a cigarette and a hat. He said, "Who's doing music? That's a New York thing. No music, no love story." This went on throughout the film. I'd repeatedly ask if he was sure he didn't want music. He would always have the same response, "No music. No love story." It was funny because his mistress was in the movie.

On the last day of shooting, as we were saying goodbye, I told him that I had a melody in my head and that I was going to go home and record a demo at my own expense. Once again he said, "No music. No love story." I spent $2,000 out of my pocket and laid down the tracks for "The Longest Day" and sent it to him.

I got a telegram from Mr. Zanuck that said: "There's going to be music — You've got it." He said that only that theme will be used and asked me, "Who would you like to work with?" Maurice Jarre. "What do you want for the song?" I told him, "Just the publishing, no money." When Twentieth Century Fox, the company putting out the film, found out that I got the publishing, they really started bugging me. Mr. Zanuck told them, "Leave him alone, I gave him my word." And they did.

The song got an Academy Award nomination. This song and *The Tonight Show* theme were great for me.

"The Longest Day"

Many men came here as soldiers
Many men will pass this way
Many men will count the hours
As they live the longest day.
Many men are tired and weary
Many men are here to stay
Many men won't see the sunset
When it ends the longest day.
The longest day, the longest day,
This will be the longest day.
Filled with hopes and filled with fears
Filled with blood and sweat and tears
Many men the mighty thousands
Many men to victory
Marching on right into battle
In the longest day in history.

Tony Asher

"Wouldn't It Be Nice"

Written by Tony Asher and Brian Wilson
Recorded by The Beach Boys

In the mid-sixties, I was working as a copywriter at an advertising agency (Carson/Roberts, Inc.) writing jingles and scoring commercials primarily for Mattel Toys. As a result, I spent a lot of time in recording studios. On one such occasion I ran into Brian Wilson whom I recognized but had never met. Brian was recording some song demos in another studio and we began to chat. Eventually Brian asked me to come listen to some of the things he had been recording. I later discovered that it was typical of Brian to do that. He loved to hear what anyone thought about the music he was working on. I remember one time he asked a FedEx delivery guy to listen to a song and give him his reaction. Brian wrote songs not to impress professional musicians but really for the average guy on the street.

After we listened to a couple of the tracks he had been recording, the engineers asked us to go out into the studio so they could finish up editing and transferring in time for the next scheduled session. So Brian and I sat at a piano in the studio — side by side on the piano bench — trading ideas. Brian started playing a rhythmic feel that he liked and asked me what I thought. I said something like, "Yeah. I love that. I started writing something sort of like that." And then I played him my idea.

Brian then said something like "Wow. That would sound great in minor!" and played a few bars in a minor key. And so it went. We kept bouncing ideas off each other for quite a while. It wasn't "one-upmanship" so much as it was really enjoying the instant connection music provided. Soon I realized I had to return to my own session down the hall and we said goodbye. I frankly wondered if I'd ever see him again.

But, as it turned out, we had a mutual friend named Loren. I didn't know he knew Brian and apparently Brian told Loren about having met me. At the time, Brian was worried about how he was going to deliver an overdue album to Capitol Records. The rest of The Beach Boys were on tour in Japan. Besides, Brian had decided he didn't want to write songs for the new album with any of the writers he had worked with previously. He really wanted to do something fresh and different this time out.

So the story goes that while Brian was agonizing over how he was going to get the album written, Loren said something along the lines of "Hey, why don't you call Tony Asher? He's a great writer and it seems like you guys got along pretty well." Brian thought it might be worth a try and fortunately Loren had my phone number.

I had already told the people I worked with about having met Brian at the recording studio. So when the phone rang and a voice said, "Hi, this is Brian Wilson," I naturally figured it was one of the guys in the office playing a prank on me. Of course I eventually realized it was, indeed, Brian Wilson and — incredibly — he was asking me if I wanted to write the next Beach Boys album with him. I was appropriately flabbergasted but wasted no time telling him "I'd LOVE to!"

I arranged to take a sabbatical from work and showed up as planned at Brian's house at 9:30 on the appointed day. Brian emerged from his bedroom at around 12:45 PM and I quickly learned that morning appointments were not going to happen.

We didn't have a specific concept for the album—or even for individual songs. Brian just said that he didn't want to do the same kind of material the group had been doing up until then. I said that was fine with me because I didn't know much about cars or surfing. I didn't own even one Beach Boys album. My first love, musically, was always jazz. I played keyboards (which in those days pretty much meant piano) and I fantasized about becoming another Bill Evans (the prodigiously talented legendary jazz pianist). When we began working together, Brian didn't even know what kind of music I liked or listened to. But we knew we were on a common wavelength. In the course of creating the album, I introduced Brian to jazz classics like "Stella by Starlight," "Lush Life" and "Sophisticated Lady" with chord and key changes that blew him away and at the same time brought me a degree of instant credibility.

The first song I started work on turned out to be "You Still Believe In Me." Brian had already recorded a complete background track for the song under the name "In My Childhood." To this day, I've never heard those original lyrics. (You can still hear the sound of the little bicycle horn in the background, particularly in the ending fade.) Brian gave me a cassette tape (remember those?) of the track and I took it home to write a lyric. Brian thought the lyric was great and after a few minor tweaks, we moved on to other songs.

Where did song ideas come from? Brian and I would talk for hours, far away from the piano, just two young guys reminiscing about early love relationships, affairs, break-ups, the pain and pleasure of love. Wondering where the ones we loved so intensely were and how they had turned out. What would we feel for that girl who seemed so easy to fall deeply in love with only a few years ago if we saw her today? At some point, we'd go to the piano and begin to write. And those conversations we'd just been having—sometimes exhilarating, other times melancholy—set the mood for the moment and profoundly influenced the kind of song we were likely to write.

During just such a conversation, one of us mentioned a girl we'd known years before whom we remembered as being nearly perfect. Beautiful. Smart. Fun. She went away for a time and when she reappeared she had changed completely. She had become a woman but she had cut her long, glamorous hair. She looked unhappy. Bitter, as though life had been giving her a bad time. The innocence we had so loved about her had disappeared.

All during the period when we were writing together, Brian kept playing little snatches of a melody I really liked. I asked him to record it for me on a cassette so that I could work on a lyric. But he protested, "It isn't finished yet" and, "It 'needs' another section which I haven't written yet." Eventually, one day he announced that it was finished and played it a couple of times all the way through. I really liked it right away. It turned out to be "Wouldn't It Be Nice." We began working on a lyric together. With the exception of "You Still Believe In Me," all the other songs we had written up until then had been collaborative efforts. By that, I mean that the two of us bounced ideas back and forth about both lyrics and melody building off each other's thoughts and suggestions. However, in the case of "Wouldn't It Be Nice," for the first time, we were working on a song for which the melody had been finished. And that proved to be a problem.

The difficulty arose from the simple fact that Brian's job was over. The melody was finished. With previous songs, we interacted a lot. However, the melody was always a work in progress. So Brian's primary attention was given to honing the melody and I was relatively free to do what I wanted with the lyrics. From time to time Brian made comments about the words I chose, of course. But, in the end, final decisions about lyrics fell to me. Now, suddenly, with "Wouldn't It Be Nice," Brian began to concentrate rather intently on the lyrics and it began to drive me a little nuts. I realized that there were lots and lots of notes in the melody of "Wouldn't It Be Nice" which meant there would be lots and lots of words in the lyric. As we worked on it together, I could see that I was going to have to negotiate virtually every line. That, I decided, would simply be untenable.

So I suggested to Brian that he make a cassette recording of the melody and let me go away and come back with an entire lyric which we could then talk about. Thankfully, he agreed. And that is how the words were written. When I returned with the completed lyric, we tinkered a bit with a word here and a word there but it remained, essentially, what I had originally intended.

It's difficult to believe today, but we were actually pushing the envelope with that song much as we did with "God Only Knows." When that one was released in 1966, we were concerned that we wouldn't get any airplay because of the word "God" in the title and lyric, although that's hard to imagine in this day and age. At the time, the only way you could get away with using "God" in a song was if it was something like "God Bless America." And in the case of "Wouldn't It Be Nice," we were talking about an unmarried young couple wishing they could sleep together which, in the day, was a fairly risqué thing to say.

Wouldn't it be nice if we could wake up
In the morning when the day is new?
And after having spent the day together
Hold each other close the whole night through?

Soon thereafter, of course, The Beatles changed all the rules and the naiveté of those days was no more.

There have been comments made by no less than Paul McCartney and George Martin to the effect that without The Beach Boys' "Pet Sounds," Sgt. Pepper would never have happened. I'm not sure if that's true. I know that both Brian and I are very flattered by such comments as are all the superb musicians who worked on the project. "Pet Sounds" is a wonderful legacy and I'm very proud of it and of having had the opportunity to work with a talent the magnitude of Brian.

"Wouldn't It Be Nice"

Wouldn't it be nice if we were older,
Then we wouldn't have to wait so long?

And wouldn't it be nice to live together
In the kind of world where we belong?

You know it's gonna make it that much better
When we can say goodnight and stay together…

Wouldn't it be nice if we could wake up
In the morning when the day is new?
And after having spent the day together
Hold each other close the whole night through?

Happy times together we've been spending
I wish that every kiss was never ending.
Wouldn't it be nice?

Maybe if we think and wish and hope and pray it might come
    true.
Baby, then there wouldn't be a single thing we couldn't do.
We could be married
And then we'd be happy.

Wouldn't it be nice?

You know, it seems the more we talk about it
It only makes it worse to live without it.
But let's talk about it.
Wouldn't it be nice?

Good night my baby.
Sleep tight my baby.

Lyrics by Tony Asher. Music by Brian Wilson. © SEA OF TUNES PUBLISHING

Photo credit Lester Cohen Archives, WireImage

Mel B

"Mama"

Written by Melanie Brown (Scary Spice), Geri Halliwell (Ginger Spice), Victoria Adams Beckham (Posh Spice), Melanie C (Sporty Spice), Emma Bunton (Baby Spice). Recorded by the Spice Girls

All of the Spice Girls wrote "Mama." It was, and is, a very special song to us. When we recorded it, we each went off to a different corner of the studio and wrote our own verses to our respective mothers. Mine was apologetic.

On the chorus, we all sang "Mama I love you, Mama I care…" It was simple and heartfelt, a universal emotion we shared. We wrote that around the piano with a guitar.

All five of us now have kids so the song has taken on a different meaning entirely. When we reunited for our last tour, we got our kids on the stage with us for that song. It crosses generations and has stood the test of time.

When we recorded it, we added a gospel choir at the end and filled it with harmonies.

I still get goose bumps when I hear it.

"Mama"

She used to be my only enemy and never let me free,
Catching me in places that I know I shouldn't be,
Every other day I crossed the line,
I didn't mean to be so bad,
I never thought you would
Become the friend I never had

Back then I didn't know why,
Why you were misunderstood,
So now I see through your eyes,
all that you did was love,
Mama I love you, Mama I care,
Mama I love you, Mama my friend,
My friend

I didn't want to hear it then but
I'm not ashamed to say it now,
Every little thing you said and did was right for me,
I had a lot of time to think about,
About the way I used to be,
Never had a sense of my responsibility.

Back then I didn't know why,
Why you were misunderstood,
So now I see through your eyes,
All that you did was love,
Mama I love you, Mama I care,
Mama I love you, Mama my friend, My friend

But now I'm sure I know why,
Why you were misunderstood,
So now I see through your eyes,

All I can give you is love,
Mama I love you, Mama I care,
Mama I love you, Mama my friend,
My friend

Mama I love you, Mama I care,
Mama I love you, Mama my friend,
You're my friend.

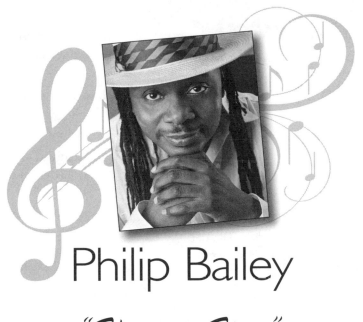

Philip Bailey

"Shining Star"

Written by Maurice White, Philip Bailey and Larry Dunn
Recorded by Earth Wind & Fire

We actually wrote "Shining Star" up at Caribou Ranch in Colorado when we were doing the "Way of the World" album. There was a lot of paranormal stuff going on there—like ghosts! We were told before we got there that they'd been there for a very long time, since the cabins were over 100 years old. I was not one to actually believe in those kinds of things but I remember seeing something in the middle of the night, being startled by it, and the image wouldn't leave. Finally I shooed it away and it went through the wall. I know it sounds crazy, but it happened.

In concert with that, we were writing "Shining Star" in Maurice White's cabin. Maurice was upstairs and I was downstairs. I was singing, ooh, aah, shouting, "I have the second verse!" He was simultaneously walking downstairs saying that *he* had it. As he got down the stairs, without having discussed the song at all, simultaneously we sang the exact same lyric. And neither of us had even written them down yet! We always remind each other of that. We wrote the lyrics in one session that morning.

We wrote this song to inspire ourselves and, therefore, everybody else as well. We were early in our success but we were very encouraged by the whole idea that our frame of mind had everything to do with how we felt about ourselves. Value is a perceived thing—it doesn't matter what your financial worth is. Everyone is a shining star no matter who they are.

It was a very spiritual recording session up there. Unusual things like that happened a lot that inspired us. It happened when Maurice and I wrote "Devotion" as well.

> *Through devotion, blessed are the children*
> *Praise the teacher, that brings true love to many.*
> *Your devotion, opens all life's treasures*
> *And deliverance, from the fruits of evil.*
> *So our mission, to bring a melody*
> *Ringin' voices sing sweet harmony.*

"Shining Star"

Yeah, hey
When you wish upon a star
Dreams will take you very far, yeah,
When you wish upon a dream
Life ain't always what it seems, oh yeah,
Once you see your light so clear
In the sky so very dear.

You're a shining star, no matter who you are
Shining bright to see what you can truly be,
That you can truly be

Shining star come into view
Shine its watchful light on you, yeah
Gives you strength to carry on
Make your body big and strong
Future roads for you to pass
Love to watch your mug past.

The shining star, lucky you
The sinful redeeming shall be true
On an adventure of the sun, yeah
Yeah it's all awake and just begun
Yeah, thought I had to stir the mood
That's it now I got my own, oh yeah.

So if you find yourself in need,
Why don't you listen to his words of heat?
Be a child free of sin
Be some place, yes I can
Words of wisdom: yes I can

You're a shining star, no matter who you are
Shining bright to see what you can truly be.
You're a shining star, no matter who you are
Shining bright to see what you can truly be.

Shining star for you to see, what your life can truly be
Shining star for you to see, what your life can truly be
Shining star for you to see, what your life can truly be

Roy Thomas Baker

"Bohemian Rhapsody"

Written by Freddie Mercury
Recorded by Queen

This is the song that keeps coming back onto the charts. It was a very unusual production. We never demo'd anything, so I'd go to Freddie's (Freddie Mercury's) place, he'd be sitting at the piano and say, "This is the beginning" and played it. Then he threw his hands in the air and said, "This is where the opera section would come in." It wasn't supposed to be an opera, per se; it was a tongue in cheek opera. He knew I would understand, because I had a background in classical music and opera. This is not like a regular pop song—there isn't even a chorus.

We recorded the song in three distinct parts—the intro and the first verse, the opera section and the end rock section. Then, in post production, we would put it together. We tested as we went along to make sure it would work. Fred was working out the words while we were recording.

This was a vision of his feelings and he brought that emotional montage into the studio. Brian (May) is a Ph.D., a true academic, scientist. He usually used his brain, however when he went in to record his solo for this song, he reached in and pulled out some emotion you wouldn't have expected. That was a direct reflection of Freddie's depth of imagination.

From the things Freddie said to me, he wanted this to have an emotional pull. That was more important to him than the words themselves. It was a story, much like Dickens, or Keats with his poetry. Freddie tended to use his life experiences and interpret them for the medium in which he worked. Dickens, for instance, was never in an orphanage, he just knew about them. Shakespeare didn't live in Cleopatra's times, but he wrote about it. This was an interpretation of a Gilbert and Sullivan opera, but we kept our sense of humor. We'd burst out laughing now and then, as people still do. We succeeded in transmitting both the emotion and the humor.

These words and phrases meant nothing or even made sense on their own, but as a whole, they had an emotional ring:

Scaramouch, Scaramouch, will you do the Fandango
Thunderbolt and lightning, very, very frightening me
(Galileo) Galileo (Galileo) Galileo, Galileo Galileo Figaro
Magnifico-o-o-o

Figaro, of course, is the opera, while Fandango is a Portuguese dance. He had some bits from the Koran as well and merged them all together as emotional outlets. That's what makes it so valuable. The impact is clear since, three decades later, there is still controversy about the lyrics and people still listen to this song. It's purely a feeling thing. It did not directly reflect what he was going through in life.

He was very particular, meticulous, the most passionate person

I've ever worked with. He knew exactly what he wanted. Even the scraps of paper he had with notes on them were meticulously written.

I've read various articles about what Freddie meant when he wrote "Bohemian Rhapsody," mostly from academics who gave definitive explanations of what each phrase meant, but I don't know that there was a direct translation from any specific experience(s). This was more a compilation of his life experiences, although he was quite young at the time. The thing about Freddie was, as flamboyant as he was on stage, that's how shy he actually was.

One night after the studio we went to dinner with Kenny Everett, the first DJ to play the record, and he asked Freddie what the lyrics in the opera section meant. Freddie responded, something like, he wrote the words that would fit the music. The truth lies somewhere in the middle, between this and the often touted academic, philosophical interpretations.

"Bohemian Rhapsody"

Is this the real life?
Is this just fantasy?
Caught in a landslide,
No escape from reality.
Open your eyes, Look up to the skies and see,
I'm just a poor boy, I need no sympathy,
Because I'm easy come, easy go, Little high, little low,
Any way the wind blows, doesn't really matter to me, to me.

Mama just killed a man,
Put a gun against his head, pulled my trigger, now he's dead.
Mama, life had just begun,
But now I've gone and thrown it all away.
Mama, ooh, Didn't mean to make you cry,

If I'm not back again this time tomorrow,
Carry on, carry on as if nothing really matters.

Too late, my time has come,
Sends shivers down my spine, body's aching all the time.
Goodbye, ev'rybody, I've got to go,
Gotta leave you all behind and face the truth.
Mama, ooh, I don't want to die,
I sometimes wish I'd never been born at all.

I see a little silhouetto of a man,
Scaramouche, Scaramouche, will you do the Fandango?
Thunderbolt and light'ning, very, very fright'ning me.
(Galileo.) Galileo. (Galileo.) Galileo, Galileo Figaro
Magnifico. I'm just a poor boy and nobody loves me.
He's just a poor boy from a poor family,
Spare him his life from this monstrosity.
Easy come, easy go, will you let me go.
Bismillah! No, we will not let you go.
(Let him go!) Bismillah! We will not let you go.
(Let him go!) Bismillah! We will not let you go.
(Let me go.) Will not let you go.
(Let me go.) Will not let you go. (Let me go.) Ah.
No, no, no, no, no, no, no.
(Oh mama mia, mama mia.) Mama mia, let me go.
Beelzebub has a devil put aside for me, for me, for me.

So you think you can stone me and spit in my eye.
So you think you can love me and leave me to die.
Oh, baby, can't do this to me, baby,
Just gotta get out, just gotta get right outta here.

Nothing really matters, Anyone can see.
Nothing really matters,
Nothing really matters to me.

Any way the wind blows.

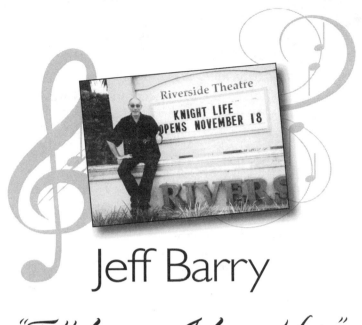

Jeff Barry

"Tell Laura I Love Her"

Written by Jeff Barry and Ben Raleigh
Recorded by Ray Peterson

This song was my first hit—in 1960. The story is about a young guy who is in love—with Laura. He has no money and he wants to be able to buy his girl some gifts. He sees a sign for a stock car race with a prize of $1,000. He joins the race to get the money and gets killed. It's a real teen angst story. I wrote it in 1959. I didn't even own a car then. I was a Brooklyn cowboy. In fact, I still wear cowboy shirts.

When I sat down to write this song, I originally saw it as a sign for a prize for winning a rodeo. Not many people know that there was a rodeo every year in Brooklyn of all places—and I went regularly.

I played the first version of the song for my very first publisher, Arnold Shaw. He said, "That's interesting, but the guy is gored to death by a Brahma bull?!" (I forgot to mention that detail.) "Who can relate to that?" That was obviously true, so I changed it. Stock car race had the same three syllables as ro-de-o and still fit in the melody—and people could relate to it.

I was told that there was a fuss in England about whether they could play it on radio because of the content but I was too excited about getting airplay in the U.S. to worry about it.

"Tell Laura I Love Her"

Laura and Tommy were lovers.
He wanted to give her everything
Flowers, presents and, most of all, a wedding ring.

He saw a sign for a stock car race
A thousand dollar price it read.
He couldn't get Laura on the phone
So to her mother Tommy said

Tell Laura I love her,
Tell Laura I need her.
Tell Laura I may be late
I have something to do
That cannot wait.

He drove his car to the racing ground,
He was the youngest driver there.
The crowd roared as they started the race,
From the track they drove at a deadly pace.

No one knows what happened that day,
How his car overturned in flames.
But as they pulled him from the twisted wreck,
With his dying breath they heard him say

Tell Laura I love her,

Tell Laura I need her.
Tell Laura not to cry,
My love for her will never die.

Now in the chapel where Laura prays
For her Tommy who passed away
It was just for Laura he lived and died.
Alone in the chapel she could hear him cry

Tell Laura I love her,
Tell Laura I need her.
Tell Laura not to cry,
My love for her will never die.

Tell Laura I love her,
Tell Laura I need her.
Tell Laura not to cry,
My love for her will never die.

Written by Jeff Barry and Ben Raleigh. © Music Sales Corporation

Jeff Barry

"Walkin' in the Sun"

Written and Recorded by Jeff Barry

Sometimes a writer's favorite song is not one of his biggest hits. That's the case with "Walkin' in the Sun." It is very meaningful to me.

My father was blind since he was about 6 years old. He was an insurance broker and did most of his work from home in Brooklyn, New York. Most of his sales were done on the phone; he was really good at it. Once in a while, though, he had to go to the office in Manhattan. Although my parents were divorced when I was 7, I still spent a lot of time with my dad.

One day, when I was about 13 or 14, I went to the city with him. We were heading to the subway and I remember it must have been the end of the day, it was kind of chilly. We talked about how the sun was on an angle jutting through the tall buildings. My dad asked if the sun was out on the other side of the street and, sure enough, it was. He said, "Let's walk there where it's warm."

Many years later, when I was probably in my early thirties, I was writing songs for myself. I had an office at A&M Records and they wanted me to record some of my songs. I thought about that day and "Walkin' in the sun." It's very simple. There are three verses and no bridge. The lyrics say that when things have been negative long enough, you need to know when they get good. The last line of the verse is:

Even a blind man can tell when he's walkin' in the sun.

I was the first person to record it but I'm very moved by the fact that it's also been covered by many cool artists, that soulful people have chosen to record this song — Glen Campbell, Percy Sledge, B.B. King, Chaka Khan, and others. I think people like it because they can tell it comes from a place of sincerity.

"Walkin' in the Sun"

Things have been goin' wrong long enough to know
Everything is right
Been walkin' in the dark long enough to know
Finally seen the light
Been losin' long enough to know when I've finally won
And even a blind man can tell when he's walkin' in the sun.

I've cried enough tears to know
This feeling's called a smile
Been bottom rung long enough to know
When I'm doin' it in style
Been run long to know
There's no more need to run
And even a blind man can tell when he's walkin' in the sun.

Oh, the wind is at my back
And I'm sailin' on a ship that's overdue.

Well I've blown so many chances
I ain't gonna blow this one with you.
I've seen enough bad times to know
Good times have begun
And even a blind man can tell when he's walkin' in the sun,
And even a blind man can tell when he's walkin' in the sun.

Lyrics and Music by Jeff Barry. © Irving Music/Jeff Barry International

Stephen Bishop

"On And On"

Written and Recorded by Stephen Bishop

It was 1975. I was walking down the street, going to the neighborhood store, and came up with the title "On and On" and wrote it on a piece of paper in my wallet. When I got back to my building, I went upstairs to my small apartment in a duplex in Silver Lake that I was sharing with my 85-year-old land lady, Violet Marshall. I went into my bedroom, sat on the edge of the bed and looked out the window at Miss Marshall's beautiful tropical garden that she was so proud of. It was made up of flowers of every conceivable color, from all over the world. They took me to thinking about being somewhere else, a getaway in the tropics. That's how I came up with Jamaica.

The song also came about because I found this chord, a special kind. I went into my wallet, where I had several song titles I had come up with and stuffed in there, and took out "On and On." I played that unusual chord over and over until the song came to me. I had this chair that I wrote all of my songs in — "Save A Rainy Day," "Careless," most of the songs from my first album. I sat there and began to work on the song. In the rough draft, you can see I went to all different places. Thank God I didn't go with some of the early lines; a few were really terrible. I kept re-writing and re-writing until I got it to where it is. One of the hardest things to do with lyric writing is editing — self-editing. It's a painful process. I wrote it in the same day and night, which was very unusual for me. It's hard to do that.

I was into very creative lyrics and colorful verses then. I think you'll find that every writer puts a piece of him or herself into each song, even if it's in a small way, and I've pulled things from my personal favorites. For instance, I'm a big fan of Sinatra so he's in there:

Poor ol' Jimmy
Sits alone in the moonlight
Saw his woman kiss another man
So he takes a ladder,
Steals the stars from the sky
Puts on Sinatra and starts to cry.

People remember that verse. I've had people come up to me in the market, while I was buying cauliflower, to tell me what a great line they think that is.

I always wondered if Sinatra ever heard it. I thought maybe one day I'd find a brand new shiny bicycle in front of my door with a big ribbon saying: "Love ya — from Frank" or something.

"On And On"

Down in Jamaica
They got lots of pretty women
Steal your money
Then they break your heart.
Lonesome Sue, she's in love with ol' Sam
Take him from the fire into the frying pan.

On and on
She just keeps on trying
And she smiles when she feels like crying
On and on, on and on, on and on.

Poor ol' Jimmy
Sits alone in the moonlight
Saw his woman kiss another man
So he takes a ladder,
Steals the stars from the sky
Puts on Sinatra and starts to cry.

On and on
He just keeps on trying
And he smiles when he feels like crying
On and on, on and on, on and on.

When the first time is the last time
It can make you feel so bad
But if you know it, show it
Hold on tight
Don't let her say goodnight.

Got the sun on my shoulders
And my toes in the sand,
My woman's left me for the some other man.
Aw, but I don't care
I'll just dream and stay tan,
Toss up my heart to see where it lands.

On and on
I just keep on trying
And I smile when I feel like dying.
On and on, on and on, on and on

On and on, on and on, on and on
On and on, on and on, on and on

Clint Black

"When I Said I Do"

Written by Clint Black
Recorded by Clint Black with Lisa Hartman Black

J was working on an album that was kind of a "trick" album. The record company wanted me to do an unplugged record but by then everyone had done one and I didn't have the heart for it anymore. I'd gotten the advance, so I had to give them what they wanted. I thought about how I could make it interesting for me. I decided I would make it not sound unplugged. I wanted it to sound electric and contemporary. The album, the first I ever produced, was titled *D'Lectrified*.

I enlisted the help of the artists who had influenced my music to be involved in the recording somehow: Steve Wariner, Waylon Jennings, Marty Stuart, Eric Idle, Edgar Winter, Kenny Loggins, Marshall Tucker Band, Leon Russell, Toy Caldwell, Bruce Hornsby, Matt Rollings, Hayden Nicholas (I hope I didn't forget anyone). And they were all a part of it. About midway through recording, I realized that the biggest influence on my life wasn't on it—my wife Lisa. I had to write a song for her. It was time to do something for us.

While Lisa was cooking, I was hanging out in the kitchen with my guitar and started writing the melody. I thought, "If we were singing in front of people and God, what would we say?" We communicate well privately but how could we express ourselves to everyone else? I started with a 3/4 feel like a wedding waltz. I had a note pad on the island in the kitchen and wrote the first half of the song. Often, she'll sing or hum along with me while I'm writing. I started teaching Lisa the chorus and had her sing it with me. The next day, I got back to work in the kitchen (I wrote the whole song in that kitchen.). By then, Lisa was locked into the harmony part.

When I wrote the bridge, I sang both parts; I hadn't told her that I wrote it for both of us to sing. After it was finished I told her she was recording it with me and she immediately said, "No." I told her that I recorded it in the key that would work for both of us. She went back and forth and kept telling me to "get a real singer." She hadn't sung in 15 years or so, and she was nervous that she didn't have the chops any more, even though I told her she was wrong. Then I resorted to guilt. I started being my lawyer, "On (such and such a date) you said you would record this song with me." She still didn't agree to do it.

Days before the album was due, I told her it would just be me on the record; if she didn't sing it with me, no one would sing that part. I asked her how she would feel if she heard it later and she wasn't on it when I wrote it for and about us. She finally agreed—FOUR days before I had to turn it in!

We recorded it and delivered it on time. The record company loved the song. I didn't tell them whose voice it was and they guessed "Martina McBride" and almost everyone but Lisa. It was the first single and they shipped it to radio without them knowing who it was.

Then I had to convince Lisa to do the music video with me. She had pretty much retired from acting when we got married, so she said no for a while and then finally did it. I directed it. It was set in a bowl, it had an amphitheater feel. She was beautiful. That's when everyone found out it was her singing with me.

We went through the same thing with *The Tonight Show*, going back and forth until she agreed to go on with me, and again for the beginning of my tour at (what is now) the Smirnoff Amphitheater in Dallas. I said, "Honey, you have to come do this with me." She said, "I'm not doing this on stage!" She did and I was thrilled. She was anxious, frightened. The song starts and, while I'm singing the first chorus, she walks around the back of the stage, and enters down a flight of stairs on the stage. 20,000 people cheered when they saw her. She felt welcome and calmed down. She realized they wanted her there and didn't resent her and whatever trepidation she had went away. She sang with me and we had the best time. From then on I couldn't get her off the stage. Seriously, it was great. She sang with me on a 75 city tour.

The record went to #1, then down to #2 and back to #1. That never happened to me before or since. It got a Grammy nomination and an Academy of Country Music Award for Vocal Event of the Year in 1999. I told her I didn't think we'd win. When they called our names, it meant something very special.

The song got a rebirth when another couple, Chanté Moore and Kenny Lattimore, did an old style R&B version of it that I loved. This is a special song for me because I've gotten so many nice letters about it. So many people tell me they played it at their weddings.

"When I Said I Do"

These times are troubled and these times are good
And they're always gonna be, they rise and they fall
We take 'em all the way that we should
Together you and me forsaking them all
Deep in the night and by the light of day.
It always looks the same, true love always does
And here by your side, or a million miles away
Nothin's ever gonna change the way that I feel,
The way it is, is the way that it was.

When I said I do, I meant that I will 'til the end of all time
Be faithful and true, devoted to you
That's what I had in mind when I said I do.

Well this old world keeps changin', and the world stays the
    same
For all who came before, and it goes hand and hand.
Only you and I can undo all that we became
That makes us so much more, than a woman and a man.
And after everything that comes and goes around
Has only passed us by, here alone in our dreams
I know there's a lonely heart in every lost and found
But forever you and I will be the ones
Who found out what forever means.

When I said I do, I meant that I will 'til the end of all time
Be faithful and true, devoted to you
That's what I had in mind when I said I do.

Truer than true, you know that I'll always be there for you.
That's what I had in mind, that's what I had in mind
When I said I do.

Lyrics and Music by Clint Black. © 1999 Blackened Music

Greg Camp

"All Star"

Written by Greg Camp
Recorded by Smash Mouth

*H*ere's how the story goes. When I was the guitarist for Smash Mouth, we'd go out on long tours and the bass player and I would take a bag of laundry and a bag of fan mail and go to a local laundromat in some of the deepest, craziest places in America. While we were doing our laundry, we would read the mail—this was when people actually still wrote letters.

We realized that a lot of kids were troubled with their family situations, parents who weren't great at parenting, older siblings, school, friends. They thanked us for our music, saying that it helped to get them through the tough times. It made us realize that we do have a voice and can help people.

This song was 100% for the fans. I wanted to give something back to them for letting us know that they were actually listening to us and I wanted them to know that we were listening to them. It was my gift to them.

We had turned in the record—*Astro Lounge*—before I wrote "All Star." The record company said they liked it, however they also said that they heard the third and fourth singles, but they didn't hear the "hit." They didn't think there was a first hot single in the songs we sent them. They (and we) felt it should be uplifting, not another "the world sucks" kind of song. We decided that it should be a song about how to get through those rough times. Because of the inspiration I had received from the fans, I said, "I can do this!"

I wrote "All Star," which became the first single, and "Then the Morning Comes" which was the second single from that album. "All Star" goes to our upbringing. It talks about our school years and how mean the world can be. In the intro, I talk about how people always tell you how you won't amount to anything and how kids later put the "L" on someone's forehead.

People used to say to me, "You're a musician?! What a pipe dream. You're never going to realize it." But *you* have to overcome negativity and make your dream a reality. Be yourself and believe in yourself and you *can* make it happen. Even if your family is no help, if your friends make fun of you or try to steer you in another direction, do what you want to do. They can't stop you unless you let them. That's how I was able to succeed at what I love and have a passion for.

It was nice to know that people appreciate it when you are positive. Those songs catapulted the album and the group and I had the fans to thank. We learned what they needed to hear and people seemed to grab a hold of the song. They heard it on the radio and it made a big impact. It was also in the movie *Shrek*, so even more people and a broader audience heard it, including kids. The next bunch of fan letters we got told us that we really helped people with those songs.

As an aside, one of the reasons I agreed to participate in this book is because a long time ago, I was in a funk. I really wasn't feeling well. Some good friends gave me a *Chicken Soup for the Soul* book and I read some of the stories and it definitely helped me. I read some of the kids' stories to my daughter, who's 10, and she really enjoys them too.

"All Star"

Somebody once told me the world is gonna roll me
I ain't the sharpest tool in the shed.
She was looking kind of dumb with her finger and her thumb
In the shape of an "L" on her forehead.

Well the years start coming and they don't stop coming
Fed to the rules and I hit the ground running
Didn't make sense not to live for fun
Your brain gets smart but your head gets dumb.

So much to do, so much to see
So what's wrong with taking the back streets?
You'll never know if you don't go
You'll never shine if you don't glow.

Hey now you're an All Star get your game on, go play.
Hey now you're a Rock Star get the show on, get paid
And all that glitters is gold
Only shooting stars break the mold.

It's a cool place and they say it gets colder
You're bundled up now but wait 'til you get older
But the meteor men beg to differ
Judging by the hole in the satellite picture.

The ice we skate is getting pretty thin
The water's getting warm so you might as well swim.
My world's on fire, how about yours?
That's the way I like it and I'll never get bored.

Hey now you're an All Star get your game on, go play.
Hey now you're a Rock Star get the show on get paid.

And all that glitters is gold
Only shooting stars break the mold.

Hey now you're an All Star get your game on, go play.
Hey now you're a Rock Star get the show on get paid.
And all that glitters is gold
Only shooting stars break the mold.

Somebody once asked could I spare some change for gas
I need to get myself away from this place.
I said yep what a concept
I could use a little fuel myself
And we could all use a little change.

Well the years start coming and they don't stop coming
Fed to the rules and I hit the ground running
Didn't make sense not to live for fun
Your brain gets smart but your head gets dumb

So much to do, so much to see.
So what's wrong with taking the back streets?
You'll never know if you don't go
You'll never shine if you don't glow.

Lyrics and Music by Greg Camp. © 2008 Warner Chappell/Squish Moth

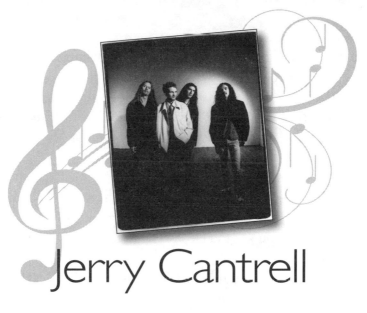

Jerry Cantrell

"Rooster"

Written by Jerry Cantrell
Recorded by Alice in Chains

The song in a nutshell is me trying to imagine my father's experience in Vietnam and to learn how it affected him—he never talked about it.

I was seven or eight when my parents were getting divorced. My dad had carried a lot back home from the war and it was translating into the family. There were some fairly difficult times early on. He moved to Oklahoma and my brother went with him. I remained in Seattle where my sister and I were raised by my mother and grandmother.

As a kid I kind of held that against him—I had a little case of hate. As I got older, in my twenties, we had made contact although I didn't see him a lot. I put part of me, as a man, in his shoes. Would I have done better? I doubt if I would have come back at all. After thinking about it more, I gained respect for him and appreciation for how he felt.

I was in between houses and staying at my manager, Susan Silver, and her husband's house. I stayed in a guest room overlooking Puget Sound. It was beautiful. I stayed up all night looking out and thinking and got a kind of epiphany about my father and the words to this song poured out. "Rooster" is the nickname my dad's grandfather gave him when he was a kid. His hair stood up like a rooster's and he was told he was a cocky strutting kid. First thing in the morning, I played the song for Susan and she loved it.

Writing this song was a big part of healing for both my father and me. I gave him the lyrics and played the song for him and told him that I was trying to get into his head. I asked if I got close. He responded, "Son, you got too close!" We're the best of friends today. That was a big turning point.

We're partners in a ranch that he runs in southeast Oklahoma. It's where we shot the video for the song. It was directed by a great filmmaker, Mark Pallington, who created a film called *Fathers' Days* about his father, a former Colts player, and his battle with Alzheimer's. Both Mark and I were dealing with acceptance so he understood this song. He had the sensitivity to interview my dad for an hour on tape. Mark was very respectful. It was a chilling interview in which my dad described what he went through. There is a clip from it at the beginning of the music video. My dad always comes to our shows now when we're in the area. He gets attention because of the video. This song means a lot to me; I tend to write about things that are important to me.

A lot of military who fought in the first Middle East war and in Iraq and Afghanistan react strongly to this song. This song translates heavily. I get a lot of feedback from people telling me how "Rooster" was helpful to them and how much they relate to it.

"Rooster"

Ain't found a way to kill me yet
Eyes burn with stinging sweat
Seems every path leads me to nowhere

Wife and kids, household pet
Army green was no safe bet
The bullets scream to me from somewhere.

Yeah they come to snuff the rooster
Yeah here come the rooster, yeah
You know he ain't gonna die
No, no, no, you know he ain't gonna die.

Here they come to snuff the rooster
Ah yeah, yeah
Yeah, here come the rooster, yeah
You know he ain't gonna die
No, no, no, you know he ain't gonna die.

Yeah they come to snuff the rooster
Yeah here come the rooster, yeah
You know he ain't gonna die
No, no, no, you know he ain't gonna die.

Walkin' tall machine gun man
They spit on me in my home land.
Gloria sent me pictures of my boy
Got my pills 'gainst mosquito death
My buddy's breathin' his dyin' breath.
Oh god please won't you help me make it through?

Yeah they come to snuff the rooster, ah yeah
Yeah here come the rooster, yeah
You know he ain't gonna die
No, no, you know he ain't gonna die.

Written by Jerry Cantrell. © 1992 Buttnugget Publishing (ASCAP). International Copyright Secured.

All Rights Reserved.

Photo credit Rocky Schenck

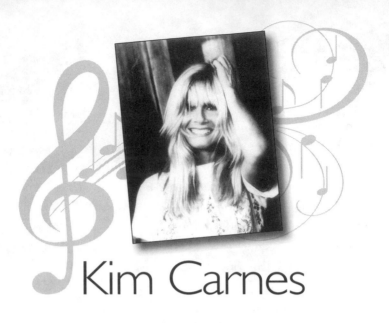

Kim Carnes

"Don't Fall In Love With A Dreamer"

Written by Kim Carnes and Dave Ellingson
Recorded by Kenny Rogers and Kim Carnes

Kenny Rogers called my husband, Dave Ellingson, and me and asked if we'd be interested in working on a concept album for him. It seemed like a daunting task but we liked the challenge and realized that we first had to formulate the characters, then conceive the story and work backwards and write the songs.

The only thing Kenny specified was that the album had a modern cowboy theme. So we created the main character, whose name was Gideon Tanner. We characterized him as a ladies man, a rogue. The character became very real to us. The story and the first song on the album, "Gideon," begins with the funeral and then flashes back to his earlier life. We've always fantasized the story with the songs as a Broadway musical. That would be cool.

"Don't Fall In Love With A Dreamer" is about the love interest of the main character in this fictional story. He is telling her, "I'm really no good for you. Don't fall in love with a dreamer, because he'll break you every time." He's letting her know that he'll be out of there. They're saying it to each other, but it's really a confessional to her on the last night they'll be together. More than anything I wanted to convey, in the way the song was written and recorded, a sense of urgency that two people feel when they know this is the very last night they'll be together. Then the harsh reality comes in the morning when people consider changing their minds because they know that once they walk away, they probably won't ever see each other again. Of all the songs on the album, this one came most quickly to us.

We were living in L.A. then. I wrote the music on my baby grand piano that has since come to Nashville with me. I'll never give it up. It's an old Mason & Hamlin that we found in a newspaper ad. I write every song on it. "Don't Fall In Love With A Dreamer" was the first single from the album and has been very good to me so the piano became my good luck charm. It has a special place in my heart. I haven't even let anyone take it away to replace its old strings. I'm afraid something will happen to it.

When we were through with all of the songs, we got some musicians together and did a demo of the album. We went to Kenny's house and played it for him. On the spot, he said that he would do the whole album. After "Dreamer," he asked if I would sing the duet with him. Of course, I agreed. Since it was my baby, it would have been hard to watch someone else sing it.

The album was recorded in Nashville and Dave and I went there for the entire process. When we recorded the duet, we realized that it was written in the key for my voice. The producer found the key for Kenny so I had to improvise the melody slightly on the spot. We recorded the vocals facing one another, live with the musicians playing with us. There were no overdubs. It turned out to be better than the original.

Kenny keeps re-packaging his greatest hits and has had several duets LP's. We've re-recorded the song, replicating the original on several occasions as Kenny's changed record labels. It is the gift that keeps on giving.

"Don't Fall In Love With A Dreamer"

Just look at you sitting there
You never looked better than tonight
And it'd be so easy to tell you I'd stay
Like I've done so many times.
I was so sure this would be the night
You'd close the door
And wanna stay with me
And it'd be so easy
To tell you I'd stay
Like I've done so many times.

Don't fall in love with a dreamer
Because he'll always take you in,
Just when you think
You've really changed him
He'll leave you again.
Don't fall in love with a dreamer
Because he'll break you every time.

So put out the light and just hold on
Before we say goodbye.
Now it's morning
and the phone rings and ya say
You gotta get your things together
You just gotta leave
Before you change your mind
And if you knew
What I was thinking girl, I'd turn around
If you'd just ask me one more time.

Don't fall in love with a dreamer
Because he'll always take you in,
Just when you think
You've really changed him
He'll leave you again.
Don't fall in love with a dreamer
Because he'll break you every time
So put out the light and just hold on
Before we say goodbye.

Written by Kim Carnes and Dave Ellingson. © APPIAN MUSIC CO; ALMO MUSIC CORP.

David Cassidy

"Stand and Be Proud"

Written by David Cassidy and Sue Shifrin-Cassidy
Recorded by The Voice of the City choir accompanied by the
Hollywood Bowl Orchestra for Rebuild LA

My wife, Sue, and I were working at the time with our friend Bob Ezrin, the renowned music producer of such artists as Pink Floyd, Alice Cooper, Kiss. He had gone through enormous changes in his life, as had we. He had helped to change the lives of many people in need.

When the riots broke out in Los Angeles in 1992, I had just come off tour. "Lyin' To Myself" was in the Top 20 and I was writing and recording my next album. "Stand and Be Proud" was in its infancy. Musically it was finished, but it hadn't been developed enough lyrically.

Bob Ezrin immediately went to the First AME Church in south central Los Angeles, in the heart of where the riots were taking place, and began helping individuals and families who had lost their businesses and homes. Amongst other things, he was directing food drives there.

Some time in the next day, Bob called us and said that we needed to do something more to help. Sue and I immediately joined him at the church. The moment that we arrived, the faces of the people and the destruction of the structures and people's lifelong possessions spawned the idea that we could make a significant contribution to help to pull the community together. The lyrics evolved from that tragedy.

Bob was mostly responsible for coordinating a much greater effort, producing an event which ultimately was filmed and recorded via generous donations from individuals and companies like John Paul DeJoria of Paul Mitchell, Jerry Moss and Herb Alpert, who gave us their studio and studio time at A&M, and lots of others. Propaganda Films donated the film crew and the helicopter, Scotti Bros. released the record.

After the event and recording were completed, the song and video were played in their entirety simultaneously on *Good Morning America* and on 5,000 radio stations! This created a great deal of awareness and stimulated donations. All of our writers and publishing royalties were donated to Rebuild LA, of which I'm very proud. I'm simply blown away by people's generosity.

The event took place at the Hollywood Bowl, which contributed the venue and their outstanding Hollywood Bowl orchestra, who participated along with various choirs and church groups of every ethnic background, representing the melting pot of those affected and who make up L.A. Many celebrities wanted to be involved but we chose to have the people from the affected area join us and make them the stars. We called them "The Voice of the City." Busses to bring the 1,000 chorus members to the Bowl were donated by the city. The Mayor of Los Angeles at the time, Tom Bradley, along with Peter Ueberroth, who headed the Rebuild LA project, was there to acknowledge our efforts, which we greatly appreciated. I was not in the video nor did I do any media about it as I didn't want anyone to misconstrue the effort as self-promotion. I was just pleased that we could help.

"Stand and Be Proud"

This is our chance
Now we gotta take it
We may never get to pass this way again.
We gotta be strong
If we're gonna make it,
Now it's time to dry the tears.
Through the ashes hope appears
And if we reach out for the sky
We might touch the stars.

Stand and be proud
Of who we are,
We've come so close
We've come so far.
Now and forever
Our light will shine,
Shout it out loud
Stand and be proud.

We have a dream
Now we gotta live it.
It's gonna take some work to make this dream come true
But this is our time.
We can't waste this moment,
We're doin' it with love
And with help from God above
Nothing in this world can take it away.

Stand and be proud
Of who we are,
We've come so close
We've come so far.

Now and forever
Our light will shine,
Shout it out loud
Stand and be proud.

Close your eyes and feel the pride inside your heart
However long the road of life may be
This is the very best of you and me!

Stand and be proud
Of who we are,
We've come so close
We've come so far.
Now and forever
Our light will shine.
Shout it out loud
Stand and be proud.

Lyrics and Music by Sue Shifrin and David Cassidy. © 1992 BeauCoo Music

Carol Connors

"With You I'm Born Again"

Written by David Shire and Carol Connors
Recorded by Billy Preston & Syreeta for the film Fast Break

Originally, David Shire and I were supposed to write the theme for *Rocky* which his wife, Talia, was co-starring in. Bill Conti, Ayn Robbins and I wound up writing that theme, but fortunately David and I worked together on "With You I'm Born Again" for the film *Fast Break*.

David played me 16 bars of the melody and I thought it was one of the most exquisitely beautiful melodies I'd ever heard. It touched my heart. I went home and sat on my bed to begin to work on the lyrics. It was like God wrote it, like I plugged into a giant socket in the sky. It came to me immediately:

> *Come bring me your softness*
> *Comfort me through all this madness...*

(I almost threw out those lines. I thought people wouldn't get it and they would hate it.) I wrote the song in 22 minutes. I couldn't write the ideas down fast enough.

At the time, I was in love with Robert Culp and he was in love with me. It was the beginning of a two and a half year relationship. All I could think about was that I wanted him to feel this way about me and me about him and we did.

The entire song was written except for two words.

Come show me your kindness
In your arms I know I'll...

Time went by and I'd go back to the song and I still couldn't come up with those two elusive words. I had a deadline and knew I had to come up with them quickly. I took a "fast break" and went to Clancy Muldoon's ice cream parlor. I loved their ice cream, especially the chocolate chip. I heard myself order "chocolate chip, paper, pencil—now!" The girl must have thought I was insane, but she got me a pencil and paper (and the chocolate chip ice cream cone) and I wrote down the elusive missing words:

Come show me your kindness
In your arms I know I'll **find this**

Berry Gordy and Suzanne de Passe, to whom I brought the idea to make this a soundtrack, became the executive producers at Motown. They approached Billy Preston and Syreeta (Stevie Wonder's ex-wife) to sing the duet, and we recorded it over New Year's.

I executive produced the record and David Shire wrote the definitive arrangement. When Billy sat at the organ in the studio and played the music for one of the instrumental tracks, David said, "Now I know why Billy is considered a genius."

When I reflect back on the song, part of me wishes I would have named it "Come Bring Me Your Softness" because in the beginning, when it was becoming a hit, so many people went into the stores and asked for that title. In fact, Berry called me himself to tell me that he heard the same thing. More importantly, he told me that when Robin Cousins skated to it in the Olympics, he and everyone else at Motown knew the song was a hit. To this day I thank God I didn't throw out those two lines. Despite the fact that the film came and went, the song became a classic.

Some of the reactions were astounding. Marvin Hamlisch was in the barber's chair when he heard it for the first time and almost got his neck cut when he jumped up in the chair.

I got a call from one of the leaders of the born again Christians who felt that the song was inspirational, and he wanted to know what my thoughts were about God when I wrote it. I told him, "I was actually thinking about Robert Culp—but he thinks he's God, so I guess it's okay." He hung up the phone on me. Over the years I've heard that the song has been played as a hymn on different religious occasions.

There have been over 90 recordings of the song, both duets and solos, including Mariah Carey and John Legend, Johnny Mathis, Michael Crawford, and a jazz version by the legendary Barbara Morrison, but in my heart the definitive recording will always be that by Billy Preston and Syreeta.

"With You I'm Born Again"

Come bring me your softness
Comfort me through all this madness.
Woman, don't you know
With you I'm born again?

Come give me your sweetness
Now there's you, there is no weakness,
Lying safe within your arms
I'm born again.

I was half, not whole
In step with none

Reaching through this world
In need of one.

Come show me your kindness
In your arms I know I'll find this.
Woman, don't you know
With you I'm born again,
Lying safe with you I'm born again?

Come bring me your softness
Comfort me through all this madness
Woman, don't you know
With you I'm born again?

Come give me your sweetness
Now there's you, there is no weakness
Lying safe within your arms
I'm born again.
Woman, don't you know
With you I'm born again?

I was half, not whole
In step with none
Reaching through this world
In need of one.

Come show me your kindness
In your arms I know I'll find this.
Woman, don't you know
With you I'm born again?
Lying safe with you I'm born again.

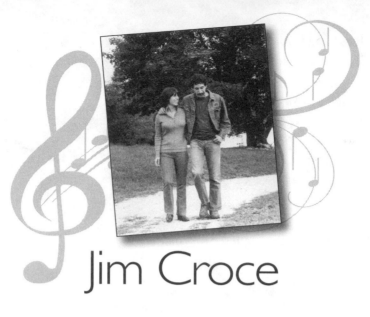

Jim Croce

"Bad, Bad Leroy Brown"

Story by Ingrid Croce

Written and Recorded by Jim Croce

This song began at Fort Dix, New Jersey and was completed at our home in Lyndell, Pennsylvania in 1971.

Since I opened Croce's Restaurant and Jazz Bar in 1985 in the Gaslamp Quarter of San Diego as a tribute to my late husband Jim Croce, 30 to 40 guys have come in over the years and claimed to be the authentic Leroy Brown. Who's to say who's the "real" Leroy Brown? But what I do know is that the real story began back in December 1966.

It was then that my father became very ill and Jim was able to get a transfer for "heart-ship" leave from Fort Jackson, South Carolina to Fort Dix, where he met Leroy Brown.

This is how Jim told his story, "Leroy Brown is somebody I met in the United States Army when I was in Basic training in the Army National Guard in Fort Dix where I had the MOS (Military

Occupational Specialty) of being a field Communications crewman, which is a wire man. That's a big long name for 'target.' I was climbing these polls and running this wire and it was a great experience. I've used it often in my daily life.

Leroy was stationed down there at Fort Dix and about a week after we got there, we were sittin' around talkin' and one night he said he didn't like it there anymore and he was gonna go home. So he did. He went AWOL. He came back at the end of the month to get his pay, which was kind of a mistake.

When he got out of the stockade, it was a lot of fun to just sit down and talk because he had opened up. It was like an enlightening experience for him and, after getting out of the cage, Leroy just turned into a completely different person. I mean he's probably doing books today or somethin', giving lectures on some corner. I used to just listen to him talk and to see how 'bad' he was, I knew someday I was gonna write a song about him...."

"Bad, Bad Leroy Brown"

Well, the South side of Chicago
Is the baddest part of town
And if you go down there
You better just beware
Of a man named Leroy Brown.

Now Leroy's more than trouble,
You see he stand 'bout six foot four.
All the downtown ladies call him Treetop Lover
All the men just call him Sir.

And it's bad, bad Leroy Brown
The baddest man in the whole damned town,
Badder than old King Kong
And meaner than a junkyard dog.

Now Leroy he's a gambler
And he likes his fancy clothes
And he likes to wave his diamond rings
In front of everybody's nose.

He's got a custom Continental
He's got an Eldorado too
He's got a 32 gun in his pocket for fun
He's got a razor in his shoe.

And it's bad, bad Leroy Brown
The baddest man in the whole damned town,
Badder than old King Kong
And meaner than a junkyard dog.

Now Friday 'bout a week ago
Leroy shootin' dice
And at the edge of the bar
Sat a girl named Doris
And ooh that girl looked nice.

Well he cast his eyes upon her
And the trouble soon began
'Cause Leroy Brown, he learned a lesson
'Bout messin' with the wife of a jealous man.

And it's bad, bad Leroy Brown
The baddest man in the whole damned town,
Badder than old King Kong
And meaner than a junkyard dog

Well the two men took to fighting
And when they pulled them off the floor
Leroy looked like a jigsaw puzzle

With a couple of pieces gone.

And it's bad, bad Leroy Brown
The baddest man in the whole damned town,
Badder than old King Kong
And meaner than a junkyard dog.

And it's bad, bad Leroy Brown
The baddest man in the whole damned town,
Badder than old King Kong
And meaner than a junkyard dog,
Yeah, badder than old King Kong
And meaner than a junkyard dog.

Jim Croce

"Operator"

Story by Ingrid Croce

Written and Recorded by Jim Croce

In 1963 Jim Croce was a clean-cut sophomore at Villanova University with a double major in psychology and modern languages. He knew over 2,000 songs that he played as a solo artist at college concerts, coffee houses and East Coast society engagements.

In addition to performing, Jim worked at the college radio station, doing a three-hour folk and blues show. He interviewed great artists like Mississippi John Hurt and Son House. Hearing this music reminded Jim of the traditional jazz and blues his father played on their old phonograph, which was seldom without a stack of Turk Murphy, Fats Waller, Bessie Smith, or Eddie Lang and Joe Venuti records.

That December I was just 16 and making the transformation from a cartwheeling cheerleader at Springfield High into a Joan Baez inspired folkie. Jim Croce was judging a folk contest I was in at Convention Hall in Philadelphia with my group "The Rumrunners" and he picked me!

After the concert, Jim asked me to perform with him and we became a duo. Our relationship grew from our love of music and an undeniable attraction we had for each other from the start.

While at Villanova, Jim had joined the Army National Guard and had waited for over two years to be called to take his basic training. Just days before our wedding on August 26, 1966 Jim finally received his orders to report for duty. Though we were madly in love and couldn't wait to move in together, sadly, 5 days after our honeymoon, Jim got his head shaved, his boots polished and gave me a teary-eyed kiss goodbye at the Pennsylvania Station. He was on his way to Boot Camp at Fort Jackson, South Carolina.

Jim wrote me wonderful love letters every day. He also wrote about his strong distaste for authority and drew pictures of his Sergeants, posting them around the barracks with quotes that said things like, "Half the army reads comic books and the other half just look at the pictures." This type of "rebelliousness" led to the necessity of Jim having to repeat basic training twice. But, as always, Jim's discontent fueled his humor and he found his wit and musical talent could be used in his favor.

At every opportunity, Jim practiced his guitar and entertained his fellow soldiers. When his superiors heard Jim's music they excused his transgressions and asked Jim to perform for them at the Officers Club. It was at Fort Jackson that Jim really started to get a lot of new ideas for his songs.

As Jim used to explain at his shows, "I got the idea for writing 'Operator' by standing outside the PX, waiting to use one of the outdoor phones. There wasn't a phone booth. It was just stuck up on the side of the building and there were about 200 guys in each line waiting to make a phone call back home, to see if their 'Dear John' letters were true. And with their raincoats over their heads, covering the telephone and everything, it really seemed surreal that so many people were going through the same experience, going through the same kind of change, and to see it happen especially on something like a telephone, talking to a long distance operator just registered...

When I got out of the Army, I was working at a bar where there was a telephone directly behind where I was playing. I couldn't help be disturbed by it all the time, and I noticed that the same kinda thing was happening, people checkin' up on somebody or finding out what was goin' on, but always talkin' to the operator, and I decided I would write a song about it."

"Operator"

Operator, oh could you help me place this call?
You see the number on the matchbook is old and faded.
She's livin' in L.A.
With my best old ex-friend Ray,
A guy she said she knew well and sometimes hated.

Isn't that the way they say it goes?
But let's forget all that
And give me the number if you can find it
So I can call just to tell them I'm fine and to show
I've overcome the blow.
I've learned to take it well
I only wish my words could just convince myself
That it just wasn't real,
But that's not the way it feels.

Operator, oh could you help me place this call,
'Cause I can't read the number that you just gave me?
There's something in my eyes,
You know it happens every time
I think about the love that I thought would save me.

Isn't that the way they say it goes?

But let's forget all that
And give me the number if you can find it
So I can call just to tell them I'm fine and to show
I've overcome the blow.
I've learned to take it well,
I only wish my words could just convince myself
That it just wasn't real
But that's not the way it feels.

Operator, oh let's forget about this call.
There's no one there I really wanted to talk to.
Thank you for your time,
Oh you've been so much more than kind
And you can keep the dime.

Isn't that the way they say it goes?
But let's forget all that
And give me the number if you can find it
So I can call just to tell them I'm fine and to show
I've overcome the blow.
I've learned to take it well
I only wish my words could just convince myself
That it just wasn't real,
But that's not the way it feels.

Hal David

"What The World Needs Now Is Love"

Written by Hal David and Burt Bacharach
Recorded by Jackie DeShannon

I was living in Roslyn, New York, on the north shore of Long Island, which is where my children were raised. I would drive into Manhattan every day to meet Burt (Bacharach) at the Brill Building in Famous Music's offices on the sixth floor, where we did our writing. Mine was a rock and roll house where each of my kids had a band that practiced there. It was hard for me to find somewhere quiet to work so I would drive into town slowly, which would give me the opportunity to think and get ideas. I would write in my head during the ride.

One day, I thought of the first two lines of this song:

What the world needs now is love, sweet love
It's the only thing that there's just too little of.

Before I got to Manhattan I had the rest of the chorus set the way it is today. Then I needed the verse section. When I began to write the first verse, everything I thought about just seemed off: *We don't need a plane to fly faster, we don't need a submarine to go deeper.…* I tried and tried, showed it to Burt, then put it away and went on to something else.

In a month or two or three, I tried again. It was always the same thing. I needed something to compare it to and everything I thought about had nothing to do with the person I was talking to—God. It took more time to write these lyrics than any other. I realized that I needed to write the antithesis—what we didn't need. One day on the ride to New York, it came to me.

> *Lord, we don't need another mountain,*
> *There are mountains and hillsides enough to climb,*
> *There are oceans and rivers enough to cross,*
> *Enough to last till the end of time.*

I knew that was it. I wrote about all of the things that had to do with nature and what God gives us. I gave the lyrics to Burt and he wrote a fabulous melody.

There were three ways Burt and I wrote together. He'd have melody ideas; I'd have lyric ideas. We'd show each other what we had, pick out what we both liked and work on it together. Sometimes we'd be writing three songs at once. Sometimes I'd take the melody home and write lyrics to it, sometimes Burt would take the lyrics home and write the melody to them.

We showed the song to Dionne Warwick, who had recorded many of our songs, and it is the only song of ours that she ever turned down. We put it aside and then received a call from Liberty Records to meet with Jackie DeShannon. We played this song for her and she wanted to do it. Burt did a great arrangement and we recorded it.

"What The World Needs Now Is Love"

What the world needs now is love, sweet love
It's the only thing that there's just too little of
What the world needs now is love, sweet love,
No not just for some but for everyone.

Lord, we don't need another mountain,
There are mountains and hillsides enough to climb
There are oceans and rivers enough to cross,
Enough to last till the end of time.

What the world needs now is love, sweet love
It's the only thing that there's just too little of
What the world needs now is love, sweet love,
No, not just for some but for everyone.

Lord, we don't need another meadow
There are cornfields and wheat fields enough to grow
There are sunbeams and moonbeams enough to shine
Oh listen, lord, if you want to know.

What the world needs now is love, sweet love
It's the only thing that there's just too little of
What the world needs now is love, sweet love,
No, not just for some but for everyone.

No, not just for some, oh, but just for everyone.

Taylor Dayne

"Beautiful"

Written by Taylor Dayne and Hitesh Ceon
Recorded by Taylor Dayne

was recording a lot in Europe at the time, which was around 2007. I was heading back to Sweden through Austria. I'd been working with some of the large number of incredible pop songwriters in Stockholm. It was mid-December and 3 below zero and it got dark very early there.

I was looking for a dance, up tempo track and had received several but when I heard Hitesh Ceon's music, I knew that was it. Although it was a mid-tempo track, it starts with the most lush string instrumental. It reminded me of some of the classic music sound-tracks from when I was a kid, like Disney movies or *Star Trek*. Then it goes into a great drum and percussion section. I wanted to write to this track.

Two days before leaving Los Angeles for Europe, I went to see some friends from E! Television at a party they were giving at Avalon. I was sitting at a table in this large club, with a bunch of my girlfriends, and saw a guy walking around. I said, "God, that's the guy for me." I told my friends how cute I thought he was. I could only see him from a distance, but it seemed as if he was working there, he seemed very authoritative.

I continued talking to the other girls and felt someone behind me. It was *the* guy, whom I heard say, "Taylor!" with a great deal of familiarity. The minute I turned around and saw him close up, I realized that I knew him. I hadn't seen him in about four years. We had a hot and heavy moment back then. He touched my arm and the minute he did, there was electricity. He moved me. I wanted to stop my life and be in his world. It was his birthday and, in fact, he was the manager of the club. He wanted to get together after he closed and asked for my number.

I left and he went into the parking lot to look for me. He remembered my car and found me there. He looked in the window and asked what was in the back seat. Two car seats—for my twins. That's a long story. I wasn't married, I used a surrogate. Let that suffice.

I never heard from him. I've seen him a bunch of times since then—in passing.

So, when I got into the studio in Stockholm, just days later, I wrote this song completely, utterly inspired by him. It's about the rush of meeting, knowing, feeling and going for it.

The song became my seventeenth Top 10 record and hit #1 on Billboard's dance charts.

"Beautiful"

Heeeey, yeahhh
Uhhmmm, Uhmmm
heeyyy
Oooh oooh oooh aah
What I say, what I say
Unh unh, yeeeah
Oooh oooh oooh aah aah aah

Yeahh
I just live for your love
The warmth of your embrace
I can't get enough.
Baby now I gotta need for your touch,
So much
I look into your eyes
I feel hypnotized, baby by you.
Darlin' you're beautiful
You give what you got
And you got a lot, baby you do.
Darling it's true 'cause
You makin' me so hot
I don't wanna stop.
It's not a fairytale the things you say
The things that you do.
Ohh
Baby you're beautiful
So give me what you got
'Cause you got a lot, baby you do.
Darling you're beautiful
So give me all you got
Don't you ever stop.
I just work for your love,
This hold that's over me
There's no better drug.
So baby I can't find the right words
To explain what it feels like to be me
When you say my name.

Baby I do what I have to because
You takin' me so high that I kiss the sky.
Baby it's true, darling I knew 'cause
You give me butterflies,
Make me wanna cry, feels so high, can't describe

This feelin' inside.
Baby you're beautiful
So give me what you got
'Cause you got a lot, baby you do.
Darling you're beautiful
So give me all you got
Don't you ever stop.
I can't explain the way I feel.
You are the answer to my dreams,
My every love inside.
I see that I was blind,
There's nothin' but blue blue skies.
(Baby you're beautiful)
So give me what you got
'Cause you got a lot, baby you do.
Darling you're beautiful
So give me all you got
Don't you ever stop.
(Beautiful Baby)
Baby you're beautiful
(Beautiful Baby)
So give me what you got
'Cause you got a lot, baby you do
(Ohh baby)
Darling you're beautiful
So give me all you got
(Give to me)
Don't you ever stop.
Baby you're beautiful
(What I say, what I say)
So give me what you got
'Cause you got a lot, baby you do.
(Don't ever stop, don't ever stop)
Darling you're beautiful

So give me all you got,
Don't you ever stop.

Howie Dorough

"What Makes You Different (Makes You Beautiful)"

Written by Howie Dorough, Andreas Carlsson, and Steve Diamond
Recorded by Backstreet Boys

I was living in Florida at the time, between relationships, and ran into a girl I'd known from church when I was growing up. I used to see her at Sunday mass all the time. I had a semi-crush on her when I was about 12 and we did a musical together, *Fame*. She was a dancer and I had one of the leads. I was too young for her. We went to confirmation classes together and then she went off to a Catholic high school. She always had jock boyfriends, which was also intimidating.

Over the years, we would see each other on holidays at church. She had a brother who was a little younger than I and one time when I saw him, he told me that she might be getting married, but he didn't think she was in love with the guy. He also told me that she had a secret crush on me. So, I intentionally tried to bump into her.

I went to the school where she taught. This was at the peak of our (Backstreet Boys) fame, so the kids were very excited when I showed up. She and I had a couple of dates after that.

She was not like the other girls I had been dating. Most of them were international, from Germany, Canada and other places. Most of them were along for the ride or to travel with us on the road, but didn't have much substance. I was finally getting over that. I realized that it was more about finding someone with a good heart rather than another trophy girl. She was even more than I thought she would be when I was younger. The words to the song came very naturally when I thought about her.

What makes you different
Makes you beautiful
What's there inside you
Shines through to me.
In your eyes I see
All the love I'll ever need.
What makes you different makes you beautiful to me.

She went from being a cheerleader in school, who could have had anyone or anything she wanted, to choosing to give back and help kids. She had a good head on her shoulders and was trying to make more of life than just a big party. I was at a point in my life when I wanted beauty that wasn't just skin deep.

You don't run with the crowd
You go your own way
You don't play after dark
You light up my day
Got your own kind of style
That set you apart
Baby that's why you capture my heart.

I was writing with Steve Diamond, a Nashville songwriter, a lot at the time. He had a great melody and this girl was definitely the inspiration for the lyrics. When I brought the song to the group, they all liked it. Brian (Littrell) suggested that we offer it to the Special Olympics, but nothing ever came of that. However, in 2008 or so, I was on tour in Canada, and I was in my bedroom at the hotel watching Jay Leno on television, and reading, and I heard this song playing on television. It was being used for a commercial for an organization creating awareness for autism. The scene was a high school prom and the previous year's prom queen was announcing the new queen. A girl with autism comes up to the stage to applause, to be crowned the new homecoming queen and the song comes on. It was a special moment for me.

"What Makes You Different (Makes You Beautiful)"

You don't run with the crowd
You go your own way,
You don't play after dark
You light up my day,
Got your own kind of style
That set you apart.
Baby, that's why you capture my heart.

I know sometimes you feel
Like you don't fit in
And this world doesn't know
What you have within.
When I look at you
I see something rare.
A rose can grow anywhere
And there's no one I know that can compare.

What makes you different

Makes you beautiful,
What's there inside you
Shines through to me.
In your eyes I see
All the love I'll ever need.
What makes you different makes you beautiful to me.

You've got something so real,
You touch me so deep
The material things
Don't matter to me.
So come as you are
You've got nothing to prove,
You won me with all that you do
And I want to take this chance to say to you

What makes you different
Makes you beautiful.
What's there inside you
Shines through to me.
In your eyes I see
All the love I'll ever need.
What makes you different makes you beautiful to me.

You don't know how you've touched my life.
Oh, there's so many ways I just can't describe.
You taught me what love is supposed to be,
It's all the little things that make you beautiful to me.

What makes you different
Makes you beautiful
What's there inside you
Shines through to me.
In your eyes I see
All the love I'll ever need.

What makes you different makes you beautiful to me.

Written by Howie Dorough, Andreas Carlsson, and Steve Diamond. ©2000 Zomba Enterprises / Universal Music—Z Tunes LLC, Real Diamonds Music, Grantsville Publishing, Ltd.

Lamont Dozier

"Stop! In The Name Of Love"

Written by Lamont Dozier, Brian Holland, Edward Holland, Jr.
Recorded by The Supremes

I was at a no-tell motel near the studio one night and someone who knew my girlfriend saw me there and told her. It must have been about 5:30 in the morning, because I remember the sun was coming up, and I heard her screaming outside the motel, "Come out of there!" She didn't know what room I was in, so she just stood out there hollering, watching people poke their heads out of their windows to see what was going on, hoping to find me. I stuck my head around the drapes to see where she was—and she saw me. She started running up the stairs, with a bat in her hands. When she started banging on the door, the girl I was with got out through the bathroom window and climbed down the fire escape. It was an escape alright. She was scared to death. She thought she was going to get killed.

I casually opened the door as if she woke me and said, "What's up?" I told her I had too much to drink, so I decided to stay there. We started arguing and, in the midst of it, she said, "Why don't you stop?" I was trying to be funny, so I said "Why don't you stop in the name of love?" She didn't think it was funny. I responded by saying, "Didn't you hear the cash register? That's a great title." She finally left and I just went to sleep.

The next morning when I went to the studio Brian was at the piano playing a hook. I told him I had the perfect title for it. We finished "Stop! In the Name Of Love" in a couple of days. Ca-ching! I definitely heard the cash register. From infidelity to #1.....

"Stop! In The Name Of Love"

Stop! in the name of love
Before you break my heart

Baby, baby
I'm aware of where you go
Each time you leave my door.
I watch you walk down the street
Knowing your other love you'll meet.
But this time before you run to her
Leaving me alone and hurt
(think it over) after I've been good to you ?
(think it over) after I've been sweet to you ?

Stop! in the name of love
Before you break my heart.
Stop! in the name of love
Before you break my heart.
Think it over,
Think it over.

I've known of your,
Your secluded nights
I've even seen her

Maybe once or twice.
But is her sweet expression
Worth more than my love and affection?
But this time before you leave my arms
And rush off to her charms
(think it over) haven't I been good to you ?   •
(think it over) haven't I been sweet to you ?

Stop! in the name of love
Before you break my heart.
Stop! in the name of love
Before you break my heart.
Think it over,
Think it over.

I've tried so hard, hard to be patient
Hoping you'd stop this infatuation,
But each time you are together
I'm so afraid I'll be losing you forever.

Stop! in the name of love
Before you break my heart.
Stop! in the name of love
Before you break my heart.
Stop! in the name of love
Before you break my heart.   .

Baby, think it over
Think it over, baby
Ooh, think it over baby...

Lamont Dozier

"Where Did Our Love Go"

Written by Lamont Dozier, Brian Holland, Edward Holland, Jr.
Recorded by The Supremes

I originally cut this track with the Marvelettes in mind. In fact, I cut it in Gladys Horton's key, the lead singer, which was much lower than Diana Ross'. At that time at Motown, the policy was that the songwriters had to pay for the tracks we cut if it didn't get recorded by one of their artists. It never entered my mind that the Marvelettes wouldn't like the song. I had the chorus and went to the office to talk with Gladys and played it for her. She said, "Oh, honey, we don't do stuff like that. And it's the worst thing I ever heard." She was adamant about it. I was shocked.

I knew I was in deep trouble if I didn't hurry and get someone to do the song because I wasn't about to pay for the track. I went through the Motown artist roster and went all the way to the bottom of the list and there were the Supremes, better known in those days as the "no hit Supremes." I told them it was tailor-made for them, knowing that they had nothing going on at the time and needed a song. Much to my surprise, they said no. Gladys (Horton of the Marvelettes) told them I was looking for someone to record it. I wasn't giving up. Brian (Holland), Eddie (Holland) and I finally persuaded them to do it, convincing them that it was their saving grace and they couldn't refuse it. We had already had Top 40 hits with Martha and the Vandellas but the Supremes hadn't had recordings of any significance yet.

They were so annoyed that they agreed to do it that, in the studio, they had a really bad attitude. Diana (Ross) said it was in the wrong key, that it was too low. (Of course it was—I wrote it in Gladys' key.) Since the track was already cut, she had to sing it in that key and she'd never sung that low before. It turned out that her bad attitude and the low key were exactly what the song needed! I'd worked out intricate background vocals but the girls refused to learn them. Finally I said, "Just sing 'Baby, baby, baby'." It worked to their advantage and worked perfectly.

They didn't necessarily agree. Diana and I were throwing obscenities back and forth and she went running to Berry (Gordy, Jr.) and told him I said something off color about him. He came down to the studio to see what was wrong and while he was there, he asked to hear the song. He thought it was really good but said that he didn't know if it was a hit, but that he thought it would be Top 10.

The song was released and flew up the charts to #1. From then on, one hit followed another. It was the first of 13 consecutive #1's we did on the Supremes. The next time the Hollands and I saw the girls was at the airport. They were getting off a plane with their Yorkshire terriers, in mink stoles. We started laughing. It was so funny to see them turn into stars overnight.

"Where Did Our Love Go"

Baby, baby
Baby don't leave me
Ooh, please don't leave me

All by myself.

I've got this burning, burning
Yearning feelin' inside me
Ooh, deep inside me
And it hurts so bad.

You came into my heart
So tenderly
With a burning love
That stings like a bee.

Now that I surrender
So helplessly
You now wanna leave
Ooh, you wanna leave me.

Ooh, baby, baby
Where did our love go?
Ooh, don't you want me,
Don't you want me no more?

Ooh, baby
Baby, baby
Where did our love go,
And all your promises
Of a love forever more?

I've got this burning, burning
Yearning feelin' inside me
Ooh, deep inside me
And it hurts so bad.

Before you won my heart
You were a perfect guy

But now that you got me
You wanna leave me behind.

Baby, baby, ooh baby
Baby, baby don't leave me,
Ooh, please don't leave me
All by myself.

Ooh, baby, baby
Where did our love go?

Melissa Etheridge

"Come To My Window"

Written and Recorded by Melissa Etheridge

*J*wrote most of this song in a hotel room, which is where I did a lot of my writing once I started touring a lot after my first album. The first three albums did fine. I was being played on radio and had a bit of a following. The hip hop beats were starting around 1990, the time of my third album, and I experimented musically with them. So for the fourth album, I was thinking of getting back to my soul—to the roots of rock and roll where I came from.

I was in a relationship at the time that was tumultuous. In my early twenties and thirties I made some poor choices and what you choose is what you get. I was struggling with fidelity, honesty and what it is that makes a relationship.

On the road as a "rock star" there's superficial attention and adulation thrown at you for a couple of hours—then you're alone in your room and it's lonely. I understand why some people turn to drugs.

I started writing in my room (I remember it was nice but can't remember where it was—Europe or America) after a show. I had a not so good phone call with my partner at the time and, out of loneliness, I sat on the phone silent:

> *I would dial the numbers*
> *Just to listen to your breath*

Because of all of the attention I was getting, I felt I needed to do something for someone else. I would sacrifice so many things, put myself through so much pain for this relationship:

> *You don't know how much I'd give*
> *Or how much I can take*
> *Just to reach you.*

The chorus is a metaphor meaning you can't come through the front door. I was telling her that we can't meet and talk in an adult fashion; we have to meet on the side and talk. And I always like a reference to the moon. It conjures up a cold, sweet image.

> *Come to my window*
> *Crawl inside, wait by the light*
> *Of the moon.*
> *Come to my window*
> *I'll be home soon.*

The last line means that I couldn't connect with her and I was longing to be home.

My friends were telling me I wasn't in a good place. They were saying, "Why are you putting up with that?" but I didn't care what they thought:

> *I don't care what they think*
> *I don't care what they say.*
> *What do they know about this*

Love anyway?

However, at the same time the album became a hit, I came out publicly. The gay community lifted me up and supported me. That bridge in the song was taken to an anthem level. It bypassed any meaning I ever put in the song and became part of a mass consciousness. It is still a huge moment when I perform it live.

I realized that I was willing to compromise my wants, wishes for someone else. The need was deeper than skin, it was in my blood. I needed to make a connection.

I need you in my blood
I am forsaking all the rest
Just to reach you

Much therapy later, I realized that the hole I felt was for me to fill, but much of our lives we try to have others do that for us. Originally, I was referring to the pain love brings when I used the metaphor "the blackness in my chest." That's where I feel my pain, where the heart chakra is. However, ten years later, in 2004 when I was diagnosed with breast cancer, my current partner asked when I last listened to my records. I couldn't remember so while I was undergoing chemotherapy, friends came over and we all listened to every album in the order in which they were released. We listened all the way through and it took about three days because we talked about the songs and each of our memories.

It hit me:

Nothing fills the blackness
That has seeped into my chest

I was sitting there with a huge scar on my chest where they literally removed the blackness from the cancer. I realized how powerful words are. As I craft songs, I have a responsibility. Words and music go beyond lyrics or thoughts—they go straight to the soul.

The cancer changed my life. It showed me the power of intention. We're all spiritual beings and there has to be a balance of the soul and the body. That is the journey I'm on now.

"Come To My Window"

Come to my window
Crawl inside, wait by the light
of the moon.
Come to my window
I'll be home soon.

I would dial the numbers
Just to listen to your breath,
I would stand inside my hell
And hold the hand of death.
You don't know how far I'd go
To ease this precious ache,
You don't know how much I'd give
Or how much I can take

Just to reach you
Just to reach you
Just to reach you.

Come to my window
Crawl inside, wait by the light
of the moon.
Come to my window
I'll be home soon.

Keeping my eyes open
I cannot afford to sleep
Giving away promises

I know that I can't keep.
Nothing fills the blackness
That has seeped into my chest,
I need you in my blood
I am forsaking all the rest

Just to reach you
Just to reach you
Oh to reach you.

Come to my window
Crawl inside, wait by the light
of the moon.
Come to my window
I'll be home soon.

I don't care what they think
I don't care what they say.
What do they know about this
love anyway?

Mick Fleetwood

"Tusk"

Written by Lindsey Buckingham
Recorded by Fleetwood Mac

"Tusk," the song, was actually born during Fleetwood Mac sound checks with Lindsey (Buckingham) playing the basic riff on stage on his guitar. He would work on it, playing it as we jammed.

Then we went into the studio and Lindsey brought out the riff and crafted the beginnings of a song. This was during the making of "Tusk," the album. Like things often happen in the studio, the song drifted off the radar and was put aside. Lindsey wasn't satisfied with where the song was going, so it was relegated to not being on the front line to be on the album.

We had a break during our recording and I went to Fleur du Cap in Bras, a fishing town in northern France. My father had just passed away and my mother was there with my sister.

A few days after I arrived, after a horrendous night with a brandy bottle, I was awakened one morning by what I came to realize was a brass band. I had a terrible hangover but gave up on sleep and went out onto the veranda to listen to the band and watch people following them as if they were the Pied Piper. The band walked around the perimeter of the town and every twenty minutes or so kids, men, women, people in wheelchairs, followed the band. That is when and where I got the crazy idea to get a brass band to play on Lindsey's song.

When I got back and went into the studio and told everyone my idea, they thought I was nuts. Lindsey, however, thought it was a cool idea. I immediately went to USC (University of Southern California) and spoke with Dr. Bartner, who was the head of the music program and the marching band. We played the song at a band meeting and asked them to come up with their own arrangement for their part, which they did. It became a very important experience for them.

There were nearly 200 kids in the USC Marching Band and we recorded them live to tape—in Dodger Stadium. It was an insane idea but we pulled it off! What's very nice is that it has become a multi-generational tradition that has made this song a staple in the USC Marching Band repertoire ever since. It is played at every game there. From time to time, I'll bang some drums with them during halftime. I keep meeting kids in school now who are still stoked about the song.

In the old days when we performed this song (which we still do) at large venues like the Forum in Los Angeles, we had the band march down the aisles, sometimes accompanied by the Trojans' horses.

More recently, Radiohead performed with the USC Marching Band on the Grammys telecast and they referenced Fleetwood Mac preceding them.

From that quirky morning in Normandie, the song lives on. It could never have seen the light of day otherwise. People react the way I imagined when I saw the people following the band when I was in Bras. My being suitably insane came off—I'm quietly happy about that.

"Tusk"

Why don't you ask him if he's going to stay?
Why don't you ask him if he's going away?
Why don't you tell me what's going on?
Why don't you tell me who's on the phone?
Why don't you ask him what's going on?
Why don't you ask him who's the latest on his throne?

Don't say that you love me!
Just tell me that you want me!
Tusk!
Just say that you love me!
Don't tell me that you...

Real savage like!

Tusk! Tusk! Tusk! Tusk!
Tusk! Tusk! Tusk! Tusk!
Tusk! Tusk! Tusk! Tusk!
Tusk! Tusk! Tusk! Tusk!
Tusk!

Written by Lindsey Buckingham. © Lindsey Buckingham

Sean Garrett

"Yeah!"

Written by Sean Garrett
Recorded by Usher featuring Lil Jon and Ludacris

This was my first big hit. I had just signed my publishing deal three months prior and, as a new writer, it was bizarre to have this opportunity. Usher was pretty much done with his album and I wanted to do a record for him so this was crazy.

L.A. Reid called to say, "You're supposed to be hot and I need a smash for Usher and you've only got a few days to do it." It was major pressure for me but I was very excited to be involved with such a big artist. I was a fan of both Usher and L.A. Reid and didn't know what I was going to do. Everyone was expecting big things from me and I didn't want to do a record for him like anything he'd already done. I wanted to give him something explosive and I was willing to win big or lose big.

I love Lil Jon beats and wanted to use them for Usher. We went to Lil Jon's lawyer and he thought I was trippin'. He said that Usher is an R&B artist and Lil Jon doesn't do R&B music.

We kept trying but everyone thought I was crazy and we couldn't get anywhere. Finally, a friend of mine who worked for him gave me ten of his tracks. The third track was exactly what I wanted. I worked on it all day, finished the song, recorded it and let my manager hear it.

He brought it to L.A. Reid, who thought it was pretty good but felt that the verses were crazy and he didn't like the hook or having Lil Jon on the chorus. It was actually me doing an interpolation of Lil Jon. I told him that having all of these elements was like a circus and it had never been done before. I wanted it to be more like a movie. L.A. asked me to tweak the words so he could get a better sense of what "Yeah, yeah, yeah" means. I did that and, although he still wasn't sure about the song, he let me cut it with Usher.

I went to Los Angeles and Usher didn't like it either at first. He said, "It's messin' up my whole plan. The first single is 'Burn' and this doesn't fit." I asked him to trust me and we cut it. His mom heard it and wasn't sure about it — but his little brother thought it was *crazy*! After Usher cut it and heard it back and heard his brother's reaction, he said this might be it.

Usher did an excellent job. Lil Jon came to the studio while we were recording and heard it for the first time. When he heard me doing a version of him on the record, he said, "Who can do me better than me?!" He wasn't happy doubling (copying) the extreme way I did his part, but finally he agreed to be featured.

I called Ludacris and put him on the record. The label still didn't want to go with it. It was during the Christmas holidays and everyone was on vacation. Luckily for me, the record got leaked to radio and it immediately got 200 spins, which is really amazing. By the time people came back from the holidays, it was chaotic — the record was flying and people were going crazy over it.

The record company sent out a cease and desist to radio anyway but they couldn't stop it. It was taking on a life of its own organically. It just exploded. It became one of the biggest records ever. It went to #1 in 42 countries and topped the charts here for 12 weeks.

Now, of course, everyone wants to take credit for the song's success but the reality is that if it hadn't been leaked, it never would have happened.

"Yeah!"

[Usher:]
Peace up! A Town Down!

[Lil Jon:]
Yeah, (Yeah!) OK!

(Usher! Usher! Usher! Usher!)

[Lil Jon:]
Lil Jon!

[Usher:]
Yeah, Yeah, Yeah! Yeah, Yeah! Yeaah!
Yeah, Yeah, Yeah! Yeah, Yeah! Yeaah!

[Usher:]
Up in the club with my homies, tryna get a li'l V-I, but keep it down on the low key, 'cause you know how it is.
I saw Shorty, she was checkin' up on me, from the game she was spittin' in my ear you would think that she knew me.
So we decided to chill.

Conversation got heavy, she had me feelin' like she's ready to blow!
(Watch Out! Oh! Watch Out!)
She's sayin', "Come get me! Come get me,"
So I got up and followed her to the floor, she said "Baby, let's go."

That's when I told her, I said,

[Usher:]
Yeah (yeah) Shorty got down low and said, "Come and get me"
Yeah (yeah) I got so caught up I forgot she told me
Yeah (yeah) Her and my girl used to be the best of homies
Yeah (yeah) Next thing I knew she was all up on me screamin'

Yeah, Yeah, Yeah! Yeah, Yeah! Yeaah!
Yeah, Yeah, Yeah! Yeah, Yeah! Yeaah!

[Usher:]
So she's all up in my head now, got me thinkin' that it might be
    a good idea to take her with me,
'Cause she's ready to leave (ready to leave)
But I gotta keep it real now, 'cause on a one to ten she's a certi-
    fied twenty, but that just ain't me. Hey.
Because I don't know if I take that chance, just where it's gonna
    lead,
But what I do know is the way she dance makes Shorty alright
    with me.
The way she (get low!)
I'm like yeah, just work that out for me.
She asked for one more dance and I'm
Like, yeah, "How the hell am I supposed to leave?"
And I said

Yeah (yeah) Shorty got down low and said, "Come and get me"
Yeah (yeah) I got so caught up I forgot she told me
Yeah (yeah) Her and my girl used to be the best of homies
Yeah (yeah) Next thing I knew she was all up on me screamin'

Yeah, Yeah, Yeah! Yeah, Yeah! Yeaah!
Yeah, Yeah, Yeah! Yeah, Yeah! Yeaah!

[Lil Jon:]
Hey, Luda!

[Ludacris:]
Watch out!
My outfit's ridiculous, in the club lookin' so conspicuous.
And Rowl! These women all on the prowl, if you hold the head
    steady I'm a milk the cow.
Forget about the game, I'm a spit the truth, I won't stop till I
    get 'em in their birthday suits.
So gimmie the rhythm and it'll be off with their clothes, then
    bend over to the front and touch your toes.
I left the Jag and I took the Rolls, if they ain't cutting then I put
    em on foot patrol.
How ya like me now, when my pinky's valued over three
    hundred thousand?
Let's drank, you the one to please. Ludacris, fill cups like
    double D's.
Me and Ush once more and we leave 'em dead, we want a lady
    in the street but a freak in the bed to say,

Yeah (yeah) Shorty got down low and said, "Come and get me"
Yeah (yeah) I got so caught up I forgot she told me
Yeah (yeah) Her and my girl used to be the best of homies
Yeah (yeah) Next thing I knew she was all up on me screamin'

Yeah, Yeah, Yeah! Yeah, Yeah! Yeaah!
Yeah, Yeah, Yeah! Yeah, Yeah! Yeaah!

[Ludacris:]
Take that and rewind it back, Lil Jon got the beat to make ya
    booty go (clap)
Take that and rewind it back, Usher got the voice to make ya
    booty go (clap)

Take that and rewind it back, Ludacris got the flow to make ya
    booty go (clap)
Take that and rewind it back, Lil Jon got the beat to make ya
    booty go (clap)

Written by Lil Jon, Sean Garrett, Patrick J. Que Smith, Ludacris, Robert McDowell, James Phillips, LaMarquis Jefferson. © SONGS OF TVT; CHRISTOPHER MATTHEW MUSIC, HITCO SOUTH; BASAJAMBA MUSIC; HITCO MUSIC; LUDACRIS MUSIC PUBLISHING INC; AIR CONTROL MUSIC; EMI APRIL MUSIC INC.; ME AND MARQ MUSIC; CHRISTOPHER GARRETT'S PUBLISHING.

Siedah Garrett

"Man In The Mirror"

Written by Siedah Garrett and Glen Ballard
Recorded by Michael Jackson

wo years before I walked into Glen Ballard's home studio, I
was in a writing session with John Beasley. He got a phone call
and I was rolling my eyes, waiting for him to return to our
writing session. I heard him say, "The man? What man? Oh, the man
in the mirror…" I thought it might be good for a song and wrote it
down and continued to seethe that he was still on the phone.

When Quincy Jones was working on Michael Jackson's album
Bad, he invited eight of us, songwriters, to his house. I was late and
when I walked in, he stopped everything to point out my tardiness.
Everyone was already seated and Quincy had begun to tell them that
he needed one more song for the record. He was looking for an up
tempo, kind of dance song like "Shake, Shake, Shake, Shake Your
Booty."

Glen and I were doing a lot of writing together and I went to his
house and told him what Quincy was looking for and he laughed. I

had a pencil, pad and my lyric book and he went to the keyboard and started playing chords. I was looking through my book and the phrase "man in the mirror" popped out at me. I started singing the beginning of the first verse and couldn't write fast enough. Writing the lyrics slowed me down, although I was writing like I was in a frenzied trance. By the end of that afternoon, we had a verse and a chorus. I knew this was an opportunity to say something important to the world because everyone would listen to Michael. I went home and finished the chorus and wrote another verse. That was Wednesday. On Thursday we knew we had it. On Friday we did a demo of the song. I couldn't wait until Monday to let Quincy hear it, so I called him and begged him to let me drop it off at his house over the weekend. I finally convinced him and went over there. I knocked on the front door and when he opened it, I saw twelve "suits" sitting there who looked extremely exasperated as if to say, "You are so interrupting us!" I handed Quincy the cassette and left quickly.

He called me two hours later and said it was the best song he'd heard in ten years. However, he went on to say that Michael had yet to record any songs he didn't write, but Quincy liked it so much that he said if Michael didn't record it, he would get someone else to use it.

A week or so later, he called to tell me that Michael really liked it (I heard whispering in the background) and that they will be recording it (I heard more whispering in the background) but that Michael said the bridge should be longer. I heard whispering in the background again and then he handed the phone to Michael. When he started talking, I was screaming in my head, "Oh my God! I'm speaking to Michael Jackson!!" but I kept a good cover and finished the conversation. I got what he was saying and I loved him, but I didn't want Michael to be a writer on the song, so I wrote six bridges for him to pick from and he found one he liked. The planets were in the right alignment, that's all I have to say.

We were in the studio and they were recording the choir with Andraé Crouch. By the third day they still hadn't finished. I was sitting on the other side of the room knitting or crocheting. Quincy had me go into the recording booth and Michael was there on one side in front of a mic stand and I was positioned facing him with my own mic. Again, my mind went to, "Oh my God—I'm doing a duet with him!" When I looked at the sheet music I realized that the lyrics were for "I Just Can't Stop Loving You" and were already noted with Michael / Siedah; Michael / Siedah.... Clearly this was not impromptu. As a result, I toured all over the world with him for the next year and a half.

I was also asked to sing in the choir for "Man In The Mirror." I also did all of the harmony with Michael. That's me above Michael singing the melody. I also sang harmony on the duet with Michael in that song. When it was finished, we listened to it over and over again and were surprised each time because we kept hearing new things.

The album was released very soon after the recording was finished. "Man In The Mirror" was the fifth single from that record and was released too late in the year to be considered for a Grammy but it's certainly been my most successful song to date.

"Man In The Mirror"

Gonna make a change for once in my life, It's gonna feel real good,
Gonna make a difference, Gonna make it right

As I, turn up the collar on, my favorite winter coat
This wind is blowing my mind
I see the kids in the street, with not enough to eat
Who am I to be blind, Pretending not to see their needs?

A summer's disregard, a broken bottle top and a one man's soul
They follow each other on the wind, ya' know
'Cause they've got nowhere to go, That's why I want you to
know...

I'm starting with the man in the mirror,

I'm asking him to change his ways
And no message could have been any clearer
If you wanna make the world a better place
Take a look at yourself, and then make a change.
Na-na-na, na-na-na, na-NAH, na-nah

I've been a victim of a selfish kind of love. It's time that I realize
there are some with no home, not a nickel to loan.
Could it be really me, pretending that they're not alone?
A willow deeply scarred, somebody's broken heart
And a washed-out dream (Washed-out dream)
They follow the pattern of the wind, ya' see
'Cause they've got no place to be, that's why I'm starting with
    me.

I'm starting with the man in the mirror (Who)
I'm asking him to change his ways (Who)
And no message could have been any clearer
If you wanna make the world a better place
Take a look at yourself, and then make a change.

I'm starting with the man in the mirror (Who)
I'm asking him to change his ways (Who)
And no message could have been any clearer
If you wanna make the world a better place
Take a look at yourself and then make that… Change.

I'm starting with the man in the mirror
(Man in the mirror—Oh, yeah)
I'm asking him to change his ways (Better change, Who-who)
No message could have been any clearer
(If you wanna make the world a better place)
(Take a look at yourself and then make a change)
(You've gotta get it right, while you got the time)
('Cause when you close your heart)

You can't close your, your mind
(Then you close your mind).

That man, that man, that man, that man
Starting with the man in the mirror
(Man in the mirror—oh, yeah)
That man, that man, that man, I'm asking him to change his
    ways
(Better change)
You know, that man
No message could have been any clearer,

(If you wanna make the world a better place)
(Take a look at yourself and then make that change)
Hoo, Hoo, Hoo, Hoo. Hoo
Na na na, na na na, na na, na nah (oh, Yeah)
Na-na-na, na-na-na, na-nah, na-nah.

Larry Gatlin

"All The Gold In California"

Written by Larry Gatlin
Recorded by Larry Gatlin & The Gatlin Brothers

My old friend Fred Foster at Monument Records in Nashville, a small independent record company, was the first one to give me a record deal. Kris Kristofferson and Dottie West introduced me to him. He discovered Roy Orbison, Dolly Parton, and Kris. Fred also became my producer and we had some hits — "Broken Lady," "I Don't Wanna Cry" and "Night Time Magic" were all #1 records. But we all knew that independent distributors weren't paying. I asked him if he would allow me to try to find a deal with a major label to get the Gatlin Brothers in the big time record business. He knew that I wouldn't throw him under the bus, and he very graciously gave me his permission.

So I went to California. I had a meeting with Jim Mazza at United Artists. My next meeting was with Mo Austin, an iconic figure at Warner Bros. On my way there, I was stuck in a terrible traffic jam—I remember I was coming from Sunset Boulevard on Highland Avenue and literally put my car in Park by the time I reached the Hollywood Bowl. It was 1979.

In front of me, as I nervously waited for the cars to move so I wouldn't be late for my next meeting, was a 1958 Mercury station wagon with Oklahoma license plates. It was filled with pots and pans, chairs, luggage, skinny kids hanging out of the windows. It looked like the *Beverly Hillbillies* meets the Joads from *The Grapes of Wrath*. All I could think was "Poor Okies!" Now don't take that the wrong way—my grandma was born on a reservation in Oklahoma—Okies are good people, hard workers and I am not saying it disparagingly at all, I say it with affection.

All I could think was that these people think they will come to California, be rich, become movie stars in the golden land of California and they'll find out very soon that "All the gold in California is in a bank in the middle of Beverly Hills in somebody else's name." I reached up on the visor and got the Hertz rental car receipt folder, grabbed a pen out of the saddle bag that I carried with me all the time back then, and wrote those two lines.

The light changed, I drove to my meeting in Burbank at Warner Bros. Mo was a gentleman, we visited for about an hour and I went back to my car in the parking lot of Warner Bros. and, in 8 minutes, wrote the song on that Hertz receipt and other scraps of paper I was able to find. It's kind of like "New York, New York"—"if you can make it there, you'll make it anywhere..." New York and California are for survivors.

The next morning I got in the airplane and flew to Houston where The Gatlin Brothers had a big concert with some folks you may have heard of—Willie Nelson and Charlie Daniels—at the Summit, a big concert venue then that is now the Joel Osteen church. I sang "All the Gold..." backstage to the Brothers and our guitar player, Steve Smith, and they all said, "That's the one!"

We went back to Nashville and signed with Bruce Lundvall at CBS Records. We recorded the song and six months later it was the #1 country song in the world. Is this a great country, or what?

P.S. We've sung that song all over the world, at the Grand Ole Opry, on *The Tonight Show*, at Carnegie Hall, but nothing is more important than singing it at school for Campbell Dale Spencer, my 3-year-old granddaughter, and her friends. And this morning my 8-year-old granddaughter showed me that she was a songwriting prodigy when we wrote, "Be careful what you pray for, your prayers just might come true." Ain't God good?!

"All The Gold In California"

All the gold in California
Is in a bank in the middle of Beverly Hills in somebody else's
    name
So if you're dreaming about California
It don't matter at all where you played before, California's a
    brand new game

Trying to be a hero, winding up a zero
Can scar a man forever, right down to your soul
Living on the spot light, can kill a man out right
Cause everything that glitters is not gold

And all the gold in California
Is in a bank in the middle of Beverly Hills in somebody else's
    name
So if you're dreaming about California
It don't matter at all where you played before, California's a
    brand new game

And all the gold in California
Is in a bank in the middle of Beverly Hills in somebody else's
    name
So if you're dreaming about California

It don't matter at all where you played before, California's a
brand new game

Macy Gray

"Sweet Baby"

Written by Macy Gray and Joe Solo
Recorded by Macy Gray

I wrote this when I was in love and none of my friends or family liked him. No one approved; no one thought he was good enough for me. I stayed with him anyway, but I was caught in the middle. It was hard to hear the negative comments people would make about him.

As a result, I spent all of my time with him. We were in a little world of our own and it's sweet when you have that and it makes a sweet love song, but there's a danger attached to it. When you're in it, you don't realize that you are alienating others. I was in a sea of denial.

I wrote this song after we had just had an argument about my being in the studio too late, and I had no one to talk to about it.

"Sweet Baby"

Many times I've been told that I should go,

But they don't know
What we got baby.
They may not see the love in you,
The love I do,
And I'll stay right here.

Ummm sweet, sweet baby,
Life is crazy
But there's one thang
I am sure of,
That I'm your lady
Always baby
And I love you now and ever.

Suga, wishes don't change what is real
Or how it feels
In the bad times
For whatever he is, he is mine all the time
And we get by with our true love.

Ummm sweet, sweet baby,
Life is crazy
But there's one thang
I am sure of,
That I'm your lady
Always baby
And I love you now and ever.

Ummm, sweet baby, life is crazy
But there's one thang
I am sure of,
See, I'm your lady
Always baby
And I love you now and ever.

Baby would I ever find, my sweet
Just a true love, my sweet
That we come this far together.
Baby, so I'm here to stay
'Cause without you baby
I can't go any further.

Ummm sweet baby
Life is crazy
But there's one thang
I am sure of.
See, I, I'm your lady
Always baby baby.
Mah mah ever
It's not that ever
Mah mah ever
It's not that ever
Mah mah sweet sweet baby,
Life is so sweet with you,
Sweet with you.

Daryl Hall

"Sara Smile"

Written by Daryl Hall
Recorded by Daryl Hall & John Oates

All of my songs are either autobiographical or sometimes I'll take bits of experiences or observations and put them together. This is one of the songs that is completely autobiographical.

I had a long relationship with Sara Allen and her family. I lived with Sara for 28 years. At the time I wrote this, we were living in a small apartment in New York City. We had no money, so John was living in the same apartment. This was at the beginning of my career with John (Oates) as Daryl Hall & John Oates.

I was on the road and inevitably, when I am on tour and writing, I tend to write about not wanting to be on the road. This is more than a love song. I like to call it a love postcard to Sara. It was like, "Having a shitty time on the road and missing you."

It's a very succinct and short lyric, but each phrase meant something to me—and still does.

The song is about living our lives together, yet individually. It's about the essence of a relationship, and at the end of the day:

And when you feel you can't go on
I'll come and hold you
It's you and me forever

The song became the third single from our first album on RCA, "Daryl Hall & John Oates" in 1975. Its success came out of the blue. Our first two singles weren't terribly successful so this was our first bona fide hit.

The record got a lot of R&B airplay, beginning on a station in Ohio and spreading throughout the country. It was a big radio hit. I was most surprised when I heard it on pop radio once it crossed over, since it didn't sound like anything else being played on pop radio at the time. That attests to its permanence.

It's a heartfelt story. It's the real thing. Time has passed and I'm not with Sara anymore and I feel badly knowing that when "Sara Smile" comes on in the supermarket, Sara has to run out of the store. Songs remain but relationships change.

"Sara Smile"

Baby hair with a woman's eyes
I can feel you watching in the night
All alone with me and
we're waiting for the sunlight.
When I feel cold you warm me
When I feel I can't go on
you come and hold me,
It's you and me forever.

Sara smile,
Won't you smile a while for me, Sara?

If you feel like leaving
you know you can go
But why don't you stay until tomorrow?
And if you want to be free
you know all you have to do is say so.
When you feel cold I'll warm you
And when you feel you can't go on
I'll come and hold you
It's you and me forever.

Sara smile,
Won't you smile a while for me, Sara?
Sara smile,
Oh won't you smile a while, Sara?

Smile,
Oh won't you smile a while, Sara?

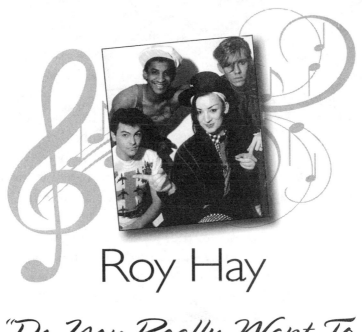

Roy Hay

"Do You Really Want To Hurt Me"

Written by M. Craig, Jon Moss, Roy Hay, George O'Dowd
Recorded by Culture Club

I was the keyboard player and guitarist for Culture Club and we had just been signed to Virgin Records. It was 1982 and "Do You Really Want To Hurt Me" was the second song we were writing for our first album. We were already a hip young band in London with that underground sound like Adam and the Ants, the Thompson Twins and Spandau Ballet. (Boy) George, of course, was big in the club scene because he was so flamboyant.

We had a big following, but we had no recording experience or success. We were in a rehearsal studio in London and made a conscious choice to try to write what *we* wanted to record, more melodic tunes, not just a "hip" sound. There's something special about the early days of a band. You do what you want and don't care because you have nothing to lose. There's usually plenty for a band to write about for the first two CDs, then there's angst that makes it difficult to have fresh ideas. We weren't thinking about writing a hit, that's the kiss of death for bands. We wanted to write what we liked and believed in.

All of the songs on our first two albums were inspired by the love affair that George was having with the drummer. When we wrote, we were like the kids from *Fame*—one person starts, then another. I started playing the chords on a Fender Rhodes and then added the rhythm box programming. It sounded good to me at the time. The bass player was a Jamaican who brought pre-programmed beats with a slow reggae groove into the band. The bass line unites the track. George started singing the melody. The song was written in 20 minutes. George went away and worked on it a little more.

It's not a conventional song since it has no real chorus. It has a long, drawn out, almost a capella, intro. George sounded like Smokey Robinson when he sang it; he had a tenor alto voice then.

We didn't consider this song a single. We already had two singles out. We were playing for about 2,000 people one night in a club and a reviewer picked up on this song and gave it attention. The head of Virgin Records then put it out. That afternoon, Radio 2 DJ in England, who largely appealed to housewives, started playing the song. We hadn't had any radio success yet, and this wasn't our audience at all, but suddenly we were popular with them and the song went to #37 on the charts.

The big television show in England for an artist to be on at the time was *Top of the Pops*. We were at the top of the waiting list to appear on the show but there was no opening. Shaky Stevens, who was like Elvis in the UK in the '80s, was scheduled to perform on the show but got the flu. When the slot opened, we were booked to go on the next day. Boy George's performance was definitely controversial, but the song went from #37 to #17 to #1 in three weeks. It was a life-changing event. But for this one fluke, it may not have happened for us. We thanked Shaky later.

Almost immediately, we doubled the size of our live audiences. In a very short time, I went from being an average guy doing music, to traveling the world. The song soon became #1 worldwide.

We were initially worried about George's image in the U.S., so we released the record in a plain white cover. With no identification or photo, Black radio thought we were a band from Jamaica and we got a lot of airplay. Once our video was released on MTV, everything changed.

We had a very successful career for a couple of years and had lots of fun. In 1999-2000 we did a reunion tour and the crowd still went mad every time we played the intro to this song. It is our musical legacy. That is the insanity and glory of this business.

There have been lots of interpretations of the lyrics. In an interview once, George was asked if it was a gay S&M (sadomasochistic) song. A TV show we did in Holland built a set that was a dentist's office and tried to put George in the chair to sing it. He threw a hissy fit and, rightfully, refused to do it. Reba McEntire has recorded it and Wyclef Jean has said it's his favorite song.

"Do You Really Want To Hurt Me"

Give me time to realize my crime
Let me love and steal
I have danced inside your eyes.
How can I be real?

Do you really want to hurt me?
Do you really want to make me cry?
Precious kisses, words that burn me
Lovers never ask you why.

In my heart the fire's burnin'
Choose my colour, find a star
Precious people always tell me
That's a step, a step too far.

Do you really want to hurt me?
Do you really want to make me cry?
Do you really want to hurt me?

Do you really want to make me cry?

Words are few, I have spoken
I could waste a thousand years
Wrapped in sorrow, words are token
Come inside and catch my tears.

You've been talkin', but believe me
If it's true you do not know
This boy loves without a reason
I'm prepared to let you go.

If it's love you want from me
Then take it away
Everything is not what you see
It's over again.

Do you really want to hurt me?
Do you really want to make me cry?
Do you really want to hurt me?
Do you really want to make me cry?

Do you really want to hurt me?
Do you really want to make me cry?
Do you really want to hurt me?
Do you really want to make me cry?

Do you really want to hurt me?
Do you really want to make me cry?

Warren Haynes

"Soulshine"

Written by Warren Haynes
Recorded by The Allman Brothers Band

I had just moved to Nashville and was going through a rough patch financially and trying to adjust to a new environment. I had not made lots of friends there yet and was in the midst of serious life changes, which happens when you make a leap like that. Everyone gets that way sometimes and has to get through it.

This is the only time I can remember that I wrote a song like this. I got the idea while I was driving my blue Datsun station wagon that I paid $750 for, which is all I could afford at the time. I didn't have a pen or paper or my guitar, so I kept singing the parts over and over so I didn't forget them. I was only about 15 minutes from home, so I turned around and went back so I could get it on tape or write it down before I forgot it. I kept singing until I got there and wrote it down. I then pulled out my guitar and started playing it in B flat, which is how I heard it in my head. I had written most of it before I got there.

I had a demo session not too long after and I was torn between an R&B version and a reggae version. I recorded both in the studio and decided on the more traditional R&B approach, which is the one people are most familiar with. It's the one that the Allman Brothers and then Gov't Mule recorded. It wasn't until about 20 years later that Phil Lesh of the Grateful Dead recorded the reggae version, which brought it all full circle, which was really nice.

The song isn't really about my dad but references him and our strong relationship. He is a huge part of my life, a huge inspiration and a great role model. It's rare to be able to have the opportunity to express that. I thought it was too simple because it came too easily, but when I tried to change it or complicate it, it seemed too contrived, so the final version is the one I wrote in the car. Some songs are better off left alone. Instead of a blues approach about how I felt, I wrote for a universal appeal. However, the more I distanced myself from it, the more I realized how personal it was.

"Soulshine"

When you can't find the light,
That got you through a cloudy day,
When the stars ain't shinin' bright,
You feel like you've lost you're way,
When those candle lights of home,
Burn so very far away,
Now you got to let your soul shine,
Just like my daddy used to say.

He used to say soulshine,
It's better than sunshine,
It's better than moonshine,
Damn sure better than rain.
Yeah now people don't mind,
We all get this way sometime,

Got to let your soul shine, shine till the break of day.

I grew up thinkin' that I had it made,
Gonna make it on my own.
Life can take the strongest man,
Make him feel so alone.
Now sometimes I feel a cold wind
Blowin' through my achin' bones,
I think back to what my daddy said,
He said "Boy, in the darkness before the dawn:"

Let your soul shine,
It's better than sunshine,
It's better than moonshine,
Damn sure better than rain.
Yeah now people don't mind,
We all get this way sometimes,
Gotta let your soul shine, shine till the break of day.

Sometimes a man can feel this emptiness,
Like a woman has robbed him of his very soul.
A woman too, God knows, she can feel like this.
And when your world seems cold, you got to let your spirit
    take control.

Let your soul shine,
It's better than sunshine,
It's better than moonshine,
Damn sure better than rain.
Lord now people don't mind,
We all get this way sometimes,
Gotta let your soul shine, shine till the break of day.

Oh, it's better than sunshine,
It's better than moonshine,

Damn sure better than rain.
Yeah now people don't mind,
We all get this way sometimes,
Gotta let your soul shine, shine till the break of day.

Howard Hewett

"Say Amen"

Written by Howard Hewett and Monty Seward
Recorded by Howard Hewett

I'm asked so many times, what my inspiration was for the song "Say Amen." I guess the curiosity stems from the fact that, through the years, this song has affected so many lives. I've had people come and tell me how "Say Amen" saved their life or how the song helped them through a most difficult time or how it simply brought them closer to an understanding or relationship with God. I know that even in my life, with the trials and obstacles that come every day living this adventure we call "Life," the words of "Say Amen" have echoed thru my mind at the perfect time to ease a pain or help me through indecisions and difficulties.

When I wrote the lyrics, it was at a time in my life when I needed to be basic with God…no frills…no bells or whistles…just clear… complete. The hook simply says:

I want to thank you God

for giving me one more chance
to raise my voice and to sing your praise
I sing it out loud
I sing it all day
This song is my prayer I give to only you
I know it can't compare to the gift from you
You gave me Your love
You gave me Your Son
And now I say Amen

It's a simple Praise song. One written to express or suggest an uncomplicated path to God's grace, His mercy. We don't need the fanfare or to stand on all the religious ceremony. We must simply state our case to our Heavenly Father with respect, reverence, and simply "Say Amen."

"Say Amen"

It's time to say goodbye for now;
We'll have our second time around
But before you go
There's something I'd like to say.

Everything's not what it seems;
There's a stronger force behind the scenes
He's in our lives every day
He's right there when you call.

In Him is where my strength lies;
I'll lift my eyes beyond the skies
Only He can save my life
And only He can hear me cry.

I wanna thank you God

For givin' me one more chance
To raise my voice and to sing Your praise,
I sing it out loud, I sing it all day.

This song is my prayer
I give to only You
I know it can't compare to the gift from You
You Gave me Your love, You gave me Your son.

I know there's some who don't believe,
Sometimes it's very hard to see
Live this old life every day,
Some things don't go your way.

But to be without is not His will;
There's cattle on a thousand hills
And they're all Yours to claim
So claim them in His Holy name.

See, you don't have to beg or crawl,
He can see you standin' proud and tall.
He'll give His everlasting love
Just come to Him as you are.

I wanna thank you God
For givin' me one more chance
To raise my voice and to sing Your praise
I sing it out loud, oh, I sing it all day.

This song is my prayer
I give to only You
I know it can't compare to the gift from You.
You gave me Your love, You gave me Your son.

I wanna thank you God

For giving me one more chance
To raise my voice and to sing Your praise;
I sing it out loud, oh, I sing it all day.

This song is my prayer
I give to only You
I know it can't compare to the gift from You
You gave me Your love, You gave me Your son.

Now I say Amen
(I say Amen)
Ah...Father, Father, Father
Father
I say Amen.

Written by Howard Hewett and Monty Seward. © 1985 LaKiva Music

Tom Higgenson

"Hey There Delilah"

Written by Tom Higgenson
Recorded by Plain White T's

The song was actually written in 2004, years before it got big on radio. I was hanging out with my friend Kim in Chicago, where we're from. She said that her friend Delilah wanted to hang out, which was fine with me. It was the last day before Delilah went back to school in New York. We picked her up and I was instantly smitten. It was like an angel walked into the room. She was gorgeous with a face you could stare at forever.

I was flirting with her all night. We (the Plain White T's) had just finished our first album, so I played some of our music for her in the car as we were driving. Delilah said she liked the CD so I gave her a copy. I told her I'd write a song for her on the next album and it became a running joke between us. We talked every day online, still flirting, and we joked back and forth when she continued to ask for *her* song. Eventually I said I really would write a song for her and kiddingly told her that it would be the one that would make us famous—and that she'd be my date for the Grammys. I knew she had a boyfriend so it was innocent flirtation and nothing happened, even though we both knew it would have if it had been up to me.

I was living with my mom in an apartment at the time. I was in my bedroom with an acoustic guitar and came up with the guitar riff that became the opening to "Hey There Delilah." It had a nice progression and I knew it could make a good song.

Since I didn't really know Delilah, I was trying to think what I could say to her after I had written the beginning of the lyrics:

> Hey there Delilah
> What's it like in New York City?
> I'm a thousand miles away
> But girl, tonight you look so pretty,
> Yes you do,
> Times Square can't shine as bright as you.

I knew I was onto something kind of special when I wrote:

> Don't you worry about the distance
> I'm right there if you get lonely
> Give this song another listen
> Close your eyes
> Listen to my voice, it's my disguise,
> I'm by your side.

I'd never gotten too poetic with lyrics before. I took my time over the next few months to make sure that every line was powerful and meant something. Writing about how I planned to pay the bills playing my guitar reflects my dreamy romantic nature.

> But just believe me, girl
> Someday I'll pay the bills with this guitar.
> We'll have it good
> We'll have the life we knew we would.

Since Delilah had two more years of school, and I knew she wasn't at all in love with me, I got a kick out of this:

If every simple song I wrote to you
Would take your breath away,
I'd write it all,
Even more in love with me you'd fall.

When I wrote the chorus, I thought it was a throwaway lyric and that I'd go back and re-do it. The more I played it, and as I was writing the rest of the song, the more I started thinking the chorus was sweet and that it worked. It turns out that it's the part that everyone sings along with.

Contact between Delilah and myself had become more sporadic. Before I finished the song, and before I'd told Delilah anything about it, the band started to tour and she came to a show in New York. She was wearing a white sweater and a big floppy hat like Audrey Hepburn and looked gorgeous.

I called Delilah when I got the first promo copy of the CD the song was on. We hadn't spoken in a few months but I wanted to tell her about it and get her a copy. I drove half an hour to her house to deliver it and was kind of nervous. At the house, we sat down in a sitting room surrounded by ceramic dolls. She didn't want to listen to the song with me there, so we had some small talk for about 20 minutes. It was very awkward. All I could say to her was, "I tried to write a song as beautiful as you are and wanted you to have one of the first copies." It turned out that she loved the song and came to a few more shows and wore an "I Am Delilah" T-shirt, which became a very popular item.

The CD came out in January on an indie label, Fearless Records. The song became an underground hit first on myspace.com and other places online. With its success, we were signed to Hollywood Records. We weren't initially sure about re-releasing the song on the new album because it was older, but the record company folks made us realize that it was good exposure to the mass market. As a bonus track, it became an immediate radio success. Delilah called me when she heard it at her gym. She got a real kick out of it.

It was #1 in ten countries including the U.S., for which we have a Billboard plaque, and it was nominated for two Grammys. During that time, I broke up with the girlfriend I had and Delilah and her boyfriend were broken up. Everything I'd foreseen came true—she actually would be my date for the Grammys. I got back with my girl-friend and she with her boyfriend before Awards night, but we still went to the show together and fulfilled the prophecy of the song.

"Hey There Delilah"

Hey there Delilah
What's it like in New York City?
I'm a thousand miles away
But girl, tonight you look so pretty,
Yes you do.
Times Square can't shine as bright as you
I swear it's true.

Hey there Delilah
Don't you worry about the distance
I'm right there if you get lonely.
Give this song another listen
Close your eyes
Listen to my voice, it's my disguise.
I'm by your side.

Oh it's what you do to me
Oh it's what you do to me
Oh it's what you do to me
Oh it's what you do to me,
What you do to me.

Hey there Delilah
I know times are getting hard
But just believe me, girl
Someday I'll pay the bills with this guitar.
We'll have it good,
We'll have the life we knew we would.
My word is good.

Hey there Delilah
I've got so much left to say.
If every simple song I wrote to you
Would take your breath away,
I'd write it all
Even more in love with me you'd fall,
We'd have it all.

Oh it's what you do to me
Oh it's what you do to me
Oh it's what you do to me
Oh it's what you do to me

A thousand miles seems pretty far
But they've got planes and trains and cars.
I'd walk to you if I had no other way
Our friends would all make fun of us
and we'll just laugh along because we know
That none of them have felt this way.
Delilah I can promise you
That by the time we get through
The world will never ever be the same
And you're to blame.

Hey there Delilah
You be good and don't you miss me
Two more years and you'll be done with school

And I'll be making history like I do.
You'll know it's all because of you.
We can do whatever we want to.
Hey there Delilah here's to you
This one's for you.

Oh it's what you do to me
Oh it's what you do to me
Oh it's what you do to me
Oh it's what you do to me
What you do to me.

Written by Tom Higgenson. © 2004 Warner Chappell

Mark Hoppus

"The Rock Show"

Written by Tom DeLonge, Mark Hoppus and Travis Barker
Recorded by Blink 182

Blink 182 had just had success with our album *Enema of the State*. It sold something like 10 million records all over the world. We became known as a silly, summertime-y, punk rock, punk punk band. We were getting ready to go into the studio and decided that we wanted to stretch our legs, grow, mature a bit as artists. We wanted to try something new.

About three weeks or a month later, we were writing and demo'ing and thought we finished the entire record and we were feeling good about it. Our manager came into the studio and we very proudly played it for him. His only comment was, "I don't hear any catchy, summertime-y Blink 182 songs." Tom (DeLonge) and I got really upset, although now we realize it was great.

I went home very angry. I went to the guest room, which was an office then, and I had decided I'd just lose everything from my head and write the catchiest, simple punk song. I was trying to think of the things that happen every summertime, like the Warped Tour, the first girlfriend of the summer, that evoke memories of summer for me. I approached it like an early Beach Boys song—a fun, catchy summertime tune. It turned into a great song, "The Rock Show." It was the first single from the CD and became a big hit for us. Tom went home and did the same thing. His result was "First Date," which was also a huge hit off the record.

There was a cool thing I learned from this—you have to get out of your own way. You have to always be who you are and grow naturally.

"The Rock Show"

Hanging out behind the club on the weekend
Acting stupid, getting drunk with my best friends.
I couldn't wait for the summer and the Warped Tour.
I remember it's the first time that I saw her—there.

She's getting kicked out of school 'cause she's failing.
I'm kinda nervous, 'cause I think all her friends hate me.
She's the one, she'll always be there.
She took my hand, and I admit it I swear

Because I fell in love with the girl at the rock show.
She said "What?" and I told her that I didn't know.
She's so cool, gonna sneak in through her window.
Everything's better when she's around.
I can't wait till her parents go out of town.
I fell in love with the girl at the rock show.

When we said we were gonna move to Vegas—
I remember the look her mother gave us.
17, without a purpose or direction
We don't owe anyone a fucking explanation.

I fell in love with the girl at the rock show.
She said "What?" and I told her that I didn't know.
She's so cool, gonna sneak in through her window.
Everything's better when she's around.
I can't wait till her parents go out of town.
I fell in love with the girl at the rock show.

Black and white picture of her on my wall
I waited for her call, she always kept me waiting.
And if I ever got another chance, I'd still ask her to dance
Because she kept me waiting.

I fell in love with the girl at the rock show.
She said "What?" and I told her that I didn't know.
She's so cool, gonna sneak in through her window.
Everything's better when she's around.
I can't wait till her parents go out of town.
I fell in love with the girl at the rock show.

With the girl at the rock show
With the girl at the rock show
(I'll never forget tonight)
With the girl at the rock show......

Janis Ian

"At Seventeen"

Written and Recorded by Janis Ian

I was 23 when I wrote "At Seventeen." I'd had to move back in with my mother because I couldn't afford to keep an apartment while I was on the road. I wasn't making much money, but I was career-building, opening for acts like Loggins and Messina and America. My previous album, *Star* (CBS Records), got critical acclaim but sold nothing. I didn't have a "career song" yet.

I've always thought that artists are outsiders by nature. One morning I was sitting at my mother's kitchen table reading a *New York Times Magazine* article entitled "I Learned the Truth At Eighteen," written by a former debutante. I'd been sitting with a guitar in my lap, playing that samba figure you hear at the beginning of the song, and I tried to work the first line in. "Eighteen" didn't scan, so it became "seventeen." The first lines came easily:

> *I learned the truth at seventeen*
> *That love was meant for beauty queens*

In the article, the girl said she thought that once she had her coming out ball, everything would be perfect—she'd have a boy who loved her, a white picket fence, 2.5 children. But once it was over, all she felt was *flat*. Instead of it being the beginning of the rest of her life, it was the end of her former life—and now she had to decide what came next.

> *And high school girls with clear skinned smiles*
> *Who married young and then retired*

Since I'd dropped out of school at 16, I had no such experience. I didn't go to a prom… but I knew what it was like to go to bed and wait for the magic moment when I'd wake up and be head-turning beautiful, and I knew what the morning let-down was like, when I woke, looked in the mirror, and realized you are what you are. I remembered that vividly as I wrote this song.

I wrote what came to me, then re-thought each line. I wondered if I could be this brutally honest. The alternative was a fluff piece that ended with the girl not caring what she looked like and meeting the man of her dreams. I couldn't do that. Instead, I followed with:

> *The valentines I never knew*
> *The Friday night charades of youth*
> *Were spent on one more beautiful*
> *At seventeen I learned the truth…*

It took three months to write this song. When I finished, I decided I was never going to play it for anyone—it was too humiliating. Still, one day I played it for my mom, who was a beautiful woman, and she wept! When I asked her why, she said, "Don't you understand, honey? That's *my* song!" What a revelation!

"At Seventeen" has taught me so much. It was a real learning curve. Even cheerleaders and captains of football teams have a hard time. And the beautiful girls have a whole different set of problems—I'd never thought about that! And I thought it was easy for guys because they were the ones who got to ask girls out for dates—what I didn't think about was the fact that they're also the ones who have to face the rejection when they're turned down and humiliated.

The song was only a hit in the United States but somehow it still endures. Now, when I tour in Japan or Europe, everyone seems to know it. It's used as a conversation topic, to bridge the gap between mothers and daughters and granddaughters. How incredible... as songwriters, we can only *dream* of writing a song that has that kind of universal impact.

"At Seventeen"

I learned the truth at seventeen
That love was meant for beauty queens
and high school girls with clear skinned smiles
who married young and then retired.
The valentines I never knew
The Friday night charades of youth
were spent on one more beautiful
At seventeen I learned the truth.

And those of us with ravaged faces
lacking in the social graces
desperately remained at home
inventing lovers on the phone
who called to say—come dance with me
and murmured vague obscenities.
It isn't all it seems at seventeen.

A brown eyed girl in hand me downs
whose name I never could pronounce
said—Pity please the ones who serve
They only get what they deserve.
The rich relationed hometown queen

marries into what she needs
with a guarantee of company
and haven for the elderly.

Remember those who win the game
lose the love they sought to gain
in debentures of quality and dubious integrity.
Their small-town eyes will gape at you
in dull surprise when payment due
exceeds accounts received at seventeen.

To those of us who knew the pain
of valentines that never came
and those whose names were never called
when choosing sides for basketball.
It was long ago and far away
The world was younger than today
when dreams were all they gave for free
to ugly duckling girls like me.

We all play the game, and when we dare
we cheat ourselves at solitaire
Inventing lovers on the phone
Repenting other lives unknown
that call and say—Come dance with me
and murmur vague obscenities
at ugly girls like me, at seventeen.

Enrique Iglesias

"Be With You"

Written by Enrique Iglesias, Paul Barry and Mark Taylor
Recorded by Enrique Iglesias

was in England finishing my first fully English speaking album, *Enrique*, recording in a studio on the outskirts of London. I was almost done with the album; this was the last song I wrote for it.

It was one of those times when everything was going so fast. Record companies were fighting to sign me, the record company I signed with wanted an album fast, there was lots of hype, it was very chaotic.

I was in my hotel room really late on a Monday night (really early Tuesday morning). I always listen to other people's music and get inspiration from them. I was listening to Tom Petty that night. Often I'd wish that I'd written a song like the one I was listening to.

I was thinking about someone I missed a lot and wished were there with me. This is autobiographical, as are most of my songs. If a story is real, the lyrics always come out a lot easier. I finished this song that night.

I never told the person I wrote it for that she was the subject. In fact, I've never told anyone I've written about them or that a song was inspired by them. That's probably why I write. It's a way to express myself whether I'm happy, angry, sad. However, I mostly write when I am sad or lonely, as I was the night I wrote this song. It seems that the sadder you are, the better the song.

I started writing when I was 14 or 15, which is a very tough age for anyone. It helped a lot. The same has carried over in my adult life. My writing has saved me a lot of money with psychologists in therapy!

The morning after I wrote "Be With You" I went to the studio and sang it for my producers—Mark Taylor (who co-wrote the music) and Brian Rawling. It got a great reaction. It has turned out to be my favorite song on the record.

"Be With You"

Monday night, and I feel so low,
I count the hours, but they go so slow.
I know the sound of your voice, can save my soul.
City lights, the streets are gold.
Looked down my window to the world below
Move so fast, but it feels so cold.
And I am all alone,
Don't let me die, I'm losing my mind,
Baby, just give me a sign.

And now that you're gone,
I just wanna be with you.
(Be with you)
And I can't go on,
I wanna be with you.

Wanna be with you…

I can't sleep, I'm up all night.
Through these tears, I try to smile.
I know, the touch of your hand, can save my life.
But don't let me down, come to me now,
I got to be with you some how.

And now that you're gone,
I just wanna be with you.
(Be with you)
And I can't go on,
I wanna be with you.
(Be with you)
Wanna be with you.

Don't let me down,
Come to me now.
I got to be with you some how.
And now that you're gone,
Who am I without you now?

I can't go on, I just wanna be with you.
And now that you're gone,
I just wanna be with you.
(Be with you)
And I can't go on,
I wanna be with you.
(Be with you)
Wanna be with you…

(Now that you're gone)
Just wanna be with you…
And I can't go on,
I wanna be with you.

Oh…
Just wanna be with you, just wanna be with you.

Iron Butterfly

Doug Ingle

"In-A-Gadda-Da-Vida"

Written by Douglas Ingle
Recorded by Iron Butterfly

In my youth, I lived in the Rocky Mountains where my father was a church pianist. I remember, when I was about 7, he played at two services a week in our hometown non-denominational community church. My mom, dad, sister, myself and our dog shared one bedroom in a house with no running water. We had a water well about the distance of two city blocks from our cottage. We would use a metal tub which was placed in the center of the living room for our family baths. We'd use two metal buckets to transport the water from the well to our place and then heat one bucket on our coal burner stove and then mix them accordingly. I'd always be the first to bathe because being the smallest person in the family I would draw less heat from the water. Every now and then, we'd get a big thrill and get a new snow sled or my grandpa would send an orange from California to put in our Christmas stocking.

My father has always been my main source for musical inspiration.

He graduated from Drake as a first string classical pianist and yet, in order to put food on the table, both he and my mother worked full time. We had an old (1908) Boston Everett, an upright acoustic piano, that my folks received as a wedding gift in 1936 from my mom's folks. Dad would play the piano a great deal of the time in the evenings. He would play Classical music, Church music, Boogie-Woogie, Post World War II standards, etc. To this day the Everett is still with me and, while it takes up a good deal of space in my music room, it also fills a big place in my heart.

The weather patterns in the Rockies played a big part in a child's play time options. During the winter months I would spend a good deal of my free time around the piano stretching an army blanket from the keyboard cover and over the piano bench to create my own tent. One of my first musical efforts was trying to emulate a thunder storm. When the thunder peals would roar, shortly after a crack of lightning, I would try to find it musically by holding down the sustain pedal while slamming both of my little hands upon the bass notes with every ounce of energy I could muster, followed with tinkering around on the high notes for simulated rain drops. While such an activity was a great adventure to this young mind, upon looking back I'm certain that it was also a great exercise in patience for the rest of the clan. When my dad would play the piano I would run and get a pencil and jump up on a chair and pretend that I was conducting my own symphony.

Another big inspiration for me was going to see Yma Sumac, a Peruvian singer, at the Red Rock Amphitheatre in Denver, Colorado. At the time, she had both the highest range of any woman and the lowest range of any man on the planet. There I was, on a beautiful evening under the stars, watching and listening to a Peruvian orchestra wearing costumes with so many great colors and such that I knew then and there that I wanted to be involved with music for the rest of my life. Thank you all...!!!

My folks had had enough of the rough living conditions in the mountains and wanted to make a new life for themselves and their children, so they began the long process of relocating to California.

My mother went first and stayed with her mother while she secured a job. Within six months, my sister and I found ourselves on a Southern Pacific train headed towards our new lives. My dad joined us about a year later after the property had been sold. Within eight days of my arrival I had already been hit by a car on the street where I lived. Other than the noticeable dent on the car's front fender, I think the car was fine. Speak of culture shock. I went from a tough little mountain boy to city slicker in less than three days. While I did enjoy the adventure of seeing California and the new states and deserts between, I was most definitely ready to go home within the first month. But it was not to be and to this day I have yet to visit my old home town of Evergreen, Colorado.

Like a lot of young people with musical aspirations, I found myself performing in a cover band during my high school years. The name of the band was "The Jeritones" named after the band leader's girlfriend, Jeri. We played a wide variety of music—our business card said "The Jeritones…We play Rock & Roll and Music." Band members Kerry Chater (the leader and bass player) went on to play bass for Gary Puckett and the Union Gap and Danny Weis (lead guitar) went on to play on the first Iron Butterfly album, *Heavy* and then on to the group Rhinoceros. He also played a starring role in Bette Midler's *The Rose*.

I moved to Los Angeles after finishing high school because I wanted to write motion picture themes like "Romeo and Juliet," "Exodus," "The Ten Commandments." Funny thing is, I didn't even know how to read music (still don't). But we can't let a little thing like that stop us!

I decided to form my own group at that time with Danny (Weis). We got paid quite well for our first efforts, come to think of it. We secured a gig at a place called "Bi-Do Li-To's" (owned by a father, mother, daughter and son (Bi = Bill = father, Do = Dorothy = mother, Li = Linda = daughter and To = Tom = son). We played about five shows per night during the week and two to three shows per night on the weekends. In return for this we each received about $25.00 per week plus we could sleep Ma & Pa Kettle style on the office floors above the club itself. We were able to transport all of our gear to Los Angeles via a 1952 Pontiac station wagon that Darryl DeLoach (I.B's other lead singer and front man) picked up for about $300.00—and he got robbed! Four bald tires with no spare, bad transmission, leaking oil, gas guzzling heap of metal.... And yet it got us there!

For my own privacy under these living arrangements, I took over the ladies restroom each night after the club had closed its doors. They had a lounge sofa-chair that I would drag up from the downstairs patio each night. The ladies room had electric lights, a door that had a lock on it from the inside, a mirror, toilet and last but not least, hot and cold running water! Let us not forget our roots! This was like going from rags to riches for me. I was finally doing what I loved best and it could only go up from here... Did I mention that we were able to practice our new material during the days? For the historians among us: The club was located in Hollywood, California on the southeast end of Cosmo Alley (appropriately enough), south of Hollywood Blvd, east of Vine St. and north of Sunset Blvd.

We continued to work our way up the Sunset Strip, opening for such acts as Arthur Lee & Love, Sky Saxon & the Seeds, Ike and Tina Turner review and by 1967 we found ourselves performing at the Whiskey A Go-Go. It was there that we began leading off for everybody and his brother and sister..... This is when the various labels began taking notice of the Iron Butterfly and making offers. While this was all very nice, it wasn't what I originally had in mind. Ultimately we signed to ATCO Records (subsidiary of Atlantic Records) and the rest is history.

It was at this time that I started experimenting in electronic sounds. Since I still wanted to write motion picture themes, I decided to write a theme that would encapsulate the different sounds I heard in my head through electronic music. I wanted to capture the full range of emotions from tranquility to rage and, as a result, crafted a basic draft that I thought might act as a good basis for such. Thus, the birth of "In-A-Gadda-Da-Vida." "In the Garden of Eden" seemed to be a suitable reference title for the moment, in that it inherently represented the field of expressions that I was pursuing. The history of man might be a good place to project from. Having said this, however, it was not my intent to actually use such a title for a number of reasons. First and foremost, to the extent that music is the international language and reflects many cultures and belief systems, it would be inappropriate for me to assign such a musical venture to one field of interpretation.

As it turns out, I didn't have to figure out a new title for the song. One night, some girls brought by a gallon of Red Mountain rose wine. Yours truly hadn't had a bite to eat in a couple of days, so the wine had a sudden and lasting effect on my ability to speak clearly. Ron (Bushy) wanted to know what I had been working on that day, at which time I directed him to go to our one and only tape recorder and take a listen to what I had recorded prior to the arrival of the wine. He listened, he liked and he wanted to know what the title was. I thought I said "In the Garden of Eden;" he thought I said "In-A-Gadda-Da-Vida." At any rate, he wrote down phonetically what he thought I had said. Hmmmm..... Funny how things work out sometimes.

As a young boy, with a child's naiveté, I always dreamed that I might one day write a song that would change this old world and make it just a little bit better place for all of us to live in. The extent to which this may or may not be true regarding any of my musical efforts is something that remains to be seen and most likely not in my lifetime. What I do know for sure is that music has taken me on many worthwhile adventures to many faraway lands and I have met many of the good people that reside in them and call their lands home. For all of the things in this world that are not quite right, it is my firm belief and conviction that there is much more that is right within the hearts of mankind than some would lead us to believe. There is hope and plenty of it!!!

I would like to take this opportunity to thank the good folks at Chicken Soup for the Soul along with a special thanks to Jo-Ann Geffen for her patience in dealing with me and those good old deadlines and, last but not least, I would like to thank you for taking the time to read this part of my story. WE ALL HAVE ONE!!! Don't we?

Always your friend in life through music, Doug Ingle

"In-A-Gadda-Da-Vida"

In-A-Gadda-Da-Vida honey,
don't ya know that I'm lovin' you?
In-A-Gadda-Da-Vida baby,
don't ya know that I'll always be true?

Oh won't ya come with me,
and ah take my hand?
Oh won't ya come with me,
and ah walk this land?

Please take my hand...

Let me tell ya now.
In-A-Gadda-Da-Vida honey,
Don't ya know that I'm lovin' you?
In-A-Gadda-Da-Vida baby,
don't ya know that I'll always be true?

Oh won't ya come with me,
and ah take my hand?
Oh won't ya come with me,
and ah walk this land?

Please take my hand...
It's alright...hut!
Alright now...come on.

(12:00 + minute instrumental break) = YES !!! ;-)

Two, three, four...hut!

In-A-Gadda-Da-Vida honey,

In-A-Gadda-Da-Vida : Doug Ingle   159

don't ya know that I'm lovin' you?
In-A-Gadda-Da-Vida baby,
don't ya know that I'll always be true?

Oh won't ya come with me,
and ah take my hand?
Oh won't ya come with me,
and ah walk this land?

Please take my hand...
Hut, hut.
Alright now.
Hut, hut.

Rodney Jerkins

"Say My Name"

Written by Rodney Jerkins, Beyoncé Knowles, LaTavia M. Roberson,
LaShawn Daniels, Fred Jerkins, LeToya Luckett, Kelendria Rowland
Recorded by Destiny's Child

This takes me back to the end of 1998 when I got called to go to London to work with the Spice Girls. While I was there, I had a chance to go out and hear different music. The big sound there at that time was Two Step Beats. I'm a person who likes new sounds and I wanted to be the first one to bring this one to America.

Me, my brother Fred, LaShawn Daniels and the girls wrote this song called "Say My Name." I wrote the track in 144 bpm (beats per minute), which is very fast for radio, compared to all the other songs out there. The two step is a fast beat and that's what I was trying to accomplish. However, this was probably the worst track I ever wrote.

After listening to it enough, I decided I liked the song, and the idea of a new sound, enough to bring it to Destiny's Child, whom I was working with at the time. They said, "What is this?!" I told them that we'd be the first to bring this sound and that I guaranteed it would be a hit. Somehow I convinced them to record it despite their misgivings.

After it was recorded, none of us really liked it. In my heart of hearts, I knew I screwed up the track. Matthew Knowles, Destiny's Child's manager, called to tell me that he didn't know if the song would make it onto the album. He said that it was totally different than the rest of the album.

They wanted to mix the album, so I was in a studio in California. I told Jean-Marie Horvat, a mix engineer on the song, to pull down all the instruments and to leave the vocals up. I approached it as if I were doing a re-mix. I began to do the track completely over. I slowed it down by one half to 72 bpm so that it had a whole different feel and sound. Now I felt confident that it was a smash! You can't have an ego about your work. If I had, the song wouldn't have even made the album. It's not just about the track, it's about the song. Because it was a great song, I was able to write a great track.

Destiny's Child's first single, "Bills, Bills, Bills" was a big hit. The second single, "Bug A Boo," didn't really make it. I spoke with Don Ienner, Tommy Mottola and Matthew Knowles who all agreed that the album had already sold almost 3 million units on the first two singles and there was no reason to release a third single. Finally, I was able to persuade them to release it and it went to #1, where it stayed for nine weeks. I won my first Grammy for this song and it is still one of my most played hits.

When I speak on panels, I tell producers and songwriters, "Never give up if you believe in a song."

"Say My Name"

Say my name, say my name
If no one is around you, say "baby I love you."
If you ain't runnin' game
Say my name, say my name.

You actin' kinda shady
Ain't callin' me baby,
Why the sudden change?
Say my name, say my name
If no one is around you, say "baby I love you."
If you ain't runnin' game
Say my name, say my name
You actin' kinda shady
Ain't callin' me baby
Better say my name.

Any other day I would call, you would say
"Baby how's your day?"
But today it ain't the same.
Every other word is uh huh, yea okay.
Could it be that you are at the crib with another lady?
If you took it there, first of all, let me say
I am not the one to sit around and be played.
So prove yourself to me,
I'm the girl that you claim.
Why don't you say the thangs
That you said to me yesterday?

I know you say that I am assuming things.
Something's going down that's the way it seems
Shouldn't be the reason why you're acting strange
If nobody's holding you back from me
'Cause I know how you usually do
When you say everything to me times two.
Why can't you just tell the truth?
If somebody's there then tell me who.

Say my name, say my name
If no one is around you, say "baby I love you."
If you ain't runnin' game

Say my name, say my name.
You actin' kinda shady
Ain't callin' me baby,
Why the sudden change?
Say my name, say my name
If no one is around you, say "baby I love you."
If you ain't runnin' game
Say my name, say my name
You actin' kinda shady
Ain't callin' me baby
Better say my name.

What's up with this?
Tell the truth, who you with,
How would you like it if I came over with my clique?
Don't try to change it now
Sayin' you gotta bounce
When two seconds ago, you said you just got in the house.
It's hard to believe that you
are at home, by yourself
When I just heard the voice,
Heard the voice of someone else.
Just this question,
Why do you feel you gotta lie?
Gettin' caught up in your game
When you can not say my name.

I know you say that I am assuming things.
Something's going down that's the way it seems
Shouldn't be the reason why you're acting strange
If nobody's holding you back from me
'Cause I know how you usually do
When you say everything to me times two.
Why can't you just tell the truth?
If somebody's there then tell me who.

Say my name, say my name
If no one is around you, say "baby I love you."
If you ain't runnin' game
Say my name, say my name.
You actin' kinda shady
Ain't callin' me baby,
Why the sudden change?
Say my name, say my name
If no one is around you, say "baby I love you."
If you ain't runnin' game
Say my name, say my name
You actin' kinda shady
Ain't callin' me baby
Better say my name.

(Where my ladies at) Yeah-yeah-yeah-yea-yeah
(Can you say that? C'mon) Yeah-yeah-yeah-yeah
Yeah-yeah-yeah-yeah
(All the girls say) Yeah-yeah-yeah-yeah
(I can't hear ya) Yeah-yeah-yeah-yeah-yeah-yeah-yeah-yeah
(All the ladies say) Yeah-yeah-yeah-yeah-yeah
Yeah-yeah-yeah-yeah
(All the girls say) Yeah-yeah-yeah-yeah
Yeah-yeah-yeah-yeah
Yeah-yeah-yeah-yeah-yeah-yeah-yeah-yeah

(Break it down) Ohh ooohh oh ooh ohhhh
(D.C., take it to the bridge c'mon)

I know you say that I am assuming things.
Something's going down that's the way it seems
Shouldn't be the reason why you're acting strange
If nobody's holding you back from me
'Cause I know how you usually do
When you say everything to me times two.

Why can't you just tell the truth?
If somebody's there then tell me who.

Say my name, say my name
If no one is around you, say "baby I love you."
If you ain't runnin' game
Say my name, say my name.
You actin' kinda shady
Ain't callin' me baby,
Why the sudden change?
Say my name, say my name
If no one is around you, say "baby I love you."
If you ain't runnin' game
Say my name, say my name
You actin' kinda shady
Ain't callin' me baby
Better say my name.

Joan Jett

"Bad Reputation"

Written by Joan Jett, Kenneth Laguna, Ritchie Cordell, and Martin Kupersmith
Recorded by Joan Jett & The Blackhearts

This was one of the first songs that Kenny (Laguna) and I wrote together. It was in 1979, the same year I recorded it and it was released. With Kenny, someone finally got it and took up the fight with me. He's my best friend; he's creative and has a business head.

When I first met Kenny, the Runaways, the first band I was in, had just broken up. We were an all girl band of teenage rock and rollers pushing the boundaries of what girls could do. The press was actually pretty good to us, but radio treated us very harshly even though we were doing the same things as punk or rock boy bands. Women in rock n' roll became a threat to the misogynists. Pop music is more tolerant of women. It's hard to live a rock n' roll lifestyle as a woman, most women can't take it.

Record companies got scared of offending radio, so they backed off—from me in particular. The double standard was frustrating. We had a "Bad Reputation" for being who we were. It affected me personally and professionally. The lyrics are pretty autobiographical. Some people thought the song was a joke, so we didn't take it too seriously.

Every member of the Runaways got a record deal at PolyGram except me. Maybe it's because I was the guitar player and considered the rock 'n roller. Kenny explains, "She was the first woman to head a rock n roll band with a #1 record and she was the first punk rocker to have a #1 record." Punk rock, in general, scared people and being a woman in leather with black hair, well.....

We wrote most of the song in London in a cool apartment (flat) that Kenny had on Kings Road. The album was almost complete. We wanted to write something fast—kind of Ramones-y. The fans got it. It was never a single, like (Led) Zeppelin's "Stairway To Heaven." People, both guys and girls, relate to the song. It has the universal theme of the underdog.

The video is really autobiographical. It showed how record companies disdained music and didn't take me seriously. Kenny played the record company guy in the video, which was filmed in London and produced by David Mallett. It had an impact on the industry. Since the song came in the wake of "I Love Rock N' Roll," MTV played the video for "Bad Reputation." However, record companies put a lot of pressure on MTV to pull it, which they did.

Our record company, Blackheart Records, is the oldest indie label in the U.S. It was founded in 1980, starting with "Bad Reputation," my first album after The Runaways. Twenty-three record labels turned down the record. We even offered it for free. The Who helped us get started by letting us use their studios and their travel agent. They fronted the money. The first album on the label was *Joan Jett* after it had been released on Ariola in Europe and became the #1 import. Kids were picking up on it in the sub-culture in the punk movement. In the beginning of Blackheart Records, Kenny and I were selling the records out of the trunk of a car at gigs.

Neil Bogart, who was a major player in the record business at the time, saw the names of the people involved in the record and got excited. He called and was coming to our show in L.A. Kenny adds, "He saw her and said she was a star." Neil helped to make it a Top 40 hit. We did a joint venture and Casablanca Records, Neil's company, distributed it until he died very young. At the funeral, his mother said that "Bad Reputation" meant more to him than any other song in his life because people said he couldn't succeed at rock n' roll. It was he who renamed the album "Bad Reputation" for his distribution.

"Do You Want To Touch Me" was a hit single from the album. It was an amazing time, an incredible time.

The most extraordinary thing was seeing Elizabeth Taylor walk on stage to "Bad Reputation" on her TV special in the late '90s. The song's had lots of interesting uses. It was the theme for *Freaks and Geeks* and for *American Chopper* and was used in *Shrek*.

"Bad Reputation"

I don't give a damn 'bout my reputation
You're living in the past it's a new generation
A girl can do what she wants to do and that's
What I'm gonna do
An' I don't give a damn 'bout my bad reputation
Oh no not me
An' I don't give a damn 'bout my reputation
Never said I wanted to improve my station
An' I'm only doin' good
When I'm havin' fun
An' I don't have to please no one
An' I don't give a damn
'Bout my bad reputation
Oh no, not me
Oh no, not me
I don't give a damn
'bout my reputation

I've never been afraid of any deviation
An' I don't really care
If ya think I'm strange
I ain't gonna change
An I'm never gonna care
'bout my bad reputation
Oh no, not me
Oh no, not me
Pedal boys!
An' I don't give a damn
'Bout my reputation
The worlds in trouble
There's no communication
An' everyone can say
What they want to say
It never gets better anyway
So why should I care
'Bout a bad reputation anyway
Oh no, not me
Oh no, not me
I don't give a damn 'bout my bad reputation
You're living in the past
It's a new generation
An' I only feel good
When I got no pain
An' that's how I'm gonna stay

An' I don't give a damn
'Bout my bad reputation
Oh no, not me
Oh no, not
Not me, not me

Jewel

"Hands"

Written by Jewel Kilcher and Patrick Leonard
Recorded by Jewel

wrote the lyrics to this song when I was 18 and homeless. I had been living in a place I was renting and had a job at a computer warehouse where I answered phones. I had no money at all and was living paycheck to paycheck and still didn't have money for food. My boss propositioned me and when I wouldn't agree, he withheld my paycheck and wouldn't even acknowledge me when I went to his office and asked for it. My landlord was nice, but said that if he didn't get paid he would have to kick me out, which he did soon after.

I thought I would sleep in my car until I could get another job. I got really sick with kidney problems and got infections because I couldn't afford medications or doctors. When I tried to go to the emergency room, I almost died in my car in the parking lot because they turned me away since I had no insurance. One nice doctor saw me and helped me and even got me the medicine I needed.

I'm not proud of this, but I was so broke that I shoplifted. The only thing I took was food—carrots and peanut butter. I couldn't keep a job because I kept getting sick. Then the car I was living in got stolen.

I was walking by a store window and saw a dress I *really* wanted. I remember it was $39. I'd never taken anything like that before and when I even considered it, I realized that I must have lost all faith in myself if I didn't think I would be able to afford $39! I knew then that I had to regain self-confidence. That's when I wrote the lyrics to this song.

> *If I could tell the world just one thing*
> *It would be, we're all okay*
> *And not to worry*
> *'Cause worry is wasteful and useless*
> *In times like these.*

Life is a calcification of your thoughts. I was watching what my hands were doing. Are they opening or closing doors? Are they shoplifting or writing songs?

> *My hands are small I know*
> *But they're not yours, they are my own*
> *But they're not yours, they are my own*
> *and I am never broken.*

I knew that even though I felt powerless, there was hope and I couldn't and wouldn't give up.

> *Poverty stole your golden shoes*
> *But it didn't steal your laughter*
> *And heartache came to visit me*
> *But I knew it wasn't ever after.*

Years later, things turned around and this song became a hit from my second album. My husband and I went camping in the mountains in northern California and as we were coming back down, we noticed an American flag at half mast. We thought a fireman may have perished because fires are not uncommon there. As we came further down, there were more flags at half mast. Finally, the radio worked and we learned that the twin towers had come down. It was surreal. Then we heard the DJ dedicate "Hands," a song I'd written at 18 at a dark time in my life, to America. It was an unbelievable experience.

You have to keep fighting for what you believe in.

"Hands"

If I could tell the world just one thing
It would be, we're all okay
And not to worry
'Cause worry is wasteful and useless
In times like these.

I won't be made useless
Won't be idle with despair
I will gather myself around my faith
For light does the darkness most fear.

My hands are small I know
But they're not yours, they are my own
But they're not yours, they are my own
and I am never broken.

Poverty stole your golden shoes
But it didn't steal your laughter
And heartache came to visit me
But I knew it wasn't ever after.

We'll fight, not out of spite

For someone must stand up for what's right
'Cause where there's a man who has no voice
There ours shall go singing.

My hands are small I know
But they're not yours, they are my own
But they're not yours, they are my own
and I am never broken.

In the end only kindness matters
In the end only kindness matters

I will get down on my knees, and I will pray
I will get down on my knees, and I will pray
I will get down on my knees, and I will pray

My hands are small I know
But they're not yours, they are my own
But they're not yours, they are my own
and I am never broken.

My hands are small I know
But they're not yours, they are my own
But they're not yours, they are my own
and I am never broken.
We are never broken.

We are God's eyes
God's hands
God's heart
We are God's eyes
God's hands
God's heart
We are God's eyes
God's hands

God's eyes
We are God's hands

Mick Jones

"Feels Like The First Time"

Written by Mick Jones
Recorded by Foreigner

"Feels Like The First Time" is the first song I'd ever written completely by myself for me with my own band in mind—before I founded Foreigner. In hindsight, I've wondered if perhaps it was a premonition. I had experience writing before that, but always for or with other artists, particularly in France, where I lived.

I was 29 or 30 and barely surviving in New York, getting by day to day, wondering what would happen with my career. I was questioning whether I had the talent to continue or if I should get a "real job."

I was in my living room and this song came out of thin air. I thought it was a breakthrough for me. I finished it in a day or two. It gave me the confidence in myself to go on and over the next two months I formed Foreigner.

It is an absolute that if you can get an idea, the song shows you the way. A phrase is the most natural beginning and usually leads to the song that you don't have to labor over.

This was Foreigner's first single, in 1977. It started the ball rolling.

"Feels Like The First Time"

I would climb any mountain
Sail across a stormy sea
If that's what it takes me baby
To show you how much you mean to me
And I guess it's just the woman in you
That brings out the man in me.
I know I can't help myself
You're all in the world to me.

It feels like the first time
Feels like the very first time
It feels like the first time
It feels like the very first time.

I have waited a lifetime
Spent my time so foolishly
But now that I've found you
Together we'll make history.

And I know that it must be the woman in you
That brings out the man in me
I know I can't help myself
You're all that my eyes can see.

And it feels like the first time
Like it never did before
Feels like the first time

Like we've opened up the door
Feels like the first time
Like it never will again, never again.

Feels like the first time, it feels like the first time
It feels like the very first time, very, very, it feels
It feels like the first time, oh it feels like the first time
It feels like the very first time.

Mick Jones

"Waiting For A Girl Like You"

Written by Mick Jones and Lou Gramm
Recorded by Foreigner

"Waiting For A Girl Like You," like many other songs I've written, came fairly easily once I had the original idea for it. At the time, I was expecting the woman I was involved with to give birth to our daughter—we had Christopher.

I wrote about half of the song and then Lou Gramm, my writing partner at the time, worked with me and we had it finished in an hour or two. We both knew it was something very special.

That's when I started to realize there was something spiritual about writing a song. It comes from somewhere above; you're just the conduit. You have to be in a space where you can accept it. The minute I wrote it, I got full of melancholy. It had sort of a strange hold over me. It made me sad when I heard it. It was very powerful. When we recorded it, I had difficulty keeping it together. I had to leave a few times during the session.

While we were recording, a girl we'd never seen before wandered into the studio. She was beautiful. She stood against the wall and when Lou went into the vocal booth, he sang for her through the glass. When we turned around, she was gone. She was the inspiration for the vocal. He captured it with such emotion, and on one take.

So many people tell me how powerful this song was for them as well. Once it was completed, we played it for several couples, all of whom were in various stages of break-up. By the end of the night, they were all cuddling. It was always very mysterious and still is for me.

I met my wife in London as this song was being released. People thought it may have been about her.

"Waiting For A Girl Like You"

So long, I've been looking too hard, I've been waiting too long
Sometimes I don't know what I will find, I only know it's a
matter of time.
When you love someone, when you love someone
It feels so right, so warm and true, I need to know if you feel it
too.

Maybe I'm wrong, won't you tell me if I'm coming on too
strong?
This heart of mine has been hurt before, this time I wanna be
sure.

I've been waiting for a girl like you to come into my life
I've been waiting for a girl like you, your loving will survive.
I've been waiting for someone new to make me feel alive,
Yeah, waiting for a girl like you to come into my life.

You're so good, when we make love it's understood
It's more than a touch or a word can say
Only in dreams could it be this way
When you love someone, yeah, really love someone.

Now I know it's right, from the moment I wake up till deep in
    the night
There's nowhere on earth that I'd rather be than holding you
    tenderly.

I've been waiting for a girl like you to come into my life
I've been waiting for a girl like you, your loving will survive.
I've been waiting for someone new to make me feel alive,
Yeah, waiting for a girl like you to come into my life.

I've been waiting, waiting for you, ooh, I've been waiting,
I've been waiting.
(I've been waiting for a girl like you, I've been waiting)
Won't you come into my life?

Words and Music by Mick Jones and Lou Gramm. © 1981 Somerset Songs Publishing, Inc.
International Copyright Secured. All Rights Reserved.

Kelly Keagy

"Sister Christian"

Written by Kelly Keagy
Recorded by Night Ranger

The song started with a visit to my sister in Oregon, where she lived. She was about 16 at the time, in high school, and hanging out as we all did at that age, on the main street of the small town. I went out with her and her friends and realized how quickly she was growing up, chasing boys, and I wanted to give her big brotherly advice.

I was in dire circumstances at the time. I was living on a buddy's couch in the San Francisco area. I had a motorcycle that had stopped running. The parts were in a box next to my "bed."

When I got home, I picked up my acoustic guitar and wrote the first lines:

Sister Christian
Oh the time has come
And you know that you're the only one
To say okay.

I wanted her to know that the boys were going to want more than she would be willing to give and it was up to her—this was me, as a big brother, sending some kind of a message to my little sister.

Where you going?
What you looking for?
You know those boys
Don't want to play no more with you,
It's true.

Once I started writing it, I realized that I was writing it for myself, too, and others in my situation. Where am I going from here? Often we write the best things when we're down and out.

The title was a working title. Once I'd written the song, I brought it to the band. They thought I said "Sister Christian" when, in fact, I had said "Sister Christy." When I corrected them, we all agreed that we preferred the new title. It was just spontaneous.

The song came out on our second album, "Midnight Madness." We hadn't had a hit single on that record yet, so when the record company released a third single, Christy heard it on the radio and she thought it was amazing. It was a big rock ballad with a simple chorus that captured people's imaginations:

You're motoring,
What's your price for flight,
In finding mister right?
You'll be alright tonight.

Once it became popular, Christy started to call herself Christian for awhile. Fans even starting writing her letters.

"Sister Christian"

Sister Christian

Oh the time has come
And you know that you're the only one
To say okay.
Where you going?
What you looking for?
You know those boys
Don't want to play no more with you.
It's true.

You're motoring
What's your price for flight
In finding Mister Right?
You'll be alright tonight.

Babe you know
You're growing up so fast
And mama's worrying
That you won't last
To say, let's play.
Sister Christian
There's so much in life.
Don't you give it up
Before your time is due.
It's true,
It's true yeah.

Motoring
What's your price for flight?
You've got him in your sight
And driving thru the night

Motoring
What's your price for flight
In finding Mister Right?
You'll be alright tonight.

Motoring
What's your price for flight
In finding Mister Right?
You'll be alright tonight.

Sister Christian
Oh the time has come
And you know that you're the only one
To say okay
But you're motoring,
You're motoring

Written by Kelly Keagy. © 1983 Figs. D Music and Rough Play Music/The Bicycle Music Company

Angélique Kidjo

"Batonga"

Written and Recorded by Angélique Kidjo

The inspiration for this song started way back when I was going to school in my country of Benin in West Africa. Two of my girlfriends and I went to school together—we were different sizes, very different types of people but the boys taunted all of us to keep us from school. When I went home and told my father, he said, "Don't get angry, you're smart. Be smarter than they are. Don't let them drag you down the alley."

So I made up the word "batonga" and told my friends that every time the boys bothered us, we must each say the word "batonga." That's exactly what we did and it drove them crazy because we wouldn't tell them what it meant and acted as if they should know. In my mind it meant, "Leave me alone. I can be whoever I want to be."

The song is about a girl with big dreams who wouldn't allow anyone to help her. She believed that "you can do as you please regardless of what anyone tells you." The girl in the song is in a rich person's house but doesn't envy them because they have no soul—all they have is their money. She is poor but has spirit and determination. Roughly translated the song says, *Beautiful child, you are so poor but you dance like a princess and you do as you please, angering the rich people in the village.*

You must be positive and find the resource inside of you to accomplish what you want and bring light to darkness. My father was a great example. He felt that the greatest wealth he could give his children was education. He also taught us that hate, violence and anger accomplish nothing. You must love even your enemy or you'll never accomplish anything.

He taught us that neither skin color nor social status nor religion defines a person and that we should never use that as an excuse for failure. He had a zero tolerance policy for racism.

As a Goodwill Ambassador for UNICEF, I have campaigned for primary education throughout the world. However, if we don't send students to secondary school, we lose the momentum. I've named my foundation the Batonga Foundation. Its mission is to further secondary education for girls in Africa. I want highly educated women to change life in Africa and beyond.

"Batonga"

Mmmmmh....
Mmmmmh....

Ovi yabada dadeh
Ovi vanvan nanbaketh
Novi yabada dadeh
Ovi vanvan nanbaketh

Batonga
Yapat'cha galwadadeh lwo
Batonga
Ankwinla djina remi (na)

Mmmmmh....
Mmmmmh....

Ovi yabada dadeh
Ovi vanvan nanbaketh
Novi yabada dadeh
Ovi vanvan nanbaketh

Batonga
Yapat'cha galwadadeh lwo
Batonga
Ankwinla djina remi (na)

Lile gogoto wemak kwon
Lilia limeto wemak kwon
Batonga
Batonga
Baton'
Batonga
Batonga

Ovi yabada dadeh
Ovi vanvan nanbaketh
Novi yabada dadeh
Ovi vanvan eloho

Batonga
Yapat'cha galwadadeh lwo
Batonga
Ankwinla djina remi na

Lile gogoto wemak kwon
Lilia limeto wemak kwon
Batonga
Batonga

Baton'
Batonga
Batonga

Mmmmmh....
Mmmmmh....

Eha ahe aghete
Eha ghete ahe aghete

Lyrics and Music by Angélique Kidjo.

© Kidjo, Angélique/Hebrail, Jean Louis Pierre Warner/Chappell Music, Inc.

Photo credit Joshua Jordan

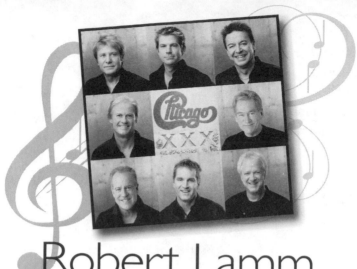

Robert Lamm

"Saturday in the Park"

Written by Robert Lamm
Recorded by Chicago

It's funny that you ask me about this song because I've been told it's on one of the Chicken Soup for the Soul CDs.

"Saturday in the Park" was written in the early '70s and is on the album *Chicago V*. I used to always travel with my movie camera, a Super 8, to document everything just for fun. In the summer of 1969, I was in New York on the way to Atlantic City. In the summers in New York City, Central Park is closed to cars. I was observing all of the people enjoying themselves on a Saturday in the park.

The following year, I was back in New York, where we cut most of our albums, recording *Chicago V*. I shot more footage then. When we finished recording, I went home and edited two years worth of color film together and came up with a short film that turned out to be what the lyrics say. There are slow motion shots of bicycles, and shots of the bronze man amongst other statues in the park like Alice in Wonderland and Hans Christian Anderson. Essentially, the song was the soundtrack to this film.

The song reflects the sense of peace common in a big city on weekends. The sense of joy, connecting with people is something we can all relate to, be they in Denmark, South America, Chicago or Nashville, or anywhere else. I'm convinced that is why the song is still so popular.

"Saturday in the Park"

Saturday in the park
I think it was the fourth of July.
Saturday in the park
I think it was the fourth of July.
People dancing, people laughing
A man selling ice cream
Singing Italian songs.
(fake Italian lyric)
Can you dig it? (Yes, I can)
And I've been waiting such a long time
For Saturday.

Saturday in the park
You'd think it was the fourth of July.
Saturday in the park
You'd think it was the fourth of July.
People talking, really smiling
A man playing guitar
Singing for us all.
Will you help him change the world?
Can you dig it? (Yes, I can)
And I've been waiting such a long time
For today.

Slow motion riders fly the colors of the day
A bronze man still can tell stories his own way
Listen children all is not lost
All is not lost.

Funny days in the park
Every day's the fourth of July,
Funny days in the park
Every day's the fourth of July.
People reaching, people touching
A real celebration
Waiting for us all
If we want it, really want it.
Can you dig it? (Yes, I can)
And I've been waiting such a long time
For the day.

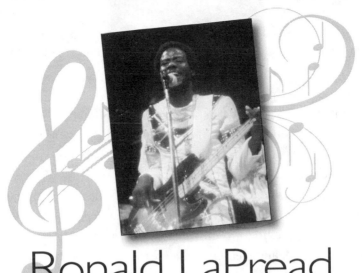

Ronald LaPread

"Zoom"

Written by Ronald LaPread and Lionel Richie
Recorded by the Commodores

We were getting ready to record the self-titled album *Commodores*. I was driving from my hometown of Tuskegee, Alabama with my wife, Cathy, riding next to me, going to gigs in Tennessee, somewhere in Kentucky, and somewhere in North Carolina, leading up to a Madison Square Garden show. On the way to Nashville, she laid down in the back seat of the car, saying that her stomach hurt. We got there, played the first gig and got back in the car right after the show to drive to Knoxville for another date. Again Cathy lay down in the back seat with stomach pains. I told her that we were going to the doctor as soon as we got back. That Monday we went to the hospital in Birmingham, where Cathy was from and her mom lived, and the doctor said that he wanted to do exploratory surgery. It was scheduled for that Friday, the day before the Madison Square Garden concert. The doctor said it would take 45 minutes so I planned to catch a plane to New York immediately after the procedure.

We left our house in Tuskegee at 6 AM for the two hour ride to Birmingham for an 8:30 AM surgery. At 9:30, I was expecting her to come out of the operating room. 9:30 came and went; 10:30 came and went; at 11:30 she was still in there. I missed two planes but wasn't leaving. About 12:10 PM the doctor came out and told me that she had massive tumors in her womb. He gave her about two months to live. She was 23 years old.

I finally left at about 3 PM for New York. The plane had to circle for an hour and when I landed, one of our crew members met me and I got dressed in my stage uniform in the car. We played that gig and another the following night and I left immediately to go get Cathy in Birmingham and take her back to Tuskegee. When we got home, she went to bed.

I sat down at the piano and started fiddling around. Cathy got out of bed and came and sat down beside me. She told me that there were nice changes but the melody should go up at a certain place. We sat there for about an hour and worked out the music.

The Commodores had a listening session soon after and I played them another song I'd written, which they didn't like. I happened to have the tape for this song on me, although it didn't have any words yet. I played it and they asked what it was called. I said, "It's like…. Zoom" and the name stuck. I played it for our producer, James Carmichael, and he said it was nice but it needed a middle. He told me that (Lionel) Richie had a song with a middle and no beginning and he put us together to combine our songs.

The group went into the studio before the words were done and we cut the track. I took the cassette home to work on, but I couldn't get Cathy out of my mind.

The first lines that came to me were:

I may be just a foolish dreamer
But I don't care
'Cause I know my happiness is waiting out there somewhere.

Richie then added:

Zoom
I'd like to fly far away from here

By then we were back in Los Angeles and Cathy was in the hospital there so I could go back and forth from the studio and spend time with her. She wasn't doing well. I told Richie that I couldn't focus on it so he finished the words and recorded the lead vocal. He captured everything I was feeling. It was very quiet in the studio when they played it for me. When the song finished, everyone was crying. They knew where it came from.

We returned to Tuskegee and the Commodores were about to go to Europe on tour. I told them I didn't want to leave and they should get a bass player to replace me during that time, but Cathy insisted that I go. She said, "I'll be here when you get back."

The tour started in the UK, in London, and then we went to Glasgow. We stayed in an old mansion that had been converted to a hotel. The rooms were huge. They had 12' ceilings and there were six windows all around the room with the bed in the center. One of the windows looked out over a cemetery that was lit at night.

At about 2 AM something woke me up. The curtains were blowing as if wind was coming in but when I went to the windows to close them, I realized they weren't open. There was a loud knock at the door and Lenny Guice, one of our crew members and a friend of mine who was very close to Cathy, was standing there. He had the same view from the window in his room down the hall. He looked shaken and said, "What's going on!?" and described the same experience I had. Then, suddenly, the lights in the cemetery went out. Two minutes later the phone rang and it was Cathy's mom telling me that Cathy was in a coma. I asked her to put the phone next to Cathy's ear and I told her I was on my way home and I'd see her the next morning. She woke up, or in her coma, she said, "I'll be waiting for you."

I got on the Concorde and was in Birmingham, Alabama in two and a half hours. I went to her mom's house and Cathy somehow got out of bed and hugged and kissed me. I put her back in bed and her mom had to give her a shot of morphine because she was in a lot of pain. She said, "I'm sorry we didn't have any kids." I responded by saying, "Don't worry, we'll do that later" and she said, "I don't think so" as she took her last breath.

The rule with the Commodores was that the best song on any given album was the single. When that album came out, they all agreed that "Zoom" was the best song, but didn't want to release it as the single so people would have to buy the album to get the song. The album did sell millions of units.

I was on stage playing with Richie not too long ago, 35 years after we wrote this song, and the excitement of 80,000 people getting up out of their seats cheering was a great tribute.

"Zoom"

I may be just a foolish dreamer
But I don't care
'Cause I know my happiness is waiting out there somewhere.
I'm searching for that silver lining
Horizons that I've never seen,
Oh I'd like to take just a moment and dream my dream
Ohhh Dream my dream.

Ohhh Zoom…
I'd like to fly far away from here
Where my mind is fresh and clear
And I'd find the love that I long to see
Where everybody can be what they wanna be.

Ohh I'd like to greet the sun each morning
And walk amongst the stars at night,
I'd like to know the taste of honey in my life, in my life.
Well, I've shared so many pains
And I've played so many games
Ohh but everyone finds the right way

Somehow
Somewhere
Someday.

Ohhh Zoom…
I'd like to fly far away from here
Where my mind can be fresh and clear
And I'll find the love that I long to see
People can be what they wanna be.

Ohhhhh I wish the world were truly happy,
Living as one.
I wish the word they call freedom someday would come
Someday would come.

Ohhh Zoom…
I'd like to fly far away from here
Where my mind can be fresh and clear
And I'd find the love that I long to see
Everybody can be what they wanna be.
Hey, Hey Hey Hey Hey Baby

Zoom
I'd like to fly away
Zoom
I'd like to fly away
Zoom
I'd like to fly away
You and me, baby
Walking free.
Don't you wanna go?
Don't you wanna go?

Lyrics by Ronald LaPread and Lionel Richie. Music by Ronald LaPread. © 1977 Cambrae Music;

Brockman Music/WB Music Corp.

Tracy Lawrence

"If The World Had A Front Porch"

Written by Tracy Lawrence, Paul Nelson and Kenny Beard
Recorded by Tracy Lawrence

y co-writers, Paul Nelson (whom I was writing with a lot those days) and Kenny Beard (who was a band member at the time) and I wrote this in my motel room when we were on the road. I can't even remember the name of the town we were in.

This song was created by recalling childhood memories. When I was very young, my mom re-married and we moved from Texas to a small town in southwest Arkansas. My grandparents lived in Atlanta and I spent every summer and a number of vacations with them. They were very poor. They lived in a "shotgun" house—that's a very small wood house with a front porch and back porch and, if you open the front door and the back door, you can shoot straight through the house!

My granddad died from emphysema when I was fourteen. He suffered with it for some time. The illness made him very weak, so he could only sit on the front porch. I spent a lot of time there with him. I would help my grandmother shuck corn, split peas, or prepare whatever she was canning. Those days are prominent in my childhood memories.

The message of the song is:

If the world had a front porch like we did back then
We'd still have our problems but we'd all be friends.

We've become a backyard nation. With all of the drive-by shootings, child abductions and other things, people are fenced in from the world—they don't sit on their front porches anymore. It's unfortunate that kids today really don't know what "front porch sittin'" means. The front porch (for children in my generation) was a place where we "learned" a lot from our parents and grandparents about communications, morals, society and the value of relationships. This song expresses the wish that we could go back in time—a time of innocence, a time spent with family and friends, and a time when people would wave to their neighbor—all from the front porch.

"If The World Had A Front Porch"

It was where my Mama sat on that old swing with her crochet,
It was where Granddaddy taught me how to cuss and how to
    pray,
It was where we made our own ice cream those sultry summer
    nights,
Where the bulldog had her puppies, and us brothers had our
    fights.
There were many nights I'd sit right there and look out at the
    stars

To the sound of a distant whippoorwill or the hum of a passin'
   car.
It was where I first got up the nerve to steal me my first kiss
And it was where I learned to play guitar and pray I had the
   gift.

If the world had a front porch like we did back then
We'd still have our problems but we'd all be friends.
Treatin' your neighbor like he's your next of kin
Wouldn't be gone with the wind
If the world had a front porch, like we did back then.

Purple hulls and pintos, I've shelled more than my share
As lightening bugs and crickets danced in the evening air.
And like a beacon that ol' yellow bulb, it always led me home
Somehow Mama always knew just when to leave it on.

If the world had a front porch like we did back then
We'd still have our problems but we'd all be friends.
Treatin' your neighbor like he's your next of kin
Wouldn't be gone with the wind
If the world had a front porch, like we did back then.

Treatin' your neighbor like he's your next of kin
Wouldn't be gone with the wind
If the world had a front porch, like we did back then.

Written by Tracy Lawrence, Paul Nelson and Kenny Beard. © Tracy Lawrence, Paul Nelson, Kenny
Beard SLL Music, Sony/ATV Tree Publishing, Warner-Tamerlane Publishing Corp, LAC Grand
Musique Inc.

John Legend

"Ordinary People"

Written by John Legend and will.i.am
Recorded by John Legend

In Spring 2004, I was going to work with will.i.am at the Hit Factory, a studio on the west side of Manhattan. We'd been writing together for the next Black Eyed Peas record. He would play me beats, see if I could come up with hooks and I'd help him write the song. We'd done it before with some success.

He started playing and eventually the chorus emerged. We had a small brainstorming session but that's all the song remained for awhile—the beat and the chorus. I liked it but the more I thought about it, I didn't think it would be a good Black Eyed Peas song. It seemed more like something for my repertoire.

I had just gotten a record deal and was on my way to finishing my first album. I decided to keep "Ordinary People" and worked on the piano to develop and mold it for myself rather than for a rap group.

I was on tour in Europe with Kanye West to help him perform

his new album. We were playing clubs and small theaters there and, at sound check each day, I worked on the song writing the lyrics and tweaking it. People around me heard me singing it and everyone seemed to feel that it was a great song. You never know. I worked on the lyrics and verses throughout the tour. I then worked on the bridge and it was pretty much finished by the time I got home.

When we decided that I would record the song, I had promised Will that I would let him produce it. I made a demo in Los Angeles at the Record Plant, just me and the piano. I sent it to Will and we, and everyone else who heard it, loved it the way it was. The demo was essentially the way it was when it was released.

The idea for the song is that relationships are difficult and the outcome uncertain. If a relationship is going to work, it will require compromise and even then, it is not always going to end the way you want it to.

No specific experience in my life led me to the lyrics for this song, although my parents were married twice to each other and divorced twice from each other. Their relationship is, of course, one of my reference points but I didn't write this to be autobiographical or biographical. It is just a statement about relationships and my view on them.

"Ordinary People"

Girl I'm in love with you
This ain't the honeymoon
Past the infatuation phase
Right in the thick of love
At times we get sick of love
It seems like we argue everyday.

I know I misbehaved
And you made your mistakes
And we both still got room left to grow.

And though love sometimes hurts
I still put you first
And we'll make this thing work
But I think we should take it slow.

We're just ordinary people
We don't know which way to go
'Cause we're ordinary people
Maybe we should take it slow.
This time we'll take it slow,
This time we'll take it slow.

This ain't a movie no,
No fairy tale conclusion ya'll
It gets more confusing everyday.
Sometimes it's heaven sent
Then we head back to hell again
We kiss and we make up on the way.

I hang up, you call
We rise and we fall
And we feel like just walking away.
As our love advances
We take second chances
Though it's not a fantasy
I still want you to stay.

We're just ordinary people
We don't know which way to go
'Cause we're ordinary people
Maybe we should take it slow
This time we'll take it slow
This time we'll take it slow
Take it slow.

Maybe we'll live and learn
Maybe we'll crash and burn
Maybe you'll stay, maybe you'll leave,
Maybe you'll return
Maybe another fight
Maybe we won't survive
But maybe we'll grow
We never know baby you and I

We're just ordinary people
We don't know which way to go
'Cause we're ordinary people
Maybe we should take it slow.
We're just ordinary people
We don't know which way to go
'Cause we're ordinary people
Maybe we should take it slow.
This time we'll take it slow
This time we'll take it slow.

Aaron Lewis

"Outside"

Written by Aaron Lewis
Recorded by Staind

We (Staind) went out with Limp Bizkit on their Family Values '99 tour, which they were recording live. There were five acts on the bill, so we were only performing five songs as the "nobody" first band. We were essentially walk-in music but it turned out the arena was full when we came out to perform at the Mississippi Coast Coliseum in Biloxi. Fifteen minutes before the show, I went into Fred Durst's dressing room and asked him if I should come out and do an acoustic song at the end of the show. It was Fred (lead singer of Limp Bizkit) who actually "discovered" us.

I suggested that I sing "Black Rain" which Fred had heard when I recorded it in the small studio in a house where he had lived in Florida. He said, "No, do the other song you did at my house and I'll come out and sing the chorus with you." He thought that "Outside" was finished, but actually all I had was a chord progression and a chorus, which is what he heard and remembered. I wasn't going to say no, since performing this song was a bonus both on stage and a bonus track on the CD. This song was really natural and accidental. Staind, after returning from the tour, recorded the full band version which was on *Break the Cycle*, our third CD.

I went on stage, in front of 14,000 people, and whatever came out of my mouth was what the audience heard—and that is the song that ended up on the radio. If they hadn't been recording the show, the song never would have survived. I made up the words to the verses as I went along, accompanied by my acoustic guitar. Fred came out and sat next to me on the steps on the stage singing the choruses with me as they came around. I couldn't have bought a better insurance policy.

On the original video, you can see how I'm sweating uncontrollably and shaking like a leaf; the camera doesn't lie. At first no words came out. In between verses, Fred must have seen my panic and screamed out to the crowd, "Biloxi! This is the real deal, y'all." He was killing time to allow me to compose some thoughts. He looked as nervous for me as I was, but it worked and I was able to carry on. I could have crashed and burned. He smiled more widely than I did when it was over. I don't know if he was more proud or relieved.

We came back from tour and the song was on the radio everywhere in heavy rotation. It was crazy. Clearly, none of this was planned.

The best part is that I can't tell you what the actual song is about. Those are just the words and phrases that came out as I sang that night.

"Outside"

And you can bring me to my knees again
All the times that I could beg you please—in vain
All the times when I felt insecure for you
And I leave my burdens at the door.

But I'm on the outside
I'm looking in.
I can see through you
See your true colors
'Cause inside you're ugly,
You're ugly like me.
I can see through you,
See to the real you.

All the times that I felt like this won't end
Was for you
And I taste what I could never have
From you.
All those times that I've tried
My intentions were full of pride
But I waste more time than anyone.

But I'm on the outside
I'm looking in.
I can see through you
See your true colors
'Cause inside you're ugly,
You're ugly like me.
I can see through you,
See to the real you

All the times that I've cried
All this wasted, it's all inside
And I feel all this pain.
I stuffed it down, it's back again
And I lie here in bed
All alone, I can't mend
But I feel tomorrow will be okay.

But I'm on the outside

And I'm looking in
I can see through you
See your true colors
'Cause inside you're ugly,
You're ugly like me.
I can see through you,
See to the real you.

Lyrics and Music by Aaron Lewis. © 1999 WB Music Corp/ Greenfund Music

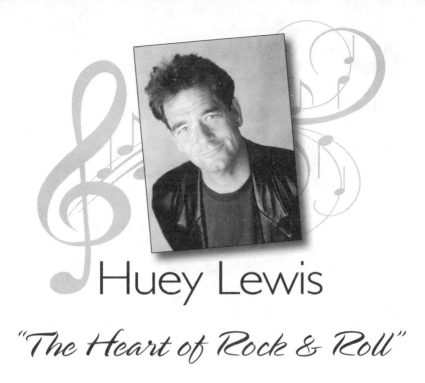

Huey Lewis

"The Heart of Rock & Roll"

Written by Huey Lewis
Recorded by Huey Lewis and the News

Our band is from northern California, Marin County, and we worked most of our lives in the Bay area. We'd always heard that Cleveland was a great rock and roll town, but I didn't really get it. We played our first gig there in 1979 or 1980 at the Agora Ballroom and it *was* a fabulous crowd. There really was something about the people in Cleveland and the way they understood the music. The next morning, driving out of town, I remarked on our tour bus, "You know, the Heart of Rock n' Roll really is in Cleveland," and the idea was born. I expanded it to include great music towns that weren't New York and L.A. but Cleveland was the genesis of the idea.

"The Heart of Rock & Roll"

New York, New York is everything they say

And no place that I'd rather be.
Where else can you do a half a million things
And all at a quarter to three?
When they play their music
Ooh, that modern music
They like it with a lot of style,
But it's still that same old back beat rhythm
That really drives them wild.

They say the heart of rock and roll is still beating
And from what I've seen I believe 'em,
Now the old boy may be barely breathin'
But the heart of rock and roll,
Heart of rock and roll is still beating.

L.A., Hollywood and the Sunset Strip
Is something everyone should see,
Neon lights and the pretty, pretty girls
All dressed so scantily.
When they play their music,
That hard rock music,
They like it with a lot of flash,
But it's still that same old back beat rhythm
That really kicks 'em in the...

They say the heart of rock and roll is still beating
And from what I've seen I believe 'em,
Now the old boy may be barely breathin'
But the heart of rock and roll,
Heart of rock and roll is still beating.

DC, San Antone and the liberty town,
Boston and Baton Rouge,
Tulsa, Austin, Oklahoma City,
Seattle, San Francisco too,

Everywhere there's music
Real live music
Bands with a million styles,
But it's still that same old rock and roll music
That really drives 'em wild.

They say the heart of rock and roll is still beating
And from what I've seen I believe 'em,
Now the old boy may be barely breathing
But the heart of rock and roll,
Heart of rock and roll is still beating, yeah.

In Cleveland,
Detroit,
Heart of rock and roll!

Lyrics and Music by Huey Lewis. © 1983 Warner Chappell

Lisa Loeb

"Stay (I Missed You)"

Written and Recorded by Lisa Loeb

*N*ormally when I write, I am primarily inspired by a word or words or a melody that comes to my mind. Usually I veer away from writing about my personal life. This song is very unusual since I was writing from personal experience.

I was having an argument with my boyfriend at the time. He and I co-produced records at the time at his small apartment on Mott Street in New York City, where we also recorded.

> *And you say, I only hear what I want to*
> *I don't listen hard, don't pay attention*
> *To the distance that you're running*
> *To anyone, anywhere.*

When you're in an argument, the other person accuses you, then turns around and says stay. Then I get the feeling that I didn't hear the person correctly.

Secondarily, it's about over-thinking situations. The song captures that as well. You ruminate about something in your head much more than necessary until it becomes something else.

At the time I was writing this, I was told by a friend that Daryl Hall was looking for music. I hadn't written for anyone else previously, but he was definitely in my mind when I wrote it. I was inspired by his style of blue eyed soul. I was thinking of those kinds of songs when I was writing the chord progression and playing it. Although it was still my signature guitar lick, there was a little bit of R&B. I learned that Hall and Oates weren't looking for songs anymore by midway through my writing, so I decided to finish the song for myself.

It's universal sounding. I recorded an earlier version with another producer as part of my demo deal. But it is the version we did at the apartment, with friends of mine on the track that made it what it is.

My friend Ethan Hawke heard it and really liked it and asked if he could pass it along to Ben Stiller, who was doing *Reality Bites* at the time. It was accepted and record company executive and producer Ron Fair finished the track, adding a tambourine and more harmonies, and it went on the soundtrack. It was finished in a two day session at a fancy Los Angeles studio. It probably cost more to record that one track than we spent on my entire album. The cartage fee on the percussion alone was as much as it cost us to record this whole song previously.

Ethan also directed the video. It was done in one take with no edits, which is very rare. Although I always play the guitar, I didn't in the video so people could relate better to the lyrics and not be distracted from them.

Structure is always important when writing. A lot of songs tend to be like a short story that unwinds then closes itself up. There was no chorus in this song but it got radio airplay anyway, which is quite unusual. It went to #1 in 1994 and got a Grammy nomination even though I was an independent artist. I am told that I am the only person who has ever been nominated without being signed to a recording contract. Luckily, the success of the song launched my career and gave me the freedom to write more of the kinds of songs I like.

"Stay (I Missed You)"

You say I only hear what I want to.
You say I talk so all the time so.
And I thought what I felt was simple,
and I thought that I don't belong,
and now that I am leaving,
now I know that I did something wrong 'cause I missed you.
Yeah yeah, I missed you.
And you say I only hear what I want to:
I don't listen hard,
don't pay attention to the distance that you're running
to anyone, anywhere,
I don't understand if you really care,
I'm only hearing negative: no, no, no.
So I turned the radio on, I turned the radio up,
and this woman was singing my song:
lover's in love, and the other's run away,
lover is crying 'cause the other won't stay.
Some of us hover when we weep for the other who was
dying since the day they were born.
Well, well, this is not that;
I think that I'm throwing, but I'm thrown.
And I thought I'd live forever, but now I'm not so sure.
You try to tell me that I'm clever,
but that won't take me anyhow, or anywhere with you.
You said that I was naive,
and I thought that I was strong.
I thought, "Hey, I can leave, I can leave."
Oh, but now I know that I was wrong, 'cause I missed you.
Yeah, I miss you.
You said, "I caught you 'cause I want you and one day I'll let
    you go."

You try to give away a keeper, or keep me 'cause you know
     you're just
scared to lose.
And you say, "Stay."
And you say I only hear what I want to.

Kenny Loggins

"Moose 'n Me"

Written by Kenny Loggins and Scott Bernard
Recorded by Kenny Loggins

started this song as an 18-year-old, about a year after I got my first dog. I had just moved out of my parents' home, and was living in East L.A., a notoriously rough part of town, renting half a duplex for $65 a month, behind a high school that had a far from stellar reputation. Coming home early one afternoon, I startled a burglar in my kitchen, who crashed his retreat out the back door. And that's how it dawned on me I wanted a dog, for both protection and companionship.

The next day, my mom and I went to the home of a friend of hers to select a puppy from a litter of new-born "beagle/mutts." I picked the biggest one, the one who climbed over his siblings to get to the food first, my logic being his natural survival instincts could serve us both, and named him Moose.

Moose and I quickly bonded, and I took him everywhere with me, even recording sessions. I confess, however, that being your basic, air-headed hippie singer/songwriter, I would sometimes forget he was with me, and leave a party at 3:00 AM without him. Moose figured out right away that one of us had to be the responsible one, and it probably wasn't going to be me, so he'd camp by the door and practically sleep with one eye open. I guess I was as much "his boy" as he was "my dog."

Back in early 1971, Jimmy Messina and I had just started picking songs for what was to be our first album together, "Sittin' In." Out of the many song ideas I showed him, Jimmy was always partial to the one about Moose and me. But I wasn't so sure. I thought it was incomplete and not quite right for Loggins and Messina. Too simple, too childlike.

37 years later, when I recently decided to do a "Family Album" for Disney, it struck me that Moose's time had finally come. I could complete it based, in hindsight, on a bittersweet memory. I wrote the new bridge and last verse remembering how, even though I had been on the road, many miles away from him when Ol' Moose passed away, I could feel in my gut the night that he left.

> But hearts stay connected wherever they roam
> One night miles away
> Somethin' told me
> He was gone.

Thus the song was reborn, this time with a subtle sense of a higher purpose.

Interestingly, just before I finished the song, my youngest son, Luke, and his little sister, Hana, lost their dog, Sprocket. The first thing I heard myself saying to my children to explain what had happened was simply, "Sprocket's gone to heaven." It was the one thought that calmed Hana the most, and I suspect what most parents say in such a moment.

I read once that the first to greet us when we pass over are our pets, then perhaps a loved one or close family member. My dad, my mom, and my big brother, Bob, have all passed away, but I know that even if no one else is there to meet me, Moose will be.

> *People talk a' how we'll all be reunited*
> *When we pass through the Pearly Gates*
> *Mom and dad and Bob 'are gonna make it*
> *'N you can bet we're gonna celebrate.*
> *We all believe we'll be meetin' our maker*
> *When it's long past time to spare*
> *(But if) His angels can't make it*
> *I know the one who'll meet me there.*
> *Moose is a good dog.*

My highest hope for this song is that parents might use it to aid their children through the mourning process, when that time inevitably comes.

"Moose 'n Me"

Me and Moose were heading down the river
Makin' for the delta line,
All our friends were back up in the mountains
Where me and Moosie had spent our lives.
Pappy say "no lazy hound dog is ever gonna
Stray from where he's born."
But moose is crazy—
Moosie thinks that I'm his home.
Moose is a good dog
Moose is a good dog,
Moose is a good dog
And I'd like to say,
A good dog Moosie is.
Captain Ferguson was waitin' by the river
Where me and Moose had planned to stay

But before Cap n' I could make a connection
Some fella' said I was in his way.
He came at me with a crazy eyed stagger
But the Moose just growled him down
And I smiled and whispered
As my foe turned around.
Moose, you're a good dog,
Moose is a good dog
Moose is a good dog
And I'd like to say
a good dog Moosie is.
Moose is a good dog
Yes he is
Moose is a good dog
Moose is a good dog
And I'd like to say
a good dog Moosie is.
Backroads and Highways
so go the years
And a young man must follow his dreams,
But hearts stay connected wherever they roam
One night miles away
Somethin' told me
He was gone.
People talk a' how we'll all be reunited
When we pass through the Pearly Gates
Mom and dad and Bob 'are gonna make it
'N you can bet we're gonna celebrate
We all believe we'll be meetin' our maker
When it's long past time to spare
(But if) His angels can't make it
I know the one who'll meet me there
Moose is a good dog
Moose is a good dog,
Moose is a good dog

And I'd like to say,
A good dog Moosie is.
Moose is a good dog
Yes he is
Moose is a good dog
Moose is a good dog
And I'd like to say
a good dog Moosie is.
Moose is a good dog
Yes he is
Moose is a good dog
Moose is a good dog
And I'd like to say
a good dog Moosie is
a good dog Moosie is.
Moose is a good dog
Yes he is
Moose is a good dog
Moose is a good dog
And I'd like to say
a good dog Moosie is.
Moose is a good dog
Moose is a good dog
Moose is a good dog
And I'd like to say
a good dog Moosie is.

Written by Kenny Loggins and Scott Bernard. © 1970 Universal Music

Shelby Lynne

"Johnny Met June"

Written and Recorded by Shelby Lynne

*J*t's really a simple story. We're all Johnny Cash fans. I've never met anyone who didn't love Johnny Cash. On the morning of September 12, 2003, I was at home, drinking my coffee, just fiddling around. I was listening to KCRW Radio in Los Angeles and Mathieu Schreyer came on and said that Johnny Cash had passed. It was earth shattering news. I got that sinking feeling you get when someone dies. I picked up my guitar and wrote "Johnny Met June" on the spot.

> *Got some news today from the radio man*
> *He spoke the words softly and as somber as he can.*
> *The world stood still and the sky opened up*
> *made my way to fill up my coffee cup.*
> *Then it occurred to me as the daylight sky shone blue*
> *Today's the day that*
> *Johnny met June.*

It was about them meeting in heaven. June Carter Cash had died four months before that. As all great loves go down, it is common that one person doesn't last too long after the person they've spent their entire life with passes.

Oh how I still love to hear you sing
And everything we ever heard about heaven is true
Today's the day that Johnny met June.

"Johnny Met June"

Got some news today from the radio man
He spoke the words softly and as somber as he can.
The world stood still and the sky opened up
made my way to fill up my coffee cup.
Then it occurred to me as the daylight sky shone blue
Today's the day that
Johnny met June.

He waited a while, he knew that he would
He was gonna hang around here for as long as he could.
The days went by and hours idly passed
He was never sure just how long he would last
But there's not much love in a lonely room.
Today's the day that
Johnny met June.

Hey my darlin', hey my sweet
I've waited on the day that I knew we would meet.
Hey my sun, hey my moon
Today's the day that
Johnny met June.

Now were starting over, it's the place that we are

You look more than pretty underneath all the stars.
Love, love is a burning thing
Oh how I still love to hear you sing
And everything we ever heard about heaven is true.
Today's the day that Johnny met June,
Today's the day that Johnny met June.

Written by Shelby Lynne. © 2003 William Boy Sound Music

Photo credit Randee St. Nicholas

Melissa Manchester

"Midnight Blue"

Written by Melissa Manchester and Carole Bayer Sager
Recorded by Melissa Manchester

Carole and I were having a conversation about our young husbands and how, as young women, we didn't know how to get through the hard times that every relationship has. This song came out of that discussion and maintains that conversational tone.

Carole and I were trying to figure out how to "do a relationship." If I had been older, I would have had more communication tools. The intimacy of the mood is what I love most about the song and I believe that's what pulls the listener into it easily. Plus, it's a love song that never uses the word "love." I like that a lot.

After we wrote it, we were thinking of a title, and thought, "One more time for all the old times," followed by "ooh, ooh, ooh," or "ahh, ahh, ahh." One of us said, "Midnight Blue." It was the perfect fit for the overall feeling of the story, which takes place during the night, after the couple has a fight, and before the morning comes and they look at their relationship through fresh eyes. I am grateful that the song and its story of gentle yearning endures.

"Midnight Blue"

Whatever it is, it'll keep till the morning.
Haven't we both got better things to do?
Midnight blue.
Even the simple things become rough.
Haven't we had enough?

And I think we can make it...
One more time... if we try...
One more time for all the old times.

For all of the times you told me you need me,
Needing me now is something I could use.
Midnight blue.
Wouldn't you give your hand to a friend?
Maybe it's not the end.

And I think we can make it...
One more time... if we try...
One more time for all the old times.
Midnight blue.

I think we can make it.
I think we can make it.
Wouldn't you give your heart to a friend?
Think of me as your friend.

And I think we can make it...
One more time... if we try...

One more time for all the old, old times.

Melissa Manchester

"The Power Of Ribbons"

Written and Recorded by Melissa Manchester

The daughter of my very dear friend, Harriet Wasserman, was told she had breast cancer. Harriet's daughter, Nancy Colton, sent out a thank you letter to all of us who supported her while she walked the Susan G. Komen Walk for the Cure. It was accompanied by photos of Nancy, Harriet, her dad Ted and the many friends who participated that sunny day. The letter thanked all of us who supported her, not only in the marathon, but throughout her battle with the disease. Nancy became my muse, living with the disease and working tirelessly to raise a family and raise money for breast cancer research. She really was a woman of valor.

I kept the simple, yet beautiful, letter in a frame and put it on my piano and looked at it every time I walked by or sat down to play. One day, I started to see the words swirl on the page and other words come from behind the printed words on the letter. I knew a song, "Power Of Ribbons," was lifting itself into being. That is one example of the exquisite mystery of songwriting. I wrote "Power Of

Ribbons" in one sitting. I wrote the melody as a walking song since the inspiration came from Nancy's walk for those with breast cancer and its fortunate survivors.

I sang the song for the first time in public on May 10, 2008 at the Revlon Run/Walk for Women event in Los Angeles. I perform it all the time and all of the royalties from the song are donated to breast cancer research. It's my first download-only song. People can buy it on Amazon.com, iTunes, revlonrunwalk.com, melissamanchester. com and other sites and all of the revenue will continue to be contributed to help to find a cure.

Nancy Colton passed away in early 2009, just a week before the next Susan G. Komen Race for the Cure. I was scheduled to perform the song before she left us. As it turned out, the "Race" landed on the last day of her mourning period (in the Jewish religion), called "shiva." I sang the song filled with gratitude for the light that Nancy brought to my life, knowing that my tears were filled with joy.

"The Power Of Ribbons"

May reminds me of spring
Spring reminds me of hope
Hope reminds me that I'm not alone.
We're connected by dreams
Dreams connected to a vision
That victory is all we know.
Can you feel it now? It's so real.

The power of ribbons to hold a million strong
The courage of women who won't wait any longer.
This is the moment, when the dream becomes the thing
There's power in ribbons the color of pink,
The color of pink, the color of pink, the color of pink.

I'm reclaiming my joy

Joy's reclaiming my life
Life begins with every step I take.
Now my spirit's flying
Love is here and I'll surrender
And take this day to celebrate
Celebrate.

The power of ribbons to hold a million strong
The courage of women who won't wait any longer.
This is the moment, when the dream becomes the thing
There's power in ribbons the color of pink,
The color of pink, the color of pink.

If we keep walking on, the winds of change will rise
And we won't stop until those blessings multiply.

The power of ribbons to hold a million strong
The courage of women who won't wait any longer.
This is the moment, when the dream becomes the thing
There's power in ribbons the color of pink,
The color of pink, the color of pink, the color of pink.

Barry Manilow

"One Voice"

Written and Recorded by Barry Manilow

This is the oddest of all of the songs that I've ever written because I wrote it in a dream. Really, in a dream. The song woke me up from my sleep. I heard the melody and the lyric all done. It was like someone was singing the whole thing to me.

I was afraid I would forget it by the morning, so I got up and ran down the very long hallway where I live, hoping that I would keep it in my head.

Even in the middle of the night, even in my sleep, I knew this was a special song. It even had a great rhyme in it.

I ran to the cassette machine, pressed play and record and, although still half asleep, I sang the whole song into it. I still have the cassette. You hear me singing in a husky, first-words-in-the-morning voice during the whole song, even that clever rhyme:

Each and every other note another octave
Hands are joined and fears unlocked

If only One Voice
Would start it on its own

The next morning I woke up and I'd forgotten that I'd done this. When I got to my cassette machine, I hit the play button and there it was—the whole song, the rhyme, the big ending, the whole thing. I played it back and just copied it down like I was taking dictation.

I'd just been beginning my spiritual work. I'd been deeply involved in reading all the books, like we all do when we turn 40 or 50. Books about channeling, I was talking with people about religion, so I guess I was receptive to the idea that it takes only one voice to inspire others to do the right thing. I was so proud of the song, I titled my album that year *One Voice*.

These days I sing the song as much as I can. Sometimes I ask a choir to sing it with me, sometimes I just stand there and sing it alone. Either way people always connect with it.

I've always believed that the public can sense when an artist has struggled to create their work. They can feel the struggle and they're uncomfortable with it. But when the work comes easily, the public can feel that too and they like it much more.

Writing a song in a dream is the purest creation I've ever been a part of. I've always been amazed.

"One Voice"

Just One Voice
Singing in the darkness,
All it takes is One Voice
Singing so they hear what's on your mind
And when you look around you'll find
There's more than

One Voice
Singing in the darkness,

Joining with your One Voice
Each and every note another octave
Hands are joined and fears unlocked
If only

One Voice
Would start it on its own
We need just One Voice
Facing the unknown
And then that One Voice
Would never be alone.
It takes that One Voice

Just One Voice
Singing in the darkness
All it takes is One Voice
Shout it out and let it ring
Just One Voice
It takes that One Voice,
And everyone will sing!

Lyrics and Music by Barry Manilow. © 1979 Universal Music Careers

Richard Marx

"Right Here Waiting"

Written and Recorded by Richard Marx

My first album was released in 1987. A promo tour was planned that turned into a 15 month tour! I got really lucky. The first single was a hit, then the second…. I was dating my wife now, Cynthia Rhodes, and had been for about two and a half years. She'd already done a couple of things, *Flashdance* and *Staying Alive*, and she got a job in South Africa. I'd been on tour for so long that we really wanted some time together. Much to the horror of my agent and manager, I took two weeks off to fly down to South Africa in the middle of her shooting schedule. She'd already been gone for five or six weeks and we really missed being together. This was before email and text messaging and with the time change, it was hard to communicate. And it would be three months since I'd seen her.

It was 1988 and there were (rightfully) sanctions against apartheid and the political situation there. Had I been asked, I would have gladly given my anti-apartheid position, but no one asked me. I got a call three days before I was going to leave that my visa had been denied. I got shut down.

So now I had two weeks off with nothing to do except be miserable and miss her. I called a friend of mine and set up a day to write a song. For a songwriter, songwriting is therapy, only cheaper. I wrote a raging rock and roll song, my version of an AC/DC song. We were just about done, and my friend's phone rang and he excused himself to take the call.

There was a baby grand in another room in the house and I went straight to the piano. I sat down and "Right Here Waiting" spilled out effortlessly. It wrote itself in 12 minutes, the only time that ever happened to me. I grabbed an envelope I found and wrote down the lyrics. My friend heard me singing it and ran and got a tape recorder. He said I had to put it on tape right then. My only mission was to send it to Cynthia in South Africa to tell her how much I missed her. When she got it, the 4 minute song took her a full day to get through. She said that after every line she stopped and cried.

A few weeks later I got a call from Barbra Streisand. She'd heard my music and asked me to write a song for her. After I went home and started thinking about it, I thought about "Right Here Waiting" and decided to give it to her. She loved the music but wanted me to re-write the lyrics. She said, "I don't want to be right here waiting for anybody!"

I told her that I didn't want to, it was too personal. She said, "Why don't you record it?" I didn't want to—it was too personal for me. I was in the studio recording my second album and everyone who heard it kept on telling me to record it. Very reluctantly, I did. Everyone who heard it said that I *had* to put it on my album.

The first single was "Satisfied," a rock and roll up tempo song that hit #1. Radio and my fans had jumped on "Right Here Waiting" immediately. That's when I realized that it is a universal song. It went to #1 and stayed there for three weeks. It was phenomenal for me. I framed the chart and sent it to Barbra with a note thanking her for turning down the song. We remind each other when we speak and laugh about it.

After all these years it's still the song in my show that pulls every-one in the room together. The audience is from 12-75 years old and they all sing every word. I start it and then just play the piano and let the audience sing. I'm thrilled to have a song that ubiquitous. Soldiers and their wives have told me, "It's our song." What a tremen-dous privilege that is!

I wrote it because I missed my wife really badly. It's not our song anymore—in a good way. It's everyone's song.

"Right Here Waiting"

Oceans apart day after day
And I slowly go insane.
I hear your voice on the line
But it doesn't stop the pain.

If I see you next to never,
How can we say forever?

Wherever you go
Whatever you do
I will be right here waiting for you.
Whatever it takes
Or how my heart breaks
I will be right here waiting for you.

I took for granted, all the times
That I thought would last somehow
I hear the laughter, I taste the tears
But I can't get near you now.

Oh, can't you see it baby?
You've got me goin' crazy.

Wherever you go
Whatever you do
I will be right here waiting for you.
Whatever it takes
Or how my heart breaks
I will be right here waiting for you.

I wonder how we can survive
This romance
But in the end if I'm with you
I'll take the chance.

Oh, can't you see it baby?
You've got me goin' crazy.

Wherever you go
Whatever you do
I will be right here waiting for you.
Whatever it takes
Or how my heart breaks
I will be right here waiting for you.

Written by Richard Marx. © 1989 Chiboy Music

Amanda McBroom

"The Rose"

Written by Amanda McBroom
Recorded by Bette Midler

Long before I had ever recorded anything, I was driving down the freeway one afternoon, sometime in 1977. I was listening to the radio when the song "Magdalena" by Danny O'Keefe, sung by Leo Sayer, came on. I liked it immediately. My favorite line was "Your love is like a razor. My heart is just a scar."

As I continued to drive down the road, I thought more about it and realized I don't agree with that sentiment. I don't think love is like a razor. (I was younger then.) What, then, do I think love is? Suddenly, it was as if someone had opened a window in the top of my head. Words came pouring in. I had to keep reciting them to myself as I drove faster and faster towards home, so I wouldn't forget them. I screeched into my driveway, ran into the house, past various bewildered dogs and cats and husbands, and sat down at the piano. Ten minutes later, "The Rose" was there.

I called my husband, George, into the room and played it for him, as I always did with my new songs. He listened, and quietly said to me, "You've just written a standard." I protested that no one but my pals would ever hear it and he said, "Mark my words. Something is going to happen with this song."

A year or so later, a professional songwriter friend of mine said, "Listen, there is this movie coming out called *The Rose*. They are looking for a title tune. Do you want me to submit this to them?" I had never really tried to submit this song to anyone. I didn't consider myself a songwriter at the time. So I said, "Sure."

She submitted the tune to the producers, who HATED it. They thought it was dull and a hymn and NOT rock and roll and totally wrong for this project. They put it in the reject box. But the divine Paul Rothchild, who was the music supervisor on the film, and had been Janis Joplin's producer, hauled it out and asked them to reconsider. They again said no. So he mailed it to Bette (Midler). She liked it, and that's how it got into the film and changed my life forever.

Originally the film had been called *The Pearl*, which was Janis Joplin's nickname. But, lucky for me, her family refused permission to use that name. "Pearl" is MUCH harder to rhyme.

I have never written another song as quickly. I like to think I was the window that happened to be open when those thoughts needed to come through. I am eternally grateful... to Bette... to Paul Rothchild... to Bill Kerby, who wrote the screenplay... to my friend who first submitted it for me... and to the Universe for speaking to me in the first place and for showing me what I truly believe.

"The Rose"

Some say love, it is a river
That drowns the tender reed.
Some say love, it is a razor
That leaves your soul to bleed.
Some say love, it is a hunger
An endless aching need.

I say love, it is a flower
And you, its only seed.
It's the heart, afraid of breaking
That never learns to dance.
It's the dream, afraid of waking
That never takes the chance.
It's the one who won't be taken
Who cannot seem to give
And the soul, afraid of dying,
That never learns to live.
When the night has been too lonely
And the road has been too long
And you think that love is only for the lucky and the strong,
Just remember in the winter
Far beneath the bitter snow
Lies the seed
That with the sun's love, in the spring
Becomes the rose.

Lyrics and Music by Amanda McBroom. © 1976 Warner-Tamerlane Publishing Corp.

Eddie Money

"Two Tickets To Paradise"

Written and Recorded by Eddie Money

When I wrote this, I was going out with a girl from college whose mother was trying to get her away from me to date a doctor, lawyer or CPA on the weekends when she went home to San Francisco. What her mom didn't know was that her daughter was living with me during the week.

I didn't have money to take her anywhere. She was from a pretty wealthy family that took her to Tahiti and Paris—I was in a rock band, going to college and living on peanut butter sandwiches and Chef Boyardee ravioli.

I was doing a show in Arcadia, which is in northern California. I decided to take her with me for a getaway and spent about $100 for Greyhound bus tickets. It was beautiful country and we went to see the redwoods and really had a wonderful time. You don't have to go to Rome or Paris or another exotic location to enjoy yourself. If you're in love, any trip is paradise.

She eventually dumped me for a lawyer, but we had a great year.

"Two Tickets To Paradise"

Got a surprise especially for you,
Something that both of us have always wanted to do.
We've waited so long, waited so long.
We've waited so long, waited so long.

I'm gonna take you on a trip so far from here,
I've got two tickets in my pocket, now baby, we're gonna
 disappear.
We've waited so long, waited so long.
We've waited so long, waited so long.

I've got two tickets to paradise,
Won't you pack your bags, we'll leave tonight,
I've got two tickets to paradise,
I've got two tickets to paradise.

I'm gonna take you on a trip so far from here,
I've got two tickets in my pocket, now baby, we're gonna
 disappear.
We've waited so long, waited so long.
We've waited so long, waited so long.

I've got two tickets to paradise,
Won't you pack your bags, we'll leave tonight,
I've got two tickets to paradise,
I've got two tickets to paradise.

Lyrics and Music by Eddie Money. © 1976 Music Sales Group

Nathan Morris

"One Sweet Day"

Written by Mariah Carey, Michael McCary, Nathan Morris, Wanya Morris,
Shawn Stockman, Walter Afanasieff
Recorded by Mariah Carey and Boyz II Men

Everything was going great for us. As an original member of
Boyz II Men, we had a very successful first CD and were
touring a lot. However, a date in Chicago was the beginning
of a very tough time for us.

We were very young, between 16 and 21 at the time. Kahlil
Roundtree was our road manager and was like a surrogate father on
the road. Our parents trusted him to handle everything, including us,
which he did very well. We had some problems with the promoter
on this particular date. Kahlil got into it with him about the hotel or
some issue in the contract, and he brought us the information in the
dressing room after the show to ask our opinion, which was odd since
he always just took care of things himself and they ran smoothly.

Later that night, after the show, he and a partner went to the front
desk of the hotel to settle the group's room charges before heading

to bed. As they entered the elevator, three men who worked in the parking structure adjacent to the hotel entered as well. Once in the elevator, there was a shootout and he was killed. This was definitely the biggest loss in our career, if not our lives.

After he died, I began working on a song for him while we were on the road. Not too long after, we got a call from Tommy Mottola asking if we'd be interested in doing a duet with Mariah Carey. We went to the studio she was recording in at the Hit Factory in New York to hear the song they had in mind. She played us the melody and the hook and it was amazing. It was almost the same song I was writing. I told her that I was working on a song with a similar melody and while the lyrics were, of course, different, the premise was the same. They complemented each other. I sang to her the melody and lyrics of what I had written and we merged the two. We switched things around to make them work and wrote it that day. The other guys in the group filled in the holes to complete it.

We came back to the studio to record it a week or so later and we only had a few hours to do everything, since we squeezed this in between dates on tour. The photo on the album cover was shot in the elevator on the way up to the studio and the video was shot during the recording session, all in those few hours that day. It entered the charts at #1 and became the longest running #1 single, keeping that position for 16 weeks, longer than any other song in billboard history.

"One Sweet Day"

I won't be afraid.
I'll be alright if you help me.
I know you're looking down from heaven
And I won't let you down.
I'll be everything you taught me
And all that I know is I'll wait
Patiently to see you in heaven...

Sorry I never told you
All I wanted to say
And now it's too late to hold you
'cause you've flown away,
So far away.

Never had I imagined
Living without your smile
Feeling and knowing you hear me.
It keeps me alive,
Alive...

And I know you're shining down on me from heaven
Like so many friends we've lost along the way.
And I know eventually we'll be together
One sweet day.
Eventually we'll sing in heaven.

Darling I never showed you,
Assumed you'd always be there
And I took your presence for granted
But I always cared
And I miss the love we shared.

And I know you're shining down on me from heaven
Like so many friends we've lost along the way.
And I know eventually we'll be together
One sweet day.
Eventually we'll sing in heaven.

Although the sun will never shine the same
I'll always look to a brighter day.
Lord I know when I lay me down to sleep
You will always listen as I pray.

And I know you're shining down on me from heaven
Like so many friends we've lost along the way.
And I know eventually we'll be together
One sweet day.
And I know you're shining down on me from heaven
Like so many friends we've lost along the way.
And I know eventually we'll be together
One sweet day
And all that I know is I'll wait
Patiently to see you in heaven...

Sorry I never told you
All I wanted to say ...

Rick Nelson

"Garden Party"

Story by Gunnar Nelson

Written and Recorded by Rick Nelson

You have to cast your mind back to the 1950s when my dad grew up on the *Ozzie and Harriet* show. While he eventually had two totally different musical careers in his life—the early "rockabilly" years were what he started with on the TV show. In those days the paradigm was that there were songwriters and artists/performers—they were separate. His early hits like "Travelin' Man," "Lonesome Town" and the others were written by other people and given to him to record.

In 1963 or so, the TV show was cancelled after fourteen and a half years and he found himself without a show to market his music. Moreover, it was a very different time politically, musically and culturally. The Eisenhower era was passé, people had moved on. It was the era of Bob Dylan, the Beatles and other great artists who wrote their own music reflecting the times… those were the ones enjoying success. Earlier artists like Elvis, Jerry Lee Lewis, Carl Perkins couldn't even get airplay at the time.

After films like *Rio Bravo*, my dad could have been a film star but he consciously chose to stick with music, his first love. He knew that he'd have to write his own songs to express himself and communicate with his listeners and audiences.

He formed a group called the Stone Canyon Band. When he was inducted into the Rock and Roll Hall of Fame, he was credited with it being the first country rock band. He had created his own genre.

The band toured little clubs for seven years without much commercial success, but he'd never had more fun. In 1970 they were invited to play Madison Square Garden, which had always been his dream. He was apprehensive but couldn't turn it down. It was originally billed as a Rock & Roll Revival, but he had it changed to a Rock & Roll Reunion since he didn't want it to sound like they were dead and needed CPR—instead they were a bunch of old friends getting back together. Some of the other people on the show were many of the greats of the old days like Chuck Berry and Bobby Darin.

While the Stone Canyon Band was touring, they had long hair and their wardrobe consisted of sequins, bell bottoms and other signature hippy attire. At the Garden, he looked out from the side of the stage and the entire audience was dressed like Sha Na Na with slicked back hair, saddle shoes—you get the picture. He didn't want to go out looking and sounding like he did now, but was assured by the promoter that he would be warmly welcomed by the audience.

When he stepped out onto that stage, however, he instantly felt uneasy. By three songs into the set, he knew the audience was not warming up to him. The fourth song was the Rolling Stones' "Honky Tonk Woman," which was a fairly new song at the time. 22,000 people booed him off the stage!

He went back to California and locked himself in his music room, which was his safe haven. He began writing, but it wasn't until three weeks later that he wrote "Garden Party." This song came to him as an inspiration during the night.

The chorus is not only catchy, it was a personal statement.

But it's all right now,
I learned my lesson well.
You see, ya can't please everyone,
So ya got to please yourself.

After a lifetime of pretending to be a character he wasn't—wearing the sweater on Monday on the set of *Ozzie and Harriet* after being a real rock star on the weekends—he was writing and performing for his own pleasure and satisfaction. The song was based on his experience at Madison Square Garden.

I went to a garden party to reminisce with my old friends
A chance to share old memories and play our songs again.
When I got to the garden party, they all knew my name
No one recognized me, I didn't look the same.

He turned what could have remained the darkest day of his life into his brightest shining moment. Just when the music industry considered him a relic, filing him away as yesterday's news, he had the biggest hit of his career and it was totally autobiographical.

As I was becoming musical as a kid, he told me that he would have given away all of his #1 records for success like this because it was a piece of his life, of his heart. The victory belonged to him alone. He told me then that the best thing in the world to be as an artist is a songwriter first and foremost. That's why I've been defiant about that very thing throughout my career. I am a songwriter. And that's what I put on the dotted line whenever I'm asked to write what my "occupation" is. And I owe it to my Pop and this one song.

I'm sorry he wasn't here to see my early success and be proud of me in person, but he was there every step of the way. Without his words of wisdom, I probably wouldn't have been nearly as committed to writing and performing my own songs.

My most prized possession is the original handwritten copy of the lyrics he wrote, which I have in a frame on the wall in my house. There are two pages side by side and you can see how he was inspired—he wrote all over the margins on the first draft because he didn't want to break the flow. The second page, which is the second draft, has the verses along with a coffee cup stain and other signs that he couldn't leave the page-notes about the arrangement (the key and ending) right there. It's funny—I do the same thing on my lyric sheets when I write them for the first time.

"Garden Party"

I went to a garden party to reminisce with my old friends
A chance to share old memories and play our songs again.
When I got to the garden party, they all knew my name
No one recognized me, I didn't look the same.

But it's all right now,
I learned my lesson well.
You see, ya can't please everyone,
So ya got to please yourself.

People came from miles around, everyone was there.
Yoko brought her walrus, there was magic in the air
'n' over in the corner, much to my surprise
Mr. Hughes hid in Dylan's shoes wearing his disguise.

But it's all right now,
I learned my lesson well.
You see, ya can't please everyone,
So ya got to please yourself.

Played them all the old songs, thought that's why they came
No one heard the music, we didn't look the same.
I said hello to "Mary Lou", she belongs to me
When I sang a song about a honky-tonk, it was time to leave.

But it's all right now,
I learned my lesson well.
You see, ya can't please everyone,
So ya got to please yourself.

Someone opened up a closet door and out stepped Johnny B.
    Goode
Playing guitar like a-ringin' a bell and lookin' like he should.
If you gotta play at garden parties, I wish you a lotta luck
But if memories were all I sang, I'd rather drive a truck.

But it's all right now,
I learned my lesson well.
You see, ya can't please everyone,
So ya got to please yourself.

'n' it's all right now, learned my lesson well
You see, ya can't please everyone, so you got to please yourself.

Written by Rick Nelson. © MATRAGUN MUSIC

Aaron Neville

"Yellow Moon"

Written by A. Neville / J. Neville
Recorded by The Neville Brothers

I was recording with the Neville Bros. at the time I wrote this. My wife was on a long anticipated cruise with her sister. They'd wanted to go for a long time and this was the only time her sister had available. Even though it was our 25th wedding anniversary, I thought it would be fun for her so I encouraged her to go. I said I'd stay home and watch the kids, and the kids thought it was pretty cool.

So I was at home in New Orleans and I was lonely. I just happened to look out of the window and there was a full moon. It looked so close—it was big and yellow. It was a personal thing, a tribute to my wife and I just started writing. When I write, it comes to me like someone is telling me the words.

I put my wife's name down as co-writer since it was definitely inspired by her and I couldn't have written it without feeling about her the way I do.

In 1989 our album was named after this title cut and we performed it in 2000 at Farm Aid and it was on the album *Farm Aid—Volume One Live*. It, of course, continues to have a very special meaning to me.

"Yellow Moon"

Oh, yellow moon, yellow moon,
Why you keep peeping in my window?
Do you know something
Do you know something I don't know?

Did you see my baby
Walking down the railroad tracks?
You can tell me
If the girl's never coming back.

Is she hid out with another
Or is she trying to get back home?
Is she wrapped up in some other's arms?
Or is the girl somewhere all alone?

Can you see if she is missing me,
Or is she having a real good time?
Has she forgotten all about,
Or is the girl still mine all mine?

With your eye so big a shiny
You can see the whole damn land
Yellow moon can you tell me
If the girl's with another man?

Oh yellow moon, yellow moon, yellow moon,
Have you seen that Creole woman?

You can tell me,
Now ain't you a friend of mine?

With your eye so big a shiny
You can see the whole damn land
Yellow moon can you tell me
If the girl's with another man?

Oh yellow moon, yellow moon, yellow moon,
Have you seen that Creole woman?
You can tell me,
Now ain't you a friend of mine?

Written by A. Neville / J. Neville. © NEVILLE MUSIC CO; APACHE RED MUSIC

John Oates

"She's Gone"

Written by John Oates and Daryl Hall
Recorded by Daryl Hall and John Oates

"She's Gone" is the quintessential Hall and Oates song for many reasons. It demonstrates the way we work together and the nature of our personalities.

Set the scene. It is December 1972 in Greenwich Village. I had been carousing in the middle of the night. It was about 3 AM in the Pink Teacup on Bleecker Street and I'm sure I was wearing some outlandish outfit of the day. Some girl came in wearing a pink tutu and cowboy boots and we had a midnight psychic contact. I started to see her and asked her out for New Year's Eve.

I was sharing an apartment with Daryl (Hall) and his longtime girlfriend Sara at the time. I was waiting for my date on New Year's Eve at the apartment. Time began ticking by, first minutes then hours. It suddenly dawned on me that she wasn't coming. I picked up my guitar and started writing:

She's Gone Oh I, Oh I'd
better learn how to face it

The next day, Daryl came back and heard it. He sat down at the piano and added his signature piano riff at the beginning of the recording. I wrote the verse in about as much time as it took him to play it. We pooled our emotions of loss at the moment and turned a simple idea into a universal expression. People relate it to their own personal losses.

Up in the morning, look in the mirror,
I'm worn as her toothbrush hanging in the stand.

The images are everyday images, using a utilitarian thing, that no one usually thinks about, in an unusual way.

The record itself took the song to another level. Arif Mardin produced it and there were great musicians on the recording. It was like a rose that bloomed in the studio. There was modulation in half steps that took it to another key and helped to bring the thought home.

It was a great marriage of music and lyrics, which is important. All of the elements came together. There's a cohesiveness that I think is very hard to capture.

"She's Gone"

Everybody's high on consolation,
Everybody's trying to tell me what's right for me.
My daddy tried to bore me with a sermon
but it's plain to see that they can't comfort me.

Sorry Charlie for the imposition
I think I've got it, got the strength to carry on.
I need a drink and a quick decision.
Now it's up to me, ooh what will be?

She's Gone Oh I, Oh I'd
better learn how to face it.
She's Gone Oh I, Oh I'd
pay the devil to replace her.
She's Gone — what went wrong?

Up in the morning, look in the mirror,
I'm worn as her toothbrush hanging in the stand,
my face ain't looking any younger
now I can see love's taken her toll on me.

She's Gone Oh I, Oh I'd
better learn how to face it.
She's Gone Oh I, Oh I'd
pay the devil to replace her.
She's Gone — what went wrong?

Think I'll spend eternity in the city
let the carbon and monoxide choke my thoughts away
and pretty bodies help dissolve the memories,
but they can never be what she was to me.

She's Gone Oh I, Oh I'd
better learn how to face it.
She's Gone Oh I, Oh I'd
pay the devil to replace her.
She's Gone — what went wrong?

Walter "Clyde" Orange

"Nightshift"

Written by Walter Orange, Dennis Lambert, Franne Golde
Recorded by the Commodores

ack in the day, whether we wrote individually or together, the Commodores always wrote the music for our songs first. I sometimes hummed a melody into a tape recorder that I always kept with me so I would remember the ideas as they came to me. Then, once I got home, or sometimes a long time after, I added the funk. In the case of "Nightshift" (which was not titled yet), I had a bunch of songs on that recorder, some just a chorus, some a verse, and some were just a thought. Most of the time, I left them on there until I had time to listen to them or I was looking for a new melody. Six to eight months after I wrote that melody the group had some time off and I listened to several ideas I had on tape. That one really stood out. I went into my studio at home in Tuskegee, Alabama, first put drums to it, then added the rhythm pattern and I finished the track.

"Nightshift" was going to be about a man and a woman—a love song on top of a funk groove, which is pretty much what I'm known for. I write up tempo, kind of promiscuous songs—"Gettin' It," "Brick House." I wrote the lyrics to "Slippery When Wet" in one and a half hours, but some of them were rejected because they needed to be cleaned up.

I liked the music, the groove of the track. It was 1983-4, Lionel (Richie) had left the group and we were recording a new CD. We had one more shot to prove ourselves.

I was on my boat in Alabama, pulling into the dock, when someone said that one of the members of my group was killed. My heart was in my stomach. It couldn't be Richie, Tommy (McClary) had already left the group—who could it be? It turned out that the guy only heard Motown on the radio, knew I was in the Commodores, and gave me the wrong information. It was Marvin Gaye who was killed by his father. Of course, we knew Marvin and admired his talent and were in shock.

About three months later, we were looking for a fresh approach for our next record and had a new producer, Dennis Lambert. Dennis brought some songs to us to consider and after our meeting I pulled out a cassette of my track. Dennis loved it. I started writing the song as a tribute to Marvin. I came up with the first verse and got stuck. Dennis asked if he could work on it with me and I was delighted. I felt good about the music but I didn't think it would be a hit anyway, since it wasn't about a woman or booty or anything popular.

The next day Dennis asked to bring in another writer, Franne Gold, and they finished the lyrics in just a few days. Franne and Dennis introduced singing about Jackie (Wilson) as well as Marvin. We threw around titles and Dennis came up with "Nightshift." I recorded the song with Dennis producing and he was happy with it and felt it was done after I finished the last lyric. I felt it needed something new. JD Nicholas was just coming into the group and I suggested that JD, another voice, sing about Jackie. It was a great way to introduce JD. Originally Dennis added him to pacify me with the stipulation that if it didn't work, we would use the version I recorded.

We brought JD in and he nailed it! Dennis really liked his voice on it and thought it would be a hit. The rest is history. It brought the Commodores our first Grammy.

"Nightshift"

Marvin, he was a friend of mine
And he could sing a song
His heart in every line.
Marvin sang of the joy and pain
He opened up our minds
And I still can hear him say…
Aw talk to me, so you can see
What's going on.
Say you will sing your songs
Forevermore (evermore).

Gonna be some sweet sounds
Coming down on the nightshift.
I bet you're singing proud
Oh I bet you'll pull a crowd.
Gonna be a long night
It's gonna be all right
On the nightshift.
Oh you found another home
I know you're not alone
On the nightshift.

Jackie (Jackie), hey what you doing now?
It seems like yesterday
When we were working out.
Jackie (Jackie, oh) you set
The world on fire.
You came and gifted us,

Your love it lifted us
Higher and higher.
Keep it up and
We'll be there
At your side,
Oh say you will sing
Your songs forevermore (evermore).

Gonna be some sweet sounds
Coming down on the nightshift.
I bet you're singing proud
Oh I bet you'll pull a crowd.
Gonna be a long night
It's gonna be all right
On the nightshift.
Oh you found another home
I know you're not alone
On the nightshift.

Gonna miss your sweet voice,
That soulful voice,
On the nightshift.
We all remember you
Ooh the songs are coming through
At the end of a long day
It's gonna be okay
On the nightshift.
You found another home
I know you're not alone
On the nightshift.

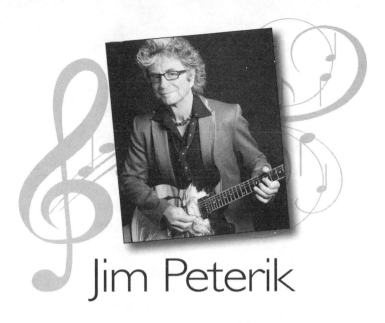

Jim Peterik

"Eye of the Tiger"

Written by Jim Peterik and Frankie Sullivan
Recorded by Survivor for Rocky III

We were asked to write this song by Sylvester Stallone. He wanted a new theme for *Rocky III* and had heard our group, Survivor, and liked our sound. I was the keyboard player and Frankie Sullivan, who wrote it with me, was the guitar player. Sly wanted "something with a pulse, something for the kids."

He sent a rough cut of the film and we immediately got fired up. These were ideas I wanted to express for so long and all I needed was an excuse to put them into a song—this was it. The story of musicians is very similar to that of prize fighters—each field is very competitive and it's a difficult struggle to win. We caught the energy for the song from the script and the film. It was my personal story and Frank's; it is about what it takes to be the best. Being from Chicago, the "second city," and not New York or Los Angeles, we had to try a little harder to be successful.

We wrote the song in my kitchen. I rented a professional Betamax machine and while we were watching the opening montage to the film, I started playing the now signature sixteenth note guitar figure. As the punches were thrown, we created the slashing chords to match the phrase "Eye of the Tiger," which was in the script. As the key to the movie, it became the title of the song. I felt it would be a hit. After all, it would have a $10 million video!

"Eye of the Tiger" took on a life of its own beyond the movie. Each generation re-discovers the song—sports competitors, people with physical or mental challenges, kids who hear it on Guitar Hero or other video games. How could we have known at the time that this song would go on to motivate generations to come?

Randy Pausch, who wrote *The Last Lecture*, cited the song. It gave me goose bumps when I saw that. Throughout my life, I've used the song to get through problems and to rise above my own challenges. That's a bonus, for sure.

"Eye of the Tiger"

Risin' up, back on the street
Did my time, took my chances
Went the distance, now I'm back on my feet
Just a man and his will to survive.
So many times, it happens too fast,
You trade your passion for glory.
Don't lose your grip on the dreams of the past
You must fight just to keep them alive.

It's the eye of the tiger,
It's the thrill of the fight
Rising up to the challenge of our rival
And the last known survivor
Stalks his prey in the night
And he's watching us all with the eye of the tiger.

Face to face, out in the heat,
Hangin' tough, stayin' hungry
They stack the odds, still we take to the street
For the kill with the skill to survive.

It's the eye of the tiger,
It's the thrill of the fight
Rising up to the challenge of our rival
And the last known survivor
Stalks his prey in the night
And he's watching us all with the eye of the tiger.

Risin' up, straight to the top
Had the guts, got the glory,
Went the distance, now I'm not gonna stop
Just a man and his will to survive.

It's the eye of the tiger,
It's the thrill of the fight
Rising up to the challenge of our rival
And the last known survivor
Stalks his prey in the night
And he's watching us all with the eye of the tiger.

Lyrics and Music by Jim Peterik and Frankie Sullivan. © 1982 Warner Chappell/Bicycle Music

Liz Phair

"Divorce Song"

Written and Recorded by Liz Phair

O ne of the things I love about songwriting is the free flow from the unconscious to the conscious state. It's like fishing—sometimes you get rare fish, other times you get the expected bass or trout.

This song was written long before I had any real understanding of divorce, with insight I couldn't have had. Although people think that I wrote this based on my own experience, it was written ten years before I was divorced.

What's funny is that the song was inspired by a drive I took when I was in college in Ohio. A guy I was casually seeing took me for a ride one night through cornfields in his bright blue Miata with the top down. That was unusual in itself since at that time we all shunned material things. Towards the end of the night, we were bickering about the most ridiculous things. We were thinking about staying in some seedy motel and he thought I was supposed to know where it was, and one thing led to another. We were like Tweedledum and

Tweedledee. It was that excursion that gave me the idea of the road trip. I wrote the song after that night and didn't record it until years later. Even then, I thought it was a sleeper; I didn't think it was that special. Every time I play it live, though, people love it. Fifteen years later, it's still always in demand, perhaps because so many people can relate to it.

The song encapsulates so many things. Most importantly, it communicates the power of words and the fact that you can't take back the things you say—and that's not only true in love.

> *But when you said that I wasn't worth talking to*
> *I had to take your word on that.*
> *But if you'd known*
> *How that would sound to me*
> *You would have taken it back*
> *And boxed it up and buried it in the ground.*

If you phrase words the right way, they have tremendous power. You can create images of cheating, arguments, money problems and all of the other issues that can destroy a relationship. But most of the time it is the little things that happen daily that build up over time and you can't come back from. It's the insidious resentments, cruelties that add up over time that create an undercurrent from which you can't escape. Watch what you say! It's a hard lesson to learn.

If you have someone's heart, you are responsible for their most valuable part and you have to be careful how you handle it.

> *You put in my hands a loaded gun*
> *And then you told me not to fire it*

You can kill with a gun or protect with it.

I believe that there are pre-figured things in life, that is, you can write about things that will happen. I will go to my grave believing that. For instance, I wrote "Whip-Smart" long before I had a child.

The song is about having a son and what I would teach him and to this day I have only one son.

> *I'm gonna tell my son to grow up pretty as the grass is green*
> *And whip-smart as the English Channel's wide*
> *And I'm gonna tell my son to keep his money in his mattress*
> *And his watch on any hand between his thighs*
> *And I'm gonna lock my son up in a tower*
> *Till I write my whole life story on the back of his big brown eyes*

There's a magic to songwriting. It usually comes in one piece, free form. It feels like you're channeling. What you write often becomes reality.

"Divorce Song"

And when I asked for a separate room
It was late at night
And we'd been driving since noon
But if I'd known
How that would sound to you
I would have stayed in your bed
For the rest of my life
Just to prove I was right
That it's harder to be friends than lovers
And you shouldn't try to mix the two
'Cause if you do it and you're still unhappy
Then you know that the problem is you.
And it's true that I stole your lighter
And it's also true that I lost the map
But when you said that I wasn't worth talking to
I had to take your word on that.
But if you'd known
How that would sound to me

You would have taken it back
And boxed it up and buried it in the ground,
Boxed it up and buried it in the ground
Boxed it up and buried it in the ground
Burned it up and thrown it away.
You put in my hands a loaded gun
And then you told me not to fire it
When you did the things you said were up to me
And then accused me of trying to fuck it up
But you've never been a waste of my time
It's never been a drag
So take a deep breath and count back from ten
And maybe you'll be alright
And the license said
You had to stick around until I was dead
But if you're tired of looking at my face I guess I already am
But you've never been a waste of my time
It's never been a drag
So take a deep breath and count back from ten
And maybe you'll be alright

Chynna Phillips

"Hold On"

Written by Chynna Phillips, Carnie Wilson and Glen Ballard
Recorded by Wilson Phillips

I remember sitting in Glen Ballard's studio and he was building the musical track for the song. I was so inspired by it. I thought it was so fresh sounding. I wasn't surprised since he's written for everyone from Aretha Franklin to Christina Aguilera, Alanis Morissette and Aerosmith.

I had a melody going on in my head as I was listening to it, but I asked Glen if I could bring a copy of the track with me. He gave me a copy on cassette and I played it over and over in the car on my way home. I was only 18 and I was living with my mom at the time. I pulled up in front of her house, took out a yellow legal pad and I didn't leave the car until I wrote both the melody and the lyrics.

It was very personal. At that time, I was struggling to stay sober and I was sort of at a crossroads in my life. I could have gone one of two ways—one was a pathway to destruction and my life would fall apart; the other road would take lots of courage and strength. I knew that if I could "Hold On" for one more day there would be a tomorrow. I also realized that it was my choice to make.

The next morning I went to Glen's studio. Carnie (Wilson) came with me, I played the song and everyone loved it. We didn't record it for about a year because we had just signed with SBK. Charles Koppelman, who was the Chairman and CEO of the label, had four songs of ours and this was one of them. After listening to them, he said that we should go back to the drawing board because we didn't have a first single. He also had us write with someone else even though we felt like Glen was the fourth member of our group.

Charles Koppelman called one day and said, "I don't know what I was thinking. We will release 'Hold On' and you should definitely work with Glen Ballard."

I remember wearing a baseball hat backwards in the studio. I didn't have a lot of vocal training before joining Wilson Phillips and I didn't have much opportunity to sing in the studio. A lot of my experience was singing the lead vocal on demos of songs that the Pointer Sisters threw in the trash can. So when we went in to do vocals on our record, I was very shaky. We were surrounded by "professional" singers and I found it very intimidating.

God let me sing this with clarity and purpose. My emotional struggle translated to the vocal. I feel like God channeled this song through me, not like I wrote it.

It's resonated with so many people. When we did interviews at radio stations, people called in and said things from "I was going to take my life when this song came on and it saved me" to "I love listening to this song when I'm driving."

It went on to be nominated for a Grammy for Song of the Year, which was very satisfying, and to selling several million singles before the album even came out, which was very unusual.

The video has been described as "the most beautiful travel brochure you've ever seen." The first half was shot in Big Bear. We were at the very peak of the mountain, on a cliff. It was so cold that Wendy (Wilson) got hypothermia and was taken down on a stretcher. What was funny is that they were doing a special effect where I had to sing about 15 times faster than the actual track. It was a chipmunk version of myself and not easy to do. The second half of the video was shot in Venice Beach where the warm beautiful weather was a welcome relief.

I'll forever be grateful for this song.

"Hold On"

I know there's pain
Why do you lock yourself up in these chains?
No one can change your life except for you.
Don't ever let anyone step all over you,
Just open your heart and your mind.
Is it really fair to feel this way inside?

Some day somebody's gonna make you want to
Turn around and say goodbye.
Until then, baby, are you going to let them
Hold you down and make you cry?
Don't you know?
Don't you know things can change?
Things'll go your way
If you hold on for one more day.
Can you hold on for one more day?
Things'll go your way,
Hold on for one more day.

You could sustain
Or are you comfortable with the pain?
You've got no one to blame for your unhappiness.
You got yourself into your own mess
Lettin' your worries pass you by.
Don't you think it's worth your time
To change your mind?

Some day somebody's gonna make you want to
Turn around and say goodbye.
Until then, baby, are you going to let them
Hold you down and make you cry?
Don't you know?
Don't you know things can change?
Things'll go your way
If you hold on for one more day.
Can you hold on for one more day?
Things'll go your way,
Hold on for one more day.

I know that there is pain
But you hold on for one more day and
Break free the chains.
Yeah, I know that there is pain
But you hold on for one more day and you
Break free, break from the chains.

Some day somebody's gonna make you want to
Turn around and say goodbye.
Until then baby are you going to let them
Hold you down and make you cry?
Don't you know?
Don't you know things can change?
Things'll go your way
If you hold on for one more day, yeah,
If you hold on.

Don't you know things can change?
Things'll go your way
If you hold on for one more day,
If you hold on.
Can you hold on?

Hold on baby.
Won't you tell me now?
Hold on for one more day
'Cause it's gonna go your way.

Don't you know things can change?
Things'll go your way
If you hold on for one more day.
Can't you change it this time?

Make up your mind.
Hold on
Hold on
Baby hold on...

Iggy Pop

"Lust For Life"

Written by Iggy Pop and David Bowie
Recorded by Iggy Pop

I was living in Berlin in the '70s. David Bowie came over to see me and stayed. The wall was still up; Berlin was an occupied zone. Every Thursday night, the Armed Forces played *Starsky and Hutch* and we could pick it up on rabbit ears. Armed Forces TV had an audio signal like the Morse Code.

David picked up his son's ukelele one day and knocked out the chord progression for this song and suggested the title. *Lust For Life* was my mom's favorite book. It is a biographical novel about Vincent Van Gogh, written by Irving Stone, that was turned into a movie. It was a metaphor for my career at that point. I wasn't enjoying success yet, much like Van Gogh who never saw any of the money or fame that his work did after he died.

Certain lyrics in the song, like "Johnny Yen" and "hypnotizing chickens," refer to Williams S. Burroughs' novel *The Ticket That Exploded*.

What the song talks about is how indispensible it is to be alive and excited but, ironically, our joys also make us vulnerable. Perhaps the people who aren't too excited about things do better.

The funny thing was that the music was very bouncy and up. The band's track had a great feel. We recorded it in a studio over there and we all hit it out of the park in one night. It was released in Holland in 1977 and became a #1 single. Then it sat on the shelf for awhile. It bubbled under the radar for about 20 years until the youth movie *Trainspotting* played the song loud in its entirety to open the movie. I was back in America then. The record became a multi-platinum soundtrack and it was a hit video here for me. It changed my life. "Lust For Life" was in other films as well, including *Desperately Seeking Susan*, but they weren't as good for the song.

The most interesting thing about it is that as time goes on, the public will make of something what they want to. It's a happy song. People don't care about the irony in the verses. Whole families come up and thank me.

"Lust For Life"

Here comes Johnny Yen again
With the liquor and drugs
And the flesh machine.
He's gonna do another striptease.
Hey man, where'd ya get that lotion?
I've been hurting since I bought the gimmick
About something called love.
Yeah, something called love
That's like hypnotizing chickens.

Well, I am just a modern guy.
Of course, I've had it in the ear before
'Cause of a lust for life
'Cause of a lust for life.

I'm worth a million in prizes
With my torture film,
Drive a G.T.O.,
Wear a uniform,
All on a government loan.
I'm worth a million in prizes.
Yeah, I'm through with sleeping on the sidewalk.
No more beating my brains
With the liquor and drugs
With the liquor and drugs.

Well, I am just a modern guy.
Of course, I've had it in the ear before
'Cause of a lust for life,
'Cause of a lust for life.

I got a lust for life,
Got a lust for life
Oh, a lust for life
Oh, a lust for life
A lust for life.
I got a lust for life
I got a lust for life.

Well, I am just a modern guy.
Of course I've had it in the ear before
'Cause of a lust for life
'Cause of a lust for life
Lust for life.

Here comes Johnny Yen again
With the liquor and drugs
And the flesh machine.
He's gonna do another striptease.

Hey man, where'd ya get that lotion?
Your skin starts itching once you buy the gimmick
About something called love.
Oh love, love, love,
That's like hypnotizing chickens.

Well, I am just a modern guy.
Of course, I've had it in the ear before
'Cause of a lust for life
'Cause of a lust for life.

Got a lust for life,
Yeah, a lust for life.
I got a lust for life
Oh, a lust for life.
I got a lust for life,
Yeah a lust for life
I got a lust for life.
A lust for life,
Lust for life,
Lust for life.

Ed Robertson

"Easy"

Written by Ed Robertson and Steven Page
Recorded by Barenaked Ladies

In the spring of 2005, there was a lot of pressure for us to write the first single of the album we were working on for our group, Barenaked Ladies. First, Steven Page and I wrote at his house and then, after the summer, we wrote another 13-15 songs in my cottage outside Toronto. All in all, the group wrote over 30 songs for this album that we had to choose from.

There were many incarnations of this song; I was happy with it lyrically but the bridge caused a lot of grief. I couldn't figure out how to approach it—so I tried it TEN different ways. I was in the studio complaining to our manager about the difficulties we were having, and he made some comment like, "The song needs a U2 sentiment." So we said, "Why don't you ask Bono?" He said that we should give him an mp3 of the song and he would.

Unbelievably, without him knowing it would happen, a friend of his was seeing Bono that night and our manager was able to have him listen to our song and give his opinion. The next day he actually had comments from him—and he was exactly right! What he suggested was similar to what we did on the very first pass, that is, a double vocal and a lower octave.

Lyrically, the song is about the complexity of relationships and how "easy" it is to make a big mistake. However, it's so hard to play on guitar that I should have called it "very hard." I came up with a contraption to put on the guitar to help me play it.

Before it was decided that it would be the first single, they wanted me to change the word "obfuscate" in this verse:

> Call it self-defense
> You can obfuscate
> And manipulate
> But it's only at your own expense.

They were concerned it sounded too much like a dictionary word, but I didn't want to change it just because some people might not get it. It is the perfect word for the scenario.

It's an amalgamation of several people—myself, friends and a mish mash of different experiences. It gets its emotional center from my own sentiments, with examples from some dear friends I won't name. The settings are changed to protect the guilty.

"Easy"

> What's a boy to do
> When you tell your tale?
> And, it never fails
> I just end up feeling bad for you.
>
> With your hang-dog eyes
> You can bring me down.
> Now I'm wrapped around your whole hand

Stop looking so surprised.

You make it easy (easy)
You make it easy (easy)

I've been burned before
You're not fooling me.
There's no mystery
You've forgotten what you're hiding for.

Call it self-defense
You can obfuscate
And manipulate
But it's only at your own expense.

You make it easy (easy)
You make it easy (easy)
You make it easy (easy)
You make it easy (easy)

Easy to be with you
Easy to obey
Easy to forgive you at the end of the day.
Easy now to judge you
Easy to betray
Easy to adore you, though you want to run away.

It's easy

Look what you have done
I can do the same
Two can play this game
You'll no longer be the only one

You make it easy (easy)

You make it easy (easy)
You make it easy (easy)
Easy (easy)

Written by Ed Robertson and Steven Page. © 2006 Treat Baker Songs

Smokey Robinson

"Cruisin'"

Written by William "Smokey" Robinson and Marvin Tarplin
Recorded by Smokey Robinson

Many, if not most, of my hits have been written based on music by Marv Tarplin and played on his guitar. He would give me a tape that I would listen to over and over until I got an idea for a song that went with that music. He's so good and so prolific. We've been working together and have been close friends since 1961. He played with Diana (Ross) and I asked if I could "borrow" him for a gig and from then on he was in my band—until 2008. Diana reminds me every time I see her.

When he gave me this particular tape of music, I loved it. It was so sensual, so sexy. It did something to my soul. I played it forever—in my car, when I got home, over and over. I wrote two or three other songs to that music but they didn't work. Nothing fit this music. This song came in bits and pieces. "Cruisin'" took five years to write. Some songs come quicker than others, like "Shop

Around." That was the first million seller at Motown and I wrote it in thirty minutes.

One night I was listening to the music again and thought about how it was ethereal, making you soar:

You're gonna fly away, glad you're going my way
I love it.....

Then I tried figuring out where to go from there—"'cause we're going together"? That wasn't it. Why do I love it?

I was driving down Sunset Boulevard, after I moved to Los Angeles, and a record I loved by a group called the Rascals came on the radio. It was "Groovin'."

Groovin'...on a Sunday afternoon

That's it!

I love it... when we're groovin' with each other?

No. I liked the sound of "groovin'." What sounds like that? Cruisin'!

I love it... when we're cruisin' together.

Then I wrote the rest of the song. I was glad that I came up with something I'd never heard before. I try to say things differently. When I wrote "Tracks Of My Tears" I listened to Marvin Tarplin's music and came up with

Take a good look at my face
You'll see my smile looks out of place

It was going to be about my smile looking out of place.

If you look closer, it's easy to trace

I was thinking, "I miss you so much." "I have to find you." "My smile is crooked." "You don't love me anymore." Nothing rang a bell. Then I realized there are many, many songs about crying, but what if a person cried so much that the tears left tracks on their face? That was it: "The Tracks of My Tears."

People always come up and ask me, "What's "Cruisin'?" What does that mean?" My reply is always the same, "Whatever you want it to be."

"Cruisin'"

Baby, let's cruise
Away from here.
Don't be confused
The way is clear.
And if you want it, you got it, forever,
This is not a one night stand, baby.
Yeah
So let the music take your mind
Just release and you will find
You're gonna fly away,
Glad you're goin' my way,
I love it when we're cruisin' together.
Music is played for love,
Cruisin' is made for love,
I love it when we're cruisin' together.
Baby, tonight
Belongs to us
Everything right
Do what you must
And inch by inch we grow closer and closer
To every little part of each other.
Oooh, baby, yeah
Sooo

Let the music take your mind
Just release and you will find
You're gonna fly away
Glad you're goin' my way,
I love it when we're cruisin' together.
Music is played for love,
Cruisin' is made for love,
I love it when we're cruisin' together.

Cruise with me baby
Ooooooooooooooooohhhhhhhh
Yeah,
Ooooooooooooooooohhhhhhhh, Oooohhh baby, let's cruise,
Let's float, let's glide.
Oooohh
Let's open up and go inside.
And if you want it, you got it, forever.
I could just stay here beside you and love you baby.
Let the music take your mind
Just release and you will find
You're gonna fly away
Glad you're goin' my way,
I love it when we're cruisin' together.
Music is played for love,
Cruisin' is made for love,
I love it when we're cruisin' together.
You're gonna fly away,
Glad you're goin my way,
I love it when we're cruisin' together.
Music is played for love,
Cruisin' is made for love,
I love it when... I love it, I love it, I love it...
Oooohh
Cruise with me baby.

I love it when we're cruisin' together.

Gavin Rossdale

"Love Remains the Same"

Written by Gavin Rossdale and Martin H. Frederiksen
Recorded by Gavin Rossdale

I wanted to write a song that expressed the alienation from someone you've lost, the big disconnect, the hostile words, the regret and ultimately the desperation of loss. It reflects the struggle to find that one person and make amends.

I wanted the song to be as simple as possible. One voice, one guitar. I wanted to describe the trailing through the streets, physically and mentally.

It is plaintive and primal. Sometimes losing someone is the quickest way to gain perspective. With love, there's no resolve—it just goes on.

I worked on the song and made a very simple demo with Marti Frederiksen. The next morning I was on a flight, back on tour, and I played the song and it really spoke to me. I had no idea how it would connect with other people, it just seemed to be very connected to me—and that made me happy.

I thought to myself, "Now that wasn't a waste of time." As song-writers, those are the moments we live for.

"Love Remains the Same"

A thousand times I've seen you standing,
Gravity like lunar landing,
You make me wanna run 'til I find you.
I shut the world away from here,
I drift to you, you're all I hear
As everything we know fades to black.

Half the time the world is ending
Truth is I am done pretending.

I never thought that I
Had anymore to give.
You're pushing me so far.
Here I am without you.
Drink to all that we have lost
Mistakes we have made.
Everything will change
But love remains the same.

I find a place where we escape
Take you with me for a space.
The city buzz sounds just like a fridge.
I walk the streets through seven bars
I have to find just where you are.
The faces seem to blur,
They're all the same.

Half the time the world is ending
Truth is I am done pretending.

I never thought that I
Had anymore to give.
You're pushing me so far.
Here I am without you.
Drink to all that we have lost
Mistakes we have made.
Everything will change
But love remains the same.

So much more to say
So much to be done
Don't you trick me out
We shall overcome.
It's all left still to play
We could have had the sun
Could have been inside,
Instead we're over here.

Half the time the world is ending
Truth is I am done pretending
Too much time, too long defending
You and I are done pretending.

I never thought that I
Had any more to give.
You're pushing me so far.
Here I am without you
Drink to all that we have lost
Mistakes we have made.
Everything will change,
Everything will change.

I, oh, I
I wish this could last forever.

I, oh I,
As if this could last forever.

Love remains the same
Love remains the same.

Darius Rucker

"It Won't Be Like This For Long"

Written by Charles Dubois, Ashley Gorley, Darius Rucker
Recorded by Darius Rucker

I was in Nashville when I first got together with my producer, Frank Rogers. He was looking for another big drinking song like Charles Dubois. Ashley Gorley and I had written, called "Drinkin' and Dialin'." When we started our writing session, Chris, Ashley and I were talking about our young kids, who are about the same age. Our stories and experiences were so similar that this song was born. During our conversation, someone said, "It Won't Be Like This For Long" and it rang true.

The song is about the most important things in my life—my three kids.

> *And when he drops her off at pre-school*
> *She's clinging to his leg*

When we wrote that line, we all three said, "Yeah."

Originally it was supposed to be a lullaby so I could tell my kids that I wrote it for them when they got older. I honestly thought it would be an album track not a single, however it was the second single from my album *Learn To Live* and became my second consecutive #1 single on the country charts, where it remained for three weeks.

The song really came out of the simplicity of everyday life. That's how all great songs happen.

"It Won't Be Like This For Long"

He didn't have to wake up,
He'd been up all night
Lying there in bed and listening
To his newborn baby cry.
He makes a pot of coffee
He splashes water on his face
His wife gives him a kiss and says,
"It's gonna be okay."

"It won't be like this for long.
One day we'll look back laughing
At the week we brought her home.
This phase is gonna fly by
So baby, just hold on
It won't be like this for long."

Four years later, 'bout 4:30
She's crawling in their bed
And when he drops her off at pre-school
She's clinging to his leg.
The teacher peels her off of him,
He says, "What can I do?"
She says, "Now, don't you worry
This'll only last a week or two."

"It won't be like this for long,
One day soon you'll drop her off
And she won't even know you're gone.
This phase is gonna fly by
If you can just hold on
It won't be like this for long."

Someday soon she'll be a teenager
And at times, he'll think she hates him
And he'll walk her down the aisle
And raise her veil,
But right now she's up and cryin'
And the truth is that he don't mind
As he kisses her goodnight
And she says her prayers.

He lays down there beside her
Till her eyes are finally closed
And just watching her it breaks his heart
'Cause he already knows

It won't be like this for long.
One day soon that little girl is gonna be
All grown up and gone
And this phase is gonna fly by
So he's trying to hold on.
It won't be like this for long,
It won't be like this for long.

Brenda Russell

"Get Here"

Written and Recorded by Brenda Russell

"Get Here" is my biggest song to date. I spent a few months living and recording in Sweden. I was under a lot of pressure to create a hit song for the album I was working on. The record company was fixated on a dance hit, which was popular in the '80s, but this melody came to mind. Since I knew that it wasn't what they were asking for, I tried to put it out of my head. Usually if I don't write it down right away, I forget it. (I don't read or write music) But the next morning, the music was still in my head. Since that never happens to me, I thought that if I worked on it right away I could let it go.

My apartment was an old penthouse and my piano was in a beautiful octagonal room with windows overlooking a spectacular view of Stockholm. I played the melody while looking out of the window, and I started thinking about all of the ways you could get to a person. It became a game:

You can reach me by railway, you can reach me by trailway

You can reach me on an airplane, you can reach me with your mind

From there, I wrote it fairly quickly. One day soon after, when my engineer came to visit, I sang it for him. I rarely do that, but I wanted his feedback. I thought it was really corny at first. He thought it was beautiful.

When I got back to Los Angeles, I dragged the song around to so many places but I was having trouble getting a record deal. I had no money, but my manager and I decided to take a risk and get a place for me to perform live in concert. We invited a lot of industry people and friends. Herb Alpert, president of A&M Records was in the audience. While I was singing "Get Here," people started yelling out loud. Melissa Manchester said that everyone at her table looked like Alice Cooper, with makeup all over their faces from crying. Herb signed me to his label because of that concert and he particularly fell in love with "Get Here."

But, if you want to hear something wild, a man came up to me that night and said that he had a new artist he'd like to record the song. It was someone by the name of Whitney Houston. If I'd known then what I know now, would I have let her record it? Probably not. I had a lot of faith that recording "Get Here" would get me the record deal I was looking for, and it did.

In 1991, Oleta Adams recorded it. The irony is that she first heard it when she was shopping in a store in Stockholm! She loved the song and as soon as she got home, she recorded it. After it was finished, my publisher played it to me over the phone and I cried. Fortunately, it became very popular.

That was around the time of the first Gulf War. So many people dedicated messages to loved ones in the Gulf on the radio playing this song for them. Some of the responses I got were the most intense I've ever had. One soldier told me, "I lost my mind and you helped me to get it back." I've never forgotten that. Someone else said he wanted to kill himself but that when he heard my song on the radio,

instead he drove 40 miles in the rain to buy the record. Unbelievable.
It gave me a great, great feeling to help to ease someone's heart.

"Get Here"

You can reach me by railway
You can reach me by trailway
You can reach me on an airplane
You can reach me with your mind.

You can reach me by caravan
Cross the desert like an Arab man
I don't care how you get here just
Get here if you can.

You can reach me by sailboat
Climb a tree and swing rope to rope
Take a sled and slide downslope
Into these arms of mine.

You can jump on a speedy colt
Cross the border in a blaze of hope
I don't care how you get here just
Get here if you can.

There are hills and mountains between us
Always something to get over
But if I had my way surely you would be closer,
I need you closer.

You can windsurf into my life
Take me up on a carpet ride,
You can make it in a big balloon
But you better make it soon.

You can reach me by caravan
Cross the desert like an Arab man,
I don't care how you get here just
Get here if you can.

Lyrics and Music by Brenda Russell. © 1984 Rutland Road Music

Carole Bayer Sager

"That's What Friends Are For"

Written by Carole Bayer Sager and Burt Bacharach
Recorded by Dionne Warwick, Stevie Wonder, Gladys Knight and Elton John

"That's What Friends Are For" was originally written in 1982 for *Night Shift*, the movie that has since become a cult classic, starring Henry Winkler and Michael Keaton. The film was directed by Ron Howard and produced by Brian Glaser. I was married to Burt Bacharach at the time and we co-wrote the song. Warner Chappell got Rod Stewart to sing it and I really liked the way it turned out. Warner Bros., however, thought it was too middle of the road to be a hit and the movie didn't do enough to trigger the song to move up the charts. "Arthur's Theme," for instance, which we also wrote, paralleled the movie's success. As the movie became more popular, so did the song and the charts and sales reflected that. Since *Night Shift* wasn't a big hit, neither was our song at the time.

Four years later, we were in the studio recording Dionne

Warwick and Burt came to me and said, "You know, Dionne wants to sing a duet with Stevie Wonder and she'd like to record 'That's What Friends Are For.'" We had never made any effort to have anyone else record it. I frankly thought that it would be difficult, if not impossible, to surpass the job that Rod did. We figured we would try it and see what happened.

The success of this record shows how important faith is. Although I wouldn't have thought to have it re-recorded, it is because I believed in Dionne and Burt that this record got made.

First we put Dionne on the track. Burt and I co-produced it — he did most of the music and I did the mixing. Stevie was coming into the studio and I knew that my good friend Elizabeth Taylor liked him and thought he was a tremendous talent, so I invited her to come and meet him. The song sounded great to me when he was recording, and it was really Elizabeth being there that inspired me to suggest that we give the money from that record to amFAR. I so admire all of the work she's done with that charity and many others. Besides, I've lost so many friends and associates to AIDS and related diseases. Peter Allen's death, in particular, touched me very deeply and made me want to help even more.

Gladys (Knight) is a friend of all of ours so she came on board for the project. We wanted Elton John but we didn't know if we could get him. Luther Vandross recorded the Elton part first. He was a great talent but, to be honest, we knew we needed a wow! We needed a heavy hitter to bring home the last chorus. Elton has all that power and we were able to get him, and replaced Luther's vocal. When Elton finished the recording and we were listening to it, he said, "If this isn't a hit, I'm going to leave the music business."

Everyone involved immediately agreed to donate their income from this project and it has made me so happy to give the money to amFAR. The cause, in fact, has become bigger than the song, which made it particularly fulfilling to be awarded the Grammy for Song of the Year.

"That's What Friends Are For"

And I, never thought I'd feel this way
And as far as I'm concerned
I'm glad I got the chance to say
That I do believe I love you.
And if, I should ever go away
Well then close your eyes and try
To feel the way we do today
And then if you can remember
Keep smiling, keep shining
Knowing you can always count on me, for sure
That's what friends are for.
For/In good times and/in bad times
I'll be on your side forever more,
That's what friends are for.
Well you came and opened me
And now there's so much more I see
And so, by the way, I thank you.
And then, for the times when we're apart,
Well then close your eyes and know
These words are coming from my hearts
And then if you can remember
Keep smiling, keep shining
Knowing you can always count on me, for sure
That's what friends are for.
For/In good times and/in bad times
I'll be on your side forever more,
That's what friends are for.

Written by Carole Bayer Sager and Burt Bacharach. © 1985 Carole Bayer Sager Music/New Hidden

Valley Music Company

Photo credit Fred Brown, AFP

Richie Sambora

"It's My Life"

Written by Jon Bon Jovi, Richie Sambora and Max Martin
Recorded by Bon Jovi

"It's My Life" is a very empowering, optimistic song. The interesting thing that I've learned about the song is that the lyric appeals to girls and guys, young and old, from age 6 to 60. Everyone can understand its essence and feel good when they hear it. I think about my daughter, Ava, and the fact that she can be empowered by it.

The idea for the chorus came about because, within the band, we identify with the Frank Sinatra, Rat Pack thing. I'm Dean, Jon (Bon Jovi) is Frank.

> *My heart is like an open highway*
> *Like Frankie said,*
> *"I did it my way."*
> *I just wanna live while I'm alive,*
> *It's my life.*

Jon and I both write music and lyrics. Our relationship is unique because we each are fortunate enough to have fame and fortune, but they came at different speeds. Jon and I naturally have a social conscience because of the modest way we grew up in New Jersey. Now, each time we write a hit song and it hits big, millions of people relate to the song all over the world, not just in America. That core, that vein of humanity we all share, is what resonates.

The important thing about songs like "It's My Life" and "Livin' On A Prayer" is that they reach everyone — even if the people hearing it don't understand the language. We've played in cities, countries, and continents around the world. When we walk on stage and everyone in the audience is singing, they're singing the lyrics in English. These songs transcend language and culture.

Early on, when we started out, only superstar acts toured globally. We were one of the first bands who actively made a point to go everywhere, including places most artists wouldn't visit. Everyone had an amazing time — the audiences and the band. We reached out to a global audience but the songs were what made it possible to have the fan base around the world we have today — because the lyrics connected to the people and the people got them.

It's a privilege to me to be able to help empower people in their lives. It makes me happy to be able to change a person's life in some way and help to make them happier, move them or help them get through a tough period and to offer them some optimism.

Both this song and "Livin' On A Prayer" accomplish that, I think. We get lots of feedback from people telling us that we've helped them. The good karma comes back to us because their support allows us to still do what it is we love to do. You get what you give. In fact, giving more to get a little is okay. In our own way, our songs allow us to all help each other.

"It's My Life"

This ain't a song for the broken-hearted

No silent prayer for the faith-departed.
I ain't gonna be just a face in the crowd
You're gonna hear my voice
When I shout it out loud.

It's my life
It's now or never
I ain't gonna live forever
I just want to live while I'm alive.
(It's my life)
My heart is like an open highway
Like Frankie said,
"I did it my way."
I just wanna live while I'm alive,
It's my life.

This is for the ones who stood their ground
For Tommy and Gina who never backed down.
Tomorrow's getting harder make no mistake
Luck ain't even lucky
Got to make your own breaks.

It's my life
And it's now or never
I ain't gonna live forever
I just want to live while I'm alive.
(It's my life)
My heart is like an open highway
Like Frankie said,
"I did it my way."
I just want to live while I'm alive
'Cause it's my life.

Better stand tall when they're calling you out
Don't bend, don't break, hell, don't back down.

It's my life
And it's now or never
'Cause I ain't gonna live forever
I just want to live while I'm alive.
(It's my life)
My heart is like an open highway
Like Frankie said,
"I did it my way."
I just want to live while I'm alive.

It's my life
And it's now or never
'Cause I ain't gonna live forever
I just want to live while I'm alive.
(It's my life)
My heart is like an open highway
Like Frankie said,
"I did it my way."
I just want to live while I'm alive
'Cause it's my life.

Richie Sambora

"Livin' On A Prayer"

Written by Jon Bon Jovi, Richie Sambora and Desmond Child
Recorded by Bon Jovi

The essence of this song comes from my mom and dad. Even though we were living through a different age and referring to a specific time and place (1986) when we wrote it, the lyric still speaks to what's happening in people's lives and in the world today.

This marked the first time Jon (Bon Jovi) and I made up characters for a song. The storyline is about working class families, much like Jon and mine as we were growing up. We were lower middle class kids in suburban New Jersey. We respect our parents and our roots so it was natural to write a song about how we grew up. In a way, the characters represented our parents and their eternal hope and optimism—"We've got a prayer." That's my specialty—I'm a very spiritual person. I'm grateful that we've gotten this far. I'm a guy who grew up on a dead-end street next to a swamp… and I literally climbed out of it. It's 25 years later and Jon and I were just inducted into the Songwriters Hall of Fame.

The song is also about survival — about the struggle of a normal blue collar family. They look at each other at the end of the day and say, "We did it."

The message is very simple — if you love each other, care about each other, and support each other, that's it, that's all that matters. At the end of the day, in a relationship, whether it's a marriage or a life situation, you're living on a prayer. It may not be the best life imaginable to others but it is one with which you're content. That's what makes the song so important. It's about an atypical relationship where people stick together no matter what. That, unfortunately, doesn't happen to most people these days.

We'd written lots of songs, many sentimental, but at that time it was unusual for two young guys to write about these kinds of real life situations, especially when you consider some of the other songs ("Thriller") that were topping the charts when "Prayer" came out.

When Jon and I write, it always begins through a conversation we're having. We talk about what's going on in our personal lives and out in the world and we use that as the basis for our ideas. "Livin' On A Prayer" was one of the songs we wrote through this process, hoping to change the world.

Human nature remains the same throughout time and will be what it's going to be. The message of "Livin' On A Prayer" still resonates today and I'm very proud of that. Songwriters are like mirrors of humanity. A songwriter wants to write songs which transcend time. We've been blessed with an amazing career and life, and these songs will live on long after we're gone.

"Livin' On A Prayer"

Once upon a time
Not so long ago

Tommy used to work on the docks
Unions been on strike

He's down on his luck...it's tough, so tough.
Gina works the diner all day
Working for her man, she brings home her pay
For love—for love.

She says, "We've got to hold on to what we've got
'Cause it doesn't make a difference
If we make it or not.
We've got each other and that's a lot."
For love—we'll give it a shot.

Whooah, were halfway there
Livin' on a prayer
Take my hand and well make it—I swear
Livin' on a prayer.

Tommy's got his six string in hock
Now he's holding in what he used
To make it talk—so tough, it's tough.
Gina dreams of running away.
When she cries in the night
Tommy whispers, "Baby it's okay, someday..."

We've got to hold on to what we've got
'Cause it doesn't make a difference
If we make it or not.
We've got each other and that's a lot
For love—we'll give it a shot.

Whooah, we're halfway there
Livin' on a prayer,
Take my hand and we'll make it—I swear
Livin' on a prayer.

We've got to hold on ready or not

You live for the fight when it's all that you've got

Whooah, we're halfway there
Livin' on a prayer,
Take my hand and we'll make it — I swear
Livin' on a prayer.

Wes Scantlin

"Blurry"

Written by Wes Scantlin and Doug Ardito
Recorded by Puddle of Mudd

I moved to Los Angeles from Kansas City, Missouri in 2000 to put together a new band and to record and put our first record out as Puddle of Mudd. I hardly knew anyone there, didn't have a lot of friends yet, and missed my son and the rest of my family and friends I had to leave behind. I was pursuing my dream and knew I had to make some sacrifices.

I was breaking up with a girl when I left home, but it was going to happen anyway. When I write, it's usually about lots of different situations that I roll into one. This was no different.

This song, however, was written primarily for my son, who was about four at the time. I missed him terribly. I wrote the song with my bass player, Doug Ardito, who was the first person I brought on board in Los Angeles to join the band. The song came out pretty quickly and was well received.

The song is quite simple—it's about missing people I love the most.

"Blurry"

Everything's so blurry
and everyone's so fake
and everybody's empty
and everything is so messed up,
pre-occupied without you
I cannot live at all.
My whole world surrounds you
I stumble then I crawl.

You could be my someone
you could be my scene
you know that I'll protect you
from all of the obscene.
I wonder what you're doing
imagine where you are
there's oceans in between us
but that's not very far.

Can you take it all away,
can you take it all away?
Well ya shoved it in my face
this pain you gave to me.
Can you take it all away,
can you take it all away?
Well ya shoved it in my face.

Everyone is changing
there's no one left that's real
to make up your own ending
and let me know just how you feel
'cause I am lost without you
I cannot live at all

My whole world surrounds you
I stumble then I crawl.

You could be my someone
you could be my scene
you know that I will save you
from all of the unclean.
I wonder what you're doing
I wonder where you are.
There's oceans in between us
but that's not very far.
Can you take it all away,
can you take it all away?
Well ya shoved it in my face
this pain you gave to me.
Can you take it all away,
can you take it all away?
Well ya shoved it in my face.

Nobody told me what you thought
nobody told me what to say.
Everyone showed you where to turn
told you when to run away.
Nobody told you where to hide
nobody told you what to say.
Everyone showed you where to turn
showed you when to run away.

Can you take it all away,
can you take it all away?
Well ya shoved it in my face
this pain you gave to me.
Can you take it all away,
can you take it all away?
Well ya shoved it in my face

This pain you gave to me.

You take it all,
You take it all away...
This pain you gave to me.
You take it all away
This pain you gave to me.
Take it all away
This pain you gave to me.

John Sebastian

"Daydream"

Written by John Sebastian
Recorded by The Lovin' Spoonful

e and The Spoonful were in the South opening for the Supremes all summer in 1965 on the heels of the success of "Do You Believe In Magic." The "tour bus" we rode on was an old school bus that broke down constantly. Along with us, it carried the Motown band and occasionally the Supremes, when they were not riding in another car.

Me and Zally (Yanovsky), our lead guitarist, were sitting on the bumper of the bus during one of those breakdowns, and we began talking about that moment when one beat goes out of style and a new beat comes in. We decided we needed some "straight 8" tunes like "Baby Love." That means a track that doesn't accentuate the backbeat. On the track of "Baby Love" and" Where Did Our Love Go?" there were people stomping on wooden choir stands in addition to the drums. That was the vibe we were imitating but, of course, it came out sounding totally different.

I pretty much wrote the lyrics for "Daydream" that afternoon. I thought we were a dead sound-alike of the Supremes. As it turned out, "Daydream" was a single and the name of our second album, which hit #2 on the American charts.

"Daydream"

What a day for a daydream
What a day for a daydreamin' boy
And I'm lost in a daydream
Dreamin' 'bout my bundle of joy

And even if time ain't really on my side
It's one of those days for taking a walk outside
I'm blowing the day to take a walk in the sun
And fall on my face on somebody's new-mown lawn.

I've been having a sweet dream
I been dreaming since I woke up today
It's starring me and my sweet thing
'Cause she's the one makes me feel this way

And even if time is passing me by a lot
I couldn't care less about the dues you say I got
Tomorrow I'll pay the dues for dropping my load
A pie in the face for being a sleepy bull toad

And you can be sure that if you're feeling right
A daydream will last long into the night.
Tomorrow at breakfast you may prick up your ears
Or you may be daydreaming for a thousand years.

What a day for a daydream
Custom made for a daydreaming boy

And now I'm lost in a daydream
Dreaming 'bout my bundle of joy.

John Sebastian

"Do You Believe In Magic"

Written by John Sebastian
Recorded by The Lovin' Spoonful

"Do You Believe In Magic" is the first visible song I ever had. In a way, The Spoonful's statement of purpose was in the song.

We were working at the Night Owl Café in Greenwich Village, on MacDougal Street. It was a "beatnik" club that usually had folk singers, poetry readings and coffee and it had a policy of no dancing. When we started our first weeks there, people in the audience began to jog around in the recesses in the back of the club where they wouldn't be noticed. The beatniks in the front would snap their fingers. Me and Zally (Zal Yanovsky) would roll our eyes.

We talked about the fact that we were waiting for "our audience" to show up. We were so certain of our success. There was no false modesty in our band. A few nights after that conversation, I had an experience that inspired this song. We were singing and playing and I saw a young girl, about 16, dancing "our way" — in a less regimented style associated more with San Francisco at the time. Zally saw her as well and we nudged each other aware that, although it was just one girl, our audience had arrived!

Do you believe in magic in a young girl's heart
How the music can free her, whenever it starts

In the next few days, I wrote the song. I began playing it on a slightly re-tuned autoharp electrified with a ukelele contact mike... It was very crude but it did the job!

In 1965, the song was released as the first single from our debut album *Do You Believe In Magic*. The song was well-received by the public and became a top ten hit on the Billboard Hot 100, peaking at #9.

It became a Top 40 Hot 100 hit again in 1978 when Shaun Cassidy recorded and released it as a single. Ironically, his older brother David Cassidy recorded it for a Christmas television advertising campaign almost three decades later. John Mellencamp is another artist who recorded it, in the '80s.

"Do You Believe In Magic"

Do you believe in magic in a young girl's heart
How the music can free her, whenever it starts?
And it's magic, if the music is groovy
It makes you feel happy like an old-time movie.
I'll tell you about the magic, and it'll free your soul
But it's like trying to tell a stranger 'bout rock and roll.

If you believe in magic don't bother to choose
If it's jug band music or rhythm and blues
Just go and listen it'll start with a smile
It won't wipe off your face no matter how hard you try.
Your feet start tapping and you can't seem to find

How you got there, so just blow your mind.

If you believe in magic, come along with me,
We'll dance until morning 'til there's just you and me
And maybe, if the music is right
I'll meet you tomorrow, sort of late at night
And we'll go dancing, baby, then you'll see
How the magic's in the music and the music's in me.

Yeah, do you believe in magic?
Yeah, believe in the magic of a young girl's soul
Believe in the magic of rock and roll
Believe in the magic that can set you free
Ohh, talking 'bout magic.

Do you believe like I believe Do you believe in magic?
Do you believe like I believe Do you believe, believer?
Do you believe like I believe Do you believe in magic?

Neil Sedaka

"Breaking Up Is Hard To Do"

Written by Neil Sedaka and Howard Greenfield
Recorded by Neil Sedaka

*I*t was 1962. I had been collaborating with Howard Greenfield for ten years. We had several songs recorded with great success by Connie Francis ("Stupid Cupid," "Where the Boys Are" & "Frankie"), Jimmy Clanton ("Another Sleepless Night"), LaVern Baker ("I Waited Too Long") and Clyde McPhatter ("Since You've Been Gone"). I also recorded several hits as a singer/songwriter ("The Diary," "Oh! Carol," "Stairway to Heaven," "Little Devil," "Happy Birthday Sweet Sixteen," "Calendar Girl").

I was traveling through California, and while I was driving in Los Angeles, I heard a local hit entitled "It Will Stand" by The Showmen. I felt that harmonically it was an exciting recording. The marriage of the voice and melody and the energy in the record inspired me.

As a result, one day, while working in The Brill Building in New York City, I came up with a title and a melody. Howie was less enchanted with it. I called it "Breaking Up Is Hard To Do." I felt it was a universal sentiment—and it's not the least bit autobiographical. Howie kept shoving it to the side, until I sat on him and made him write the lyric. It's a unique song because it has a happy melody and an emotional and sad lyric.

When it was finished, I played a few songs on the piano for Barry Mann, a great songwriter. Amongst them was "Breaking Up." It was his least favorite. (Songs are so subjective!)

I was recording at RCA Victor on East 24th Street in New York. Al Nevins and Don Kirshner were my producers. The night before the session, I came up with the obbligato line, "Down Doo Be Doo Down Down." I called the arranger and sang it over the phone. The rest is history. It became my first #1 record in America. I had four more after that. It also made me the first and, I believe, only artist to have a #1 record twice for the same song. I re-recorded it 14 years later as a ballad and still perform it both ways in my shows.

I knew it was a hit when I heard it for the first time on the radio. My son, however, had a much more impactful experience when he heard it years later. He was going out with a lovely girl at the time and she gave him an ultimatum—marry me or we're breaking up. He left to determine his future and, when he got in the car, he heard my song. He married her and they're still very happy.

Carole King said that "Breaking Up" was so fresh and innovative that it inspired her for a couple of her songs. What really makes me feel good is when I receive emails telling me how the song has helped get people through their emotional difficulties. Music touches everyone and I'm pleased that this song seems to continue to have universal appeal.

"Breaking Up Is Hard To Do"

Don't take your love away from me,
Don't you leave my heart in misery
If you go then I'll be blue
'Cause breaking up is hard to do.

Remember when you held me tight
And you kissed me all through the night?
Think of all that we've been through,
Breaking up is hard to do.
They say that breaking up is hard to do
Now I know, I know that it's true.
Don't say that this is the end,
Instead of breaking up I wish that we were making up again.
I beg of you, don't say goodbye.
Can't we give our love another try?
Come on baby, let's start anew
'Cause breaking up is hard to do.

Carly Simon

"Let the River Run"

Written and Recorded by Carly Simon

ike Nichols called one day and asked me if I'd score a movie he was doing—it was *Working Girl*. It didn't really matter what it was, because anything he does is so classy, funny, I'd drop anything for him. He sent a script to me but I didn't get much of a sense of it until I read through it a couple of times. On the first read, I knew it was about a girl in the tough world of Wall Street, a man's world. Then I saw the story emerge. The essence of it is that New York, and Wall Street in particular, is the jungle so I thought of a jungle beat.

Ironically, the character Melanie Griffith plays worked in the Twin Towers. My skin gets crawly when I think about it. When she takes the ferry in the film, you see the Towers. Of course, that was before 9/11. It's so profound to see it now.

I wanted the irony of a jungle hymn (this is the one and only hymn I've ever written). This is about beasts killing other beasts, what Wall Street is in a covert way, although not so covert anymore.

When I thought about the lyrics and the title, "river" came to mind. Almost every song I've ever written has the words *river* and *dream* in them. I owe much of the concept to Jim Hart, my husband at the time and still a great friend. It was he who suggested that I consult with Walt Whitman to get a feel of a hymn and I got an understanding of Old Amsterdam from "Leaves of Grass," which I read quite a lot. Old Amsterdam, too, was a jungle and man has always been a bit of a beast.

It was Jim who said I should use "River Run" in the title. He's a poet (and a good one) and appreciates the way words are put together. I was thinking of the Hudson River in real terms and, metaphorically, the universal river that runs through all of our lives. Although this is the only song Jim ever helped me with, he pointed me in all of the right directions from Whitman to William Blake, who referenced New Jerusalem. Jim is much more knowledgeable about the Bible than I.

I wrote most of the song in the living room of my house on Martha's Vineyard. The words came first and I just kept going back to the piano until I was happy with the melody. For the power of the song, I wanted the bridge to have a different tempo than the choruses. The varied rhythm built the tension—it pulls away then comes back for the choruses.

When I was ready to make the demo, I called my lawyer, friends, my kids and their friends, rented a studio, and taught them all the melody and the words and everyone sang it together. There were 7 voices on 8 tracks and we kept doubling them until I got a choir sound. When it was finished, I invited Mike (Nichols) and Diane (Sawyer) over—they came to dinner a lot—and played it for them while I sang and played it on the piano in my living room over the recording.

Mike was thrilled and I've seen him when something wasn't right! You can tell when a song works—and this one did. It is one of my most requested and most played songs. Mike reacted like that when I wrote "Itsy Bitsy Spider" as the theme for *Heartburn*. Mike, Meryl Streep and Jack Nicholson called me from their trailer crying. I knew that was right and it was the same with this. Although I wrote several other songs for *Working Girl*, this one worked so well that we just used various versions of it 15 times throughout the film.

One of the most meaningful applications of the song was right after 9/11. The Post Office asked me to sing it for a TV spot praising the postal workers, for which I re-recorded some of it.

Although I did a video with Melanie Griffith and Joan Cusack for the song, unfortunately, with questionable judgment from the record company, it wasn't released as a soundtrack until four or five months after the film was released and it had already lost its impetus for radio. I tried to promote it myself and have radio play it, but it was a daunting task and not my forté. The song has certainly taken on a life of its own, however, and there are even arrangements now for school choirs.

Winning all of the accolades, from the Oscar and Golden Globe to the Grammy and British awards, was the icing on the cake.

"Let the River Run"

We're coming to the edge,
Running on the water,
Coming through the fog,
Your sons and daughters.

Let the river run,
Let all the dreamers
Wake the nation.
Come, the New Jerusalem.

Silver cities rise,
The morning lights
The streets that meet them,
And sirens call them on
With a song.

It's asking for the taking.
Trembling, shaking.
Oh, my heart is aching.

We're coming to the edge,
Running on the water,
Coming through the fog,
Your sons and daughters.

We the great and small
Stand on a star
And blaze a trail of desire
Through the dark'ning dawn.

It's asking for the taking.
Come run with me now,
The sky is the color of blue
You've never even seen
In the eyes of your lover.

Oh, my heart is aching.
We're coming to the edge,
Running on the water,
Coming through the fog,
Your sons and daughters.

It's asking for the taking.
Trembling, shaking.
Oh, my heart is aching.

We're coming to the edge,
Running on the water,
Coming through the fog,
Your sons and daughters.

Let the river run,
Let all the dreamers
Wake the nation.
Come, the New Jerusalem.

Rick Springfield

"Jessie's Girl"

Written and Recorded by Rick Springfield

I was in between writing songs and, as I usually do during those times, I wanted to do something with my hands—work with clay, paint, draw. I decided to take a stained glass class in Pasadena, California.

There was a girl in the class I really fell for—until I found out that her boyfriend was also in the class. His name wasn't Jessie, it was actually Gary but that name didn't fit in the song. Besides, Jessie is tougher sounding....

Nothing happened with her, and the song lasted longer than the relationship would have, I'm sure.

I generally have my writing sessions at home. I was in my music room and originally was going to title this song "Don't Talk To Strangers." After I changed the title to "Jessie's Girl," I wrote another song entitled "Don't Talk To Strangers" that also became well known, fortunately.

I wrote "Jessie's Girl" in pieces and held on to it a bit, then put the pieces together over time. I thought it would only be an album track, but I played several cuts for Keith Olsen, who produced Fleetwood Mac, Foreigner, Pat Benatar and many others, because he expressed interest in doing a song with me. "Jessie's Girl" stuck out to him, so that's the one we worked on together. It's hard for me to select a song—they're all my babies. I had recorded the demo in my home studio and we followed it pretty closely except there was a long guitar solo part in the demo that we took out.

The song took a long time to become a hit. It took a year to reach #1 on the charts. Those were the days when songs were still meaningful to record companies and they stayed on them.

It was a serendipitous time of my life. "Jessie's Girl" was a catalyst for me and my career. It has become my "Thanks For the Memories" that I'll be performing until I'm 106.

"Jessie's Girl"

Jessie is a friend.
Yeah, I know he's been
A good friend of mine
But lately something's changed
That ain't hard to define.
Jessie's got himself a girl
And I want to make her mine
And she's watching him with those eyes
And she's lovin' him with that body,
I just know it.
Yeah, he's holding her in his arms late,
Late at night.

You know, I wish that I had Jessie's girl
I wish that I had Jessie's girl.
Where can I find a woman like that?
I'll play along with the charade,

There doesn't seem to be a reason to change.
You know, I feel so dirty
When they start talking cute.
I wanna tell her that I love her
But the point is probably moot
'Cause she's watching him with those eyes
And she's lovin' him with that body,
I just know it
And he's holding her in his arms late, late at night.

You know, I wish that I had Jessie's girl
I wish that I had Jessie's girl.
Where can I find a woman,
Where can I find a woman like that?
And I'm lookin' in the mirror all the time
Wondering what she don't see in me.
I've been funny
I've been cool with the lines.
Ain't that the way
Love supposed to be?
Tell me, where can I find a woman like that?

You know, I wish that I had Jessie's girl,
I wish that I had Jessie's girl,
I want Jessie's girl.
Where can I find a woman like that, like
Jessie's girl?
I wish that I had Jessie's girl,
I want,
I want Jessie's girl.

Mervin and Melvin Steals

"Could It Be I'm Falling In Love"

Written by Mervin Steals and Melvin Steals, the Steals Brothers
Recorded by The Spinners

Melvin:

My twin brother, Mervin, and I met my high school sweetheart through a friend when we were in the 11th grade. We flipped a coin outside her door to see who would stay. I won. It was love at first sight. Adrena's angelic qualities inspired the following lyrics for "Could It Be I'm Falling In Love":

Since I met you, I've begun to feel so strange
Every time I speak your name.

After graduation Mervin and I went to Cheyney University, the oldest black college in America. Adrena remained behind and took a job in the City of Pittsburgh. We had planned to wed after my senior year, but two weeks before our August 10th wedding date, I sent a telegram stating that I did not want to get married. College life and the civil unrest of the 1960's had dramatically altered my perceptions of reality.

My fiancée returned all the wedding gifts, quit her job and moved to Chicago where she promptly found new employment. She lived with her grandma. Because the Bible she had given me contained her grandma's address, I was able to track her down. Although her parents told her grandma not to let me see her, one weekend I took three Greyhound busses from Pennsylvania, where I was teaching, and arrived in Chicago at 5:30 AM. Her grandma told Adrena to follow her heart and see me. This wonderful woman had been in love with someone when she was younger and didn't marry him and always regretted it.

Upon seeing each other we immediately decided to get married. After getting a license, we tied the knot in a makeshift chapel on the 17th floor of a skyscraper. The next weekend I returned and brought Adrena home with me. That was over forty years ago and we've been together ever since. This was a love song to her, telling her how I truly felt.

Mervin:

This song was originally written for Tammi Terrell, who was a good friend of my brother and me and Marvin Gaye. We met her when she had just gotten out of the hospital where she was treated for a brain tumor. We wanted to do something special for her.

Tommy Bell, whom I first met when I was in college, taught me a lot about playing music. One day I was fooling around with the key changes that this highly successful songwriter/producer had shown me, and I came up with the music to "Could It Be I'm Falling In Love." We tried to get it to Tammy and Marvin but couldn't get through the Motown ranks, so we tried to have Peaches and Herb record it but they didn't like it.

Tommy was producing the Stylistics and (unbeknown to us) The Spinners at the time, but he didn't like the original lyrics to the song so we had to go back and re-write them. The Spinners then recorded it and it became a hit.

"Could It Be I'm Falling In Love"

Since I met you I've begun to feel so strange
Every time I speak your name.
That's funny, you say that you are so helpless too
That you don't know what to do.

Each night I pray there will never come a day
When you up and take your love away.
Say you feel the same way too
And I wonder what it is I feel for you.

Could it be I'm falling in love [with you baby]?
Could it be I'm falling in love?
Could it be I'm falling in love?
With you, with you, with you, with you

I don't need all those things that used to bring me joy
You make me such a happy boy
And honey, you'll always be the only for me,
Meeting you was my destiny.

You can be sure I will never let you down
When you need me I'll be around
And darling, you'll always be the only one for me
Heaven made you specially.

Could it be I'm falling in love [with you baby]?
Could it be I'm falling in love?

Could It Be I'm Falling In Love : Mervin and Melvin Steals   331

Could it be I'm falling in love?
With you, with you, with you, with you

And darling you'll always be the only for me
Heaven made you specially.

Could it be I'm falling in love [With you baby]?
Could it be I'm falling in love? [I wanna know now baby]
Could it be I'm falling in love?
With you, with you, with you, with you

I walk around with my heart in my hands hey,
Walk the street as long as I can baby.
I used to sing fa fa fa fa
But right now I feel so good I sing la la la la.

Once you get me up
Won't let me down,
Just let this feeling carry me on,
Skip the beats with my heart girl.

Could it be I'm falling in love?
Could it be I'm falling in love?
Could it be I'm falling in love?
Could it be I'm falling in love?
Could it be I'm falling in love?

Written by Mervin Steals and Melvin Steals. © 1972 Bellboy Music Warner Chappell Music

Billy Steinberg

"True Colors"

Written by Billy Steinberg and Tom Kelly
Recorded by Cyndi Lauper

"True Colors" was written in September 1985. Originally, I had a verse and a chorus lyric:

> *You've got a long list with so many choices*
> *A ventriloquist with so many voices*
> *And your friends in high places say where the pieces fit*
> *You've got too many faces in your make-up kit*
> *But I see your true colors shining through*
> *I see your true colors and that's why I love you*
> *Don't be afraid to let them show*
> *Your true colors are as beautiful as a rainbow*

That was the original lyric that I took to my songwriting partner, Tom Kelly. Tom sat down at the piano and wrote a beautiful melody to it with a gospel flavor. We did something that we didn't ordinarily do—we made a demo of the unfinished song. The original lyric had been written about my mother. It started out abstractly:

You've got a long list with so many choices
A ventriloquist with so many voices

And then it starts to get more focused about her:

And your friends in high places say where the pieces fit
You've got too many faces in your make-up kit

Then it goes into the chorus:

But I see your true colors shining through

Tom said to me sometime after we had written it, "You know, the chorus of 'True Colors' is so universal and so powerful. It could be from a husband to a wife, a mother to a daughter, or a friend to a friend." On the other hand, Tom pointed out that the verse was very specific, about a person with friends in high places. He acknowledged that the verse was poetic and well-written, but felt that it detracted from the great universal chorus. I reluctantly agreed with him and my reluctance was enormous because I knew I would have to face that demon that I had been avoiding for many years: my difficulty with rewriting something that I had already written. I really believed in my stream-of-consciousness method and felt that if something just poured out, it would have veracity and some intrinsic honesty. I felt that if I had to go back and tinker with it, that it would lose that truth. But I did see that if we wanted to make this song have a larger life, we needed to have verses that matched the chorus. But agreeing with him didn't accomplish much because I really had writer's block about doing the re-write.

Whenever Tom and I would get together to write, he would sit down at the piano and play the intro to "True Colors." I would get agitated and insist that we work on something else. Finally, after that happened four or five times, Tom got the message that I wasn't going to go off on my own and re-write the verse lyrics. In the meantime, I don't know if Tom just met George Martin, the Beatles' producer, or if he was invited to submit something to him, but Tom played him the demo of "True Colors." George thought it was a great song, which really spurred Tom's eagerness to finish it. So Tom suggested that we sit and write it together. I think I had scribbled something about "sad eyes" and I think Tom phrased the first line:

You with the sad eyes

instead of the original lyric, which said:

You've got a long list

He probably liked the way it sounded starting with "you." I pretty much took it from there writing the first verse lyric. I always felt it was sort of patched together and that it wasn't fluid or cohesive. It never felt finished to me, although now I accept it. Of all the songs in my catalog, "True Colors" has earned the most money. It seems to be our best loved song.

I was happy with the second verse:

Show me a smile then, don't be unhappy
Can't remember when I last saw you laughing

Classic songs don't have to have a lot of lyrics. It's simply two verses and a chorus.

When we made the demo, we were very much enamored with the idea that the song had a gospel feel to it. We brought in Bob Carlisle and Julie Christensen to sing background vocals. They both have very strong, soulful voices that enhanced that feel. Tom played a piano solo that was very much in the style of the instrumental piano break of "In My Life" by The Beatles—more classical than gospel. We finished the demo and that's when Lady Luck got involved because when you write a song, no matter how good it is, you are somewhat at the mercy of the artist or producer who records the song.

Tom and I were beginning to be successful, but we weren't in a position to pick any artist in the world and tell them we had this wonderful brand new song. We did what we usually did—finished the demo and started sending it around to every credible artist who was looking for a song at that time. I remember one of the artists we sent it to was Kim Carnes. Her A&R person told us that she wrote her own ballads, and passed on the song. Of course, in the end, that turned out to be a favor to us. Cyndi Lauper had released her first album, *She's So Unusual*. It was a real breakthrough, from the album cover with the Van Gogh painting on the soles of her shoes, to brilliant songs like "Girls Just Wanna Have Fun," "All Through the Night" and "Time After Time." Cyndi would have been at the top of any writer's list of who they would want to record a song. Number one, even ahead of Madonna. At that time, the perception was that Cyndi Lauper was a real artist who would last and Madonna was just a sexy girl, singing dance-pop songs, who would vanish from the scene.

Tom and I were over the moon with excitement when we heard that Cyndi Lauper wanted to record the song and we anxiously waited to hear what she would do with it. Cyndi's first album had been produced by Rick Chertoff and he had done an impeccable job. With some concern, we learned that she was going to be producing her second album by herself. But when we got a copy of her version of "True Colors," it took our breath away because Cyndi's recording was simply brilliant and original. And it was a huge departure from our demo. Madonna had copied our demo of "Like A Virgin," but Cyndi had really reinvented "True Colors." Usually, in those days, a demo was kind of basic and a record would have been a more full-blown production. But in this case, Tom and I had done this rather grand production for the demo of "True Colors" and Cyndi's version was much more sparse. I remember thinking it had an Oriental quality to it—it felt like a Japanese haiku, fragile and delicate.

Cyndi's vocal is beautiful. I was told that when she was in the studio, she sang a guide vocal for the musicians. Then later, when she went back to record the final vocals, she wasn't able to match the emotional quality of the guide vocal, so they decided to keep her original one take vocal. On the B-section of the verse, she changed the phrasing:

If this world makes you crazy and you've taken all you can
*   bear*
Call me up, because you know I'll be there

Just like Madonna had titled her second album "Like A Virgin," Cyndi Lauper titled her second album "True Colors." So, both "True Colors" and "Like A Virgin" were first singles, title cuts and #1 songs. That got Tom and me a lot of attention in the music industry.

Shortly after "True Colors" was a big hit for Cyndi, Kodak requested to use the song for a big advertising campaign. Believe it or not, at the time Tom and I were kind of torn about whether or not to allow the usage. We were worried that Cyndi might be angry about it and we didn't want to damage our relationship with her. We were also concerned that a commercial use of the song might damage its integrity. But we saw a sample of what Kodak planned to do, and in thinking about the product, photography and pictures, it seemed okay. In fact, besides earning us a lot of money, it introduced the song to a huge audience who didn't know the Cyndi Lauper record.

It is gratifying to know that "True Colors" has become a standard. In addition to Cyndi Lauper, it has been recorded by Phil Collins, Kasey Chambers, Eva Cassidy, Ane Brun and many others. It was also featured in the movie, *Save the Last Dance*.

"True Colors"

You with the sad eyes
Don't be discouraged.
Oh, I realize
It's hard to find courage

In a world full of people.
You can lose sight of it all
And the darkness inside you
Makes you feel so small.

But I see your true colors shining through.
I see your true colors and that's why I love you.
Don't be afraid to let them show
Your true colors
True colors are beautiful like a rainbow.

Show me a smile then
Don't be unhappy,
Can't remember when
I last saw you laughing.
If this world makes you crazy
And you've taken all you can bear
You call me up
Because you know I'll be there.

And I'll see your true colors shining through,
I'll see your true colors and that's why I love you.
Don't be afraid to let them show
Your true colors
True colors are beautiful like a rainbow.

Lyrics and Music by Billy Steinberg and Tom Kelly. © 1986 Sony Music Publishing

Ray Stevens

"The Streak"

Written and Recorded by Ray Stevens

ome years ago I was on a plane coming home to Nashville from Los Angeles when I read an article in a news magazine about a new trend at American colleges they called "STREAKING." Kids were taking off all their clothes and running across the campus for no particular reason. I tore the article out, took it home, did a rough draft of a song and put it in my piano bench. I thought, "I'll get to that later." It wasn't much later at all. "Streaking" caught fire across the country so I hastily finished my song, booked in a session (studio and musicians) and recorded "The Streak."

By the time I made my record, there were already a dozen or so "streaking" records on the market. It seemed everybody wanted to get in on this phenomenon. "Streaking" was a hot topic. Even Walter Cronkite mentioned it on his newscast and a guy ran across the stage naked behind host David Niven on the Academy Awards Show on national TV.

The day of the session, I got instant feedback on the projected success of the record. I ran a rough demo over to a local radio station and asked them to play it on the air. Their phone lit up immediately! The studio microphones were still warm and we were still packing up our instruments in the recording studio when the disc jockey called to report the listeners' response. Needless to say, at that moment I was pretty sure "THE STREAK" would be a hit! I had no idea, however, how huge it would become.

During the weeks that followed, there would be 30 or 40 recordings about "streaking" released on the market. But none of the others caught the imagination of the public like Ethel and her poor boyfriend who kept yelling... "Don't look Ethel!!!" That phrase, along with "Yeah I did!", "Boogity-Boogity" and the whistle became a part of the whole "streaking" phenomenon.

This was in the days of the "single" record and "The Streak" sold over 4 million of these little 45 RPM pieces of vinyl in less than 6 weeks. Those were great days in the record business… when you could write and record a song and get it to the market quickly to take advantage of national fads before they faded from the scene. Later, albums became the standard. You didn't just cut a single anymore. You had to take the time and bear the expense of recording 10 or 12 songs to compete in the marketplace. It looks like things are about to come full circle in that regard now because with digital downloading we are once again able to get a single topical song out to the public in a flash via the Internet.

"The Streak" had a new life with the release of my *Comedy Video Classics* video package when I sold direct through television ads and catalogues, and then again when I produced it for my stage act complete with a Wagnerian Opera singer. The stage show was also released on a video… *Ray Stevens Live*.

I don't know how many million recordings of the song have been sold by now but it is no doubt one of the best selling songs I have ever written or recorded!!

"The Streak"

(Reporter)

Hello, everyone, this is your action news reporter with all the
    news
that is news across the nation, on the scene at the supermarket.
    There
seems to have been some disturbance here. Pardon me, sir, did
    you see
what happened?

(Witness)
Yeah, I did. I's standin' overe there by the tomaters, and here he
come, running through the pole beans, through the fruits and
    vegetables,
nekkid as a jay bird. And I hollered over t' Ethel, I said, "Don't
look, Ethel!" But it's too late, she'd already been incensed.

(Chorus)
Here he comes, look at that, look at that
There he goes, look at that, look at that
And he ain't wearin' no clothes.

Oh, yes, they call him the Streak
Look at that, look at that
Fastest thing on two feet.
Look at that, look at that
He's just as proud as he can be
Of his anatomy
He goin' give us a peek.

Oh, yes, they call him the Streak
Look at that, look at that
He likes to show off his physique.
Look at that, look at that
If there's an audience to be found
He'll be streakin' around
Invitin' public critique.

(Reporter)
This is your action news reporter once again, and we're here at
    the gas
station. Pardon me, sir, did you see what happened?

(Witness)
Yeah, I did. I's just in here I' my car checked, he just appeared
out of the traffic. Come streakin' around the grease rack there,
    didn't
have nothin' on but a smile. I looked in there, and Ethel was I'
her a cold drink. I hollered, "Don't look, Ethel!" But it was too
late. She'd already been mooned. Flashed her right there in
    front of
the shock absorbers.

(Chorus)
He ain't crude, look at that, look at that
He ain't lewd, look at that, look at that
He's just in the mood to run in the nude.

Oh, yes, they call him the Streak
Look at that, look at that
He likes to turn the other cheek.
Look at that, look at that
He's always makin' the news
Wearin' just his tennis shoes
Guess you could call him unique.

(Reporter)
 Once again, your action news reporter in the booth at the gym,
    covering
the disturbance at the basketball playoff. Pardon me, sir, did
    you see
what happened?

(Witness)
Yeah, I did. Half time, I's just goin' down thar to get Ethel a
    snow
cone. And here he come, right out of the cheap seats, dribbling,
    right
down the middle of the court. Didn't have on nothing but his
    PF's.
Made a hook shot and got out through the concessions stand. I
    hollered up
at Ethel, I said, "Don't look, Ethel!" But it was too late. She'd
already got a free shot. Grandstandin', right there in front of
    the
home team.

(Chorus) (Witness)
Oh, yes, they call him the Streak. Here he comes again.
Look at that, look at that. Who's that with him?
The fastest thing on two feet. Ethel? Is that you, Ethel?
Look at that, look at that. What do you think you're…
He's just as proud as he can be… doin'? You git your…
Of his anatomy… clothes on!
He's gonna give us a peek.

Oh, yes, they call him the Streak. Ethel! Where you goin'?
Look at that, look at that Ethel, you shameless…
He likes to show off his physique… hussy! Say it isn't so.
Look at that, look at that Ethel! Ethelllllll!!!
If there's an audience to be found
He'll be streakin' around
Invitin' public critique.

Written by Ray Stevens. © 1974 Ahab Music Company, Inc. © Renewed 2002

Joss Stone

"Music"

*Written by Wyclef Jean, Joss Stone, Samuel Michel, Alonzo Stevenson,
Lauryn N. Hill, Tony Reyes
Recorded by Joss Stone featuring Lauryn Hill*

This is actually my favorite song. It's my love letter to music as
if it were a boyfriend. I'm in love with my music and there's
nothing else.

> *Nothing in this world got me like you do baby*
> *I'd give up my soul if I couldn't sing with you daily*

The track is almost completely a replica of the Fugees' "The Mask." I
loved the track as soon as I heard it but I knew that I couldn't write a
song about "nothing." I was in Barbados and thought about what the
concept should be for a week. Usually it only takes me one to three
hours to write lyrics to a song. Once I got the idea and started to
write, it took no time at all. "Novel" helped me. The Fugees brought
music to my life and I wanted to show my respect and admiration

for them. Clearly inspired by their song, and therefore the track to "Music," is the verse:

> *So bring me back to the day when tape decks press play*
> *DJ drop the needle 'til the record just break*
> *You are my sunlight, you are the one mic*
> *That sound so sweet because the beat just inspires me.*

Unlike a boyfriend, music will never hurt you. If you don't like a track, you can skip over it. You can't do that with a man, you have to deal with the situation.

Songs are usually inspired by everyday life. My friend Betty Wright, a songwriter and amazing soul singer, told me that she heard that the song "Call Me" was written because there was a couple parting—one was walking away and the other was in the car leaving. One said, "Call me, call me" and they told each other "I love you." It's as simple as that.

The songs already exist. You just have to be open enough to let them come. It's really not about you.

"Music" was missing a bridge and there was nothing I could add. It needed to be filled in by a poet, a rapper. The person I thought of was, of course, Lauryn Hill. When I suggested her, everyone laughed at me. No one thought that I would get someone of her stature to be featured on the record. I believed that Lauryn loves music as much as I do and might be interested. She's given so much light to people. Luckily, she didn't disappoint me. It took me awhile to find a direct route to her and I finally got her mom's number and called her. She was so sweet. I called her every two days, sometimes daily, for two months. I apologized but told her I wouldn't quit until I got a final yes or no from Lauryn. She said that Lauryn was busy and that she was interested. I prayed on it a lot and remained confident. Time went by and by then I was in the studio recording. Everyone was still laughing at the idea that Lauryn would do this. I didn't want to hear negativity. One comment was, "You have more of a chance of getting the Pope." It only made me push harder. In the end, her mom gave me her manager's number and I got her to do it. She even did two different versions. I think she liked the concept.

Lauryn Hill and Melissa Etheridge are my favorite lyricists. Melissa has an amazing way with words. Lauryn and Aretha Franklin are my favorite vocalists. If I were stranded on an island, I could listen just to them for a year. There are two things I've always wanted to do — sing with Lauryn Hill and sing with Aretha Franklin. I can tick one off now. I'm very grateful. It was a big moment for me.

"Music"

Nothing in this world got me like you do baby
I'd give up my soul if I couldn't sing with you daily.
I'm not the only girl in love with you it's crazy,
I appreciate your groove now I know I owe everything to you.

Music, I'm so in love with my music
The way you keep me movin'
Ain't nobody doing what you're doing
Doing, doing.

So bring me back to the day when tape decks press play,
DJ drop the needle 'til the record just break.
You are my sunlight, you are the one mic
That sound so sweet because the beat just inspires me.
Ooh

No limit to your mind
Your endless love is open
To every race and kind.
Could it be your blood runs golden?

Baby if this world were mine
We would be singing in the Key of Life.

When you're gone I can't survive
'Cause I just can't be without my

Music, I'm so in love with my music,
The way you keep me movin'
Ain't nobody doing what you're doing
Doing, doing.

So bring me back to the day when tape decks press play
DJ drop the needle 'til the record just break.
You are my sunlight, you are the one mic
That sound so sweet because the beat just inspires me.
Ooh

[Lauryn Hill]
Colours of sound, scales and beauty
Audio scenery, electric love and
Rhythmic symmetry written in memory
Beautifully crafted scenery
Complex or simplicity, sonic energy.

Piercing insensitivity, sympathetic poetry
For some even identity collective entity
Something to belong to a source of energy
The possibilities, wave lengths and bandwith
Higher vibration energizing entire lands with

Something to stand with or stand for
Lovers to walk hand in hand with, then plan for
Sanctuary chords, harmony, melodies, even riffs can be
Disguised human essence, sonically bottled ecstasy
Or melancholy agony blues angst

Exercising anxieties, fueling entire societies
Making economies, stimulating generating

Inspiration synonymously, entertaining expression
Intangible invisible but undeniable

Plays the language of excitement on survival
Some call it tribal
But perspective is everything, connected to everything
Some say collectively everything

Music, I'm so in love with my music
The way you keep me movin'
Ain't nobody doing what you're doing
Doing, doing.

So bring me back to the day when tape decks press play
DJ drop the needle 'til the record just break
You are my sunlight, you are the one mic
That sound so sweet because the beat just inspires me.
Ooh

Corey Taylor

"Duality"

Written by Corey Taylor and Slipknot
Recorded by Slipknot

The song itself is basically inspired by my life at the time. I was trying to figure out the struggle within myself, the duality of the soul. This was my way of figuring out how one's good half lives with the bad half. I've struggled my whole life to be a good person and to make the right decisions yet there's something inside of me that's okay with making bad decisions. I realized it was me learning about the different territories in myself and that I would rather be a good person who's done some bad things than a bad person who's prone to doing good things at times.

I'm hoping I can look back and realize that I've made mistakes but I was a good person. The point of the song is to figure out how the two halves within me can co-exist to give power to the half I feel the most comfortable with yet let the other half have its way.

The song has a coming of age feel. You have to attach yourself to the qualities you want to have in order to inspire others and to pass on to your children.

The lyrics came quite easily after the first line of the chorus:

I push my fingers into my eyes
It's the only thing that slowly stops the ache

The headaches wouldn't go away. They weren't stress headaches, they were life headaches. You have to live with yourself and make the right decisions or nothing will change. You take the first step and hope that the other foot will follow.

"Duality"

I push my fingers into my eyes
It's the only thing that slowly stops the ache
But it's made of all the things I have to take.
Jesus it never ends, it works its way inside
If the pain goes on.

I have screamed until my veins collapsed,
I've waited as my time's elapsed.
Now all I do is live with so much fate.

I wished for this, I bitched at that
I've left behind this little fact
You cannot kill what you did not create.

I've gotta say what I've gotta say
And then I swear I'll go away
But I can't promise you'll enjoy the noise.

I guess I'll save the best for last
My future seems like one big past.

You're left with me 'cause you left me no choice.

I push my fingers into my eyes
It's the only thing that slowly stops the ache
If the pain goes on, I'm not gonna make it.

Put me back together or separate the skin from bone
Leave me all the pieces
Then you can leave me alone.

Tell me the reality is better than the dream
But I've found out the hard way
Nothing is what it seems.

I push my fingers into my eyes
It's the only thing that slowly stops the ache
But it's made of all the things I have to take.
Jesus it never ends, it works its way inside.
If the pain goes on, I'm not gonna make it.

All I've got, all I've got is insane
All I've got, all I've got is insane
All I've got, all I've got is insane
All I've got, all I've got is insane

All I've got, all I've got is insane
All I've got, all I've got is insane

I push my fingers into my eyes
It's the only thing that slowly stops the ache
But it's made of all the things I have to take.
Jesus it never ends, it works its way inside.
If the pain goes on, I'm not gonna make it.

All I've got, all I've got is insane

All I've got, all I've got is insane
All I've got, all I've got is insane
All I've got, all I've got is insane

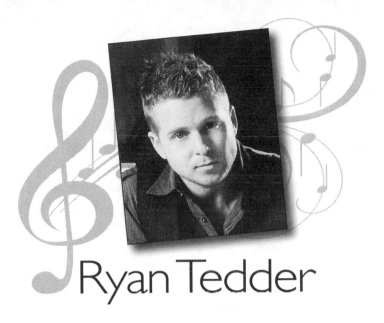

Ryan Tedder

"Apologize"

Written by Ryan Tedder
Recorded by One Republic

I won a record deal in a singer-songwriter competition on MTV when I was 20 and went from being a college student to a professional in two months. It turned into a bunch of nothing but hype. I was broke, frustrated and generally disgusted with the music industry, so I went back home to Oklahoma.

For the next three years, I started searching for the type of music that was the best fit for me. I tried everything from hip hop to pop, rock, R&B, everything, and I kept going back to British rock. I started working a little—I did a record with Timbaland and a few others.

I wanted to start a band and I had a name—Republic. So I moved to Colorado Springs, where I had gone to high school and a lot of my old band mates still lived, and formed One Republic. I stayed with my dad. He had just gotten a grand piano and I sat down to work at it. "Apologize" just kind of popped up. I was 23 at the time. I was writing about relationships, like almost every songwriter does. It's instinctive. I had no luck in relationships from the time I was in middle school through college. Every relationship blew up in my face. I had no girlfriend for more than four or five months. I had become the definitive lonely heart.

My family couldn't figure me out. I could always get girls, I just couldn't keep them. I attracted the flavor of the month (or week) but I wore my heart on my sleeve, a set-up for disaster. I became totally disenchanted with women and wrote "Apologize" as the ultimate kiss-off song. It was the last song I was going to dedicate to relationships and it summarizes all of the relationships I had.

I was always the nice guy and treated girls really well. They'd break up with me and go off with some badass. Then I'd get a call six months later and the girl would tell me she realized how well I treated her and that she was sorry and wanted to get back together. I got tired of hearing "I'm sorry" and realized I value myself more than that.

When I finished the song, I was so convinced that it was a hit that I said I would get a new job if I was wrong. One Republic was signed to Columbia at the time but they dropped us despite hearing this song. Of course, it was the same week they dropped the Jonas Brothers and Katy Perry.

All the labels passed on us, but I still believed in the song. It sat on the shelf for five years until Interscope Records heard it and got it. Ironically, Interscope was the first label I did a showcase for when I moved to Los Angeles and I told friends that it was the label I wanted to be at. The rest is definitely history. It was very vindicating. The song was not only #1 in countries all over the world, it made history by getting the most airplay ever for a song in one week and it sold over 10 million singles.

I've cornered the market on breakup songs, so I'm trying to write more positive songs now. They come more naturally now that I'm happily married.

"Apologize"

I'm holding on your rope,

Got me ten feet off the ground.
I'm hearin' what you say but I just can't make a sound.
You tell me that you need me
Then you go and cut me down, but wait
You tell me that you're sorry
Didn't think I'd turn around, and say...

It's too late to apologize, it's too late.
I said it's too late to apologize, it's too late.

I'd take another chance, take a fall,
Take a shot for you

And I need you like a heart needs a beat
But it's nothin' new.
I loved you with a fire red—
Now it's turning blue, and you say...
"Sorry" like the angel heaven let me think was you.
But I'm afraid...

It's too late to apologize, it's too late
I said it's too late to apologize, it's too late.

It's too late to apologize, it's too late.
I said it's too late to apologize, it's too late.
It's too late to apologize, yeah
I said it's too late to apologize, yeah—
I'm holdin' on your rope, got me ten feet off the ground...

Written by Ryan Tedder. © MIDNITE MIRACLE MUSIC; VELVET HAMMER MUSIC;
SONY/ATV TUNES LLC

Ryan Tedder

"Bleeding Love"

Written by Ryan Tedder and Jesse McCartney
Recorded by Leona Lewis

was introduced to Jesse McCartney by his manager, whom I met through Greg Wells, who was producing Jesse. His manager wanted me to work with him, so we met and I played Jesse some songs. He said that he was taking a new direction for his new album and I went home and started writing.

I always like to deliver at least one hit for anyone I work with. I was getting ready to go to meet Jesse and I didn't feel like I had that one smash. I write my best songs like this, under pressure. I heard a Hammond B3 organ sound. Jesse had told me that Prince was his biggest influence, so I started thinking, "What would Prince do?" I worked on a repetitious chord change with lots of emotion. I added the drum beat, guitar and strings (I really like strings and use them in all of my records).

I went to the studio with the track and Jesse got it. We knew we had something special; even the engineer was freaking out and it's not easy to impress an engineer who hears music all day long every day. Jesse and I finished writing the song in a small 9' x 10' room in my apartment in Los Angeles. Lyrically, I wanted something visceral, visual, almost scary. I can't remember who thought of the title, but we were both captivated with it.

When you're burned enough in relationships, it takes someone extraordinary to re-open the veins to your heart.

But something happened
For the very first time with you,
My heart melts into the ground,
Found something true.

I was inspired by my wife. I had just gotten married and she was the first person I was able to let my guard down with in a long time.

When Jesse and I finished the song, I thought it was at least as good as "Apologize," which I'd written a few years before. Although "Apologize" hadn't been recorded or released yet, I was staking my career on its ultimate success, so the comparison was really saying something.

The demo for "Bleeding Love" sounded great. Jesse is a vocal perfectionist. We took the record to Hollywood Records, Jesse's label, but they didn't get it. They didn't think it was a hit. Two months went by so I pitched it, along with four other songs on one CD, to Simon Cowell's company and Clive Davis' company for Leona Lewis. Both of them listened to it and flipped out. I wrote "Take A Bow" for Leona but both Simon and Clive thought that "Bleeding Love" was the first single. No one knew who Leona was yet but I thought she had a great voice and believed she'd be successful.

I knew that Jesse really wanted the song on his album, so before I agreed to give it to Leona, I went back to Jesse's record company and gave them the opportunity to have it. They still wouldn't let

Jesse release it, so Leona cut it in June 2007. I got to write the video treatment as well.

One Saturday, not long after that, was possibly the craziest day in my career. "Apologize," recorded by my group One Republic, was just coming out and I got a call from Sony that I got the first Jennifer Lopez single for "Do It Well" and that I had Natasha Bedingfield's first single, "Love Like This." Three hours later, Simon Cowell called and said that he'd gone over every song on Leona's album and that "Bleeding Love" was going to be the first single. I had the first singles across the board—and found out all in one day!

"Bleeding Love" came out about two months after "Apologize" and broke my own record for the most radio airplay in a week, and it sold 9 million singles. It seems to be a pattern for me—all of my biggest songs get passed on by record labels before they become hits.

"Bleeding Love"

Closed off from love
I didn't need the pain,
Once or twice was enough
And it was all in vain.
Time starts to pass
Before you know it you're frozen.

But something happened
For the very first time with you.
My heart melts into the ground,
Found something true,
And everyone's looking round
Thinking I'm going crazy.

But I don't care what they say
I'm in love with you.
They try to pull me away

But they don't know the truth.
My heart's crippled by the vein
That I keep on closing.
You cut me open and I

Keep bleeding,
Keep, keep bleeding love.
I keep bleeding
I keep, keep bleeding love.
Keep bleeding
Keep, keep bleeding love.
You cut me open

Trying hard not to hear
But they talk so loud
Their piercing sounds fill my ears,
Try to fill me with doubt
Yet I know that the goal
Is to keep me from falling.

But nothing's greater than the risk that comes with your
        embrace
And in this world of loneliness
I see your face,
Yet everyone around me
Thinks that I'm going crazy, maybe, maybe.

But I don't care what they say
I'm in love with you.
They try to pull me away
But they don't know the truth.
My heart's crippled by the vein
That I keep on closing.
You cut me open and I

Keep bleeding
Keep, keep bleeding love.
I keep bleeding
I keep, keep bleeding love,
Keep bleeding
Keep, keep bleeding love.
You cut me open

And it's draining all of me.
Oh, they find it hard to believe.
I'll be wearing these scars
For everyone to see.

I don't care what they say
I'm in love with you.
They try to pull me away
But they don't know the truth.
My heart's crippled by the vein
That I keep on closing.
You cut me open and I

Keep bleeding
Keep, keep bleeding love.
I keep bleeding
I keep, keep bleeding love,
Keep bleeding
Keep, keep bleeding love.
You cut me open and I

Keep bleeding
Keep, keep bleeding love.
I keep bleeding
I keep, keep bleeding love
Keep bleeding
Keep, keep bleeding love.

You cut me open and I
Keep bleeding
Keep, keep bleeding love.

Jack Tempchin

"Peaceful Easy Feeling"

Written by Jack Tempchin
Recorded by the Eagles

I was playing the coffee house circuit, folk music clubs, in San Diego where I grew up. A friend made a poster with quotes about me, all lies that he made up and attributed to various famous people. The poster found its way to a coffee house in El Centro, California. I guess the owner believed it, because he hired me.

It was a small club in a mini mall. It was my first time in the desert and the view of the stars was amazing. I was attracted to a waitress there, but unfortunately I guess she didn't feel the same way about me because she went home—without me. I wound up sleeping on the floor in the club with my guitar instead of the girl. It was then that I started writing "Peaceful Easy Feeling" on the back of the poster my friend made. Some verses weren't good at all, but I did get the phrase "peaceful easy feeling."

I went back to San Diego where I was living in a big house with a lot of other guys, music hippies like myself. We'd sit in front of the picture window and watch the beautiful girls on the bus stop bench and fall in love with them until their bus came. We talked in those days about how love never seems to show up until you stop looking for it. But, as young guys, we were unable to stop looking for love even for one day.

I went to a street fair in Old Town and saw a girl with turquoise earrings against her dark skin. I never spoke with her but I put her in the first line of the song. I guess I was trying to distill the beauty of every girl I saw into words on paper and then into a song.

In those days I carried my $13 Stella guitar (that I bought in a pawn shop) with me everywhere I went. I wrote the last verse of the song in the parking lot of the Der Wienerschnitzel fast food restaurant on Washington Street in San Diego, which is still there today 37 years later.

Jackson Browne, Glenn Frey and J.D. Souther were helping me to hook up in L.A. I was staying at Jackson's and sitting in his piano room playing my new song. Glenn Frey heard it and asked what it was. He said he had a new band (the Eagles) that had only been together for eight days and he wanted to know if I'd mind if they worked it up.

The next day he brought me a cassette of what they had done with it. It was so good I couldn't believe it. A few months later, they went to the UK and recorded their first album. When they got back, Glenn played some of the cuts for me, "Take It Easy," "Witchy Woman," and "Peaceful Easy Feeling." I knew it was the best record I had ever heard.

That same year, in 1972, my girlfriend and I traveled in a Volkswagen bus across the U.S. Halfway up the California Coast, in somebody's kitchen that we met on the road, I heard "Peaceful Easy Feeling" playing over the airwaves for the first time. It was coming out of a small transistor radio that was sitting on top of the refrigerator.

Since then the song has found a life of its own in the big world, like a kid who leaves home and does great things.

"Peaceful Easy Feeling"

I like the way your sparkling earrings lay
against your skin, it's so brown
and I wanna sleep with you
in the desert tonight
with a billion stars all around
'cause I gotta peaceful easy feeling
and I know you won't let me down
'cause I'm already standing on the ground.

And I found out a long time ago
what a woman can do to your soul
Ah, but she can't take you anyway
You don't already know how to go

and I gotta peaceful, easy feeling
and I know you won't let me down
'cause I'm already standing on the ground.

I get this feeling I may know you
as a lover and a friend
but this voice keeps whispering
in my other ear, tells me
I may never see you again.

'cause I get a peaceful, easy feeling
and I know you won't let me down
'cause I'm already standing on the ground
'cause I'm already standing...
on the ground.

Lyrics and Music by Jack Tempchin. © Warner Bros Publishing

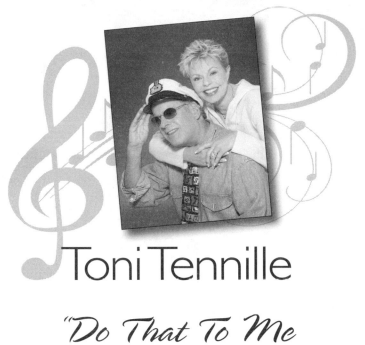

Toni Tennille

"Do That To Me One More Time"

Written by Toni Tennille
Recorded by Captain & Tennille

inety percent of the love songs I've written over the years were inspired by Daryl (Dragon), my husband (and the "Captain" of Captain & Tennille). In 1969 I wrote the music for a new show called *Mother Earth*, which premiered in 1970 at South Coast Repertory Theatre in southern California. In 1971 *Mother Earth* was staged in San Francisco at the Marines' Memorial Theatre. Later that summer we needed a new keyboard player for the show and Daryl (nicknamed "Captain Keyboard" because he always wore a skipper's cap) applied for the job. He was on a break from touring with the Beach Boys. When he auditioned, he made me laugh. He plays kind of quirky things when he improvises on the piano. I hired him on the spot. The show closed a couple of months later, and Daryl asked me to join

The Beach Boys as their only female member. We toured with them for about a year and then Daryl and I returned to Los Angeles and started performing as a duo. We've been together ever since. We lived together for three illegal years then got married, much to my mother's joy.

When I was writing this song, I thought back to the first time Daryl and I met and the first time he kissed me and how much I liked it and wanted him do that again. I thought, "Once is never enough with a man like you…" It took about twenty minutes to write the song. All of my best songs come to me quickly like that.

Most people think the title is "Do *It* To Me One More Time" with the implication of doing "it," although no one banned the song as far as I know. On the other hand, "The Way I Want To Touch You," the first song I wrote for Daryl, was banned on many radio stations even though the lyrics meant that I wanted to touch Daryl emotionally. I was saying, "I want you to understand I love you." I prefer to keep my romantic lyrics subtle. For example, films of the last two or three decades tend to show everything, but I prefer when whatever happens after "the kiss" is left to the imagination—like in the film *From Here To Eternity* when the waves washed over Deborah Kerr and Burt Lancaster as they kissed on the beach, and left the rest to your imagination.

In 1979, we had just changed from our original record label, A&M, to Casablanca. Neil Bogart, the president of the company, and the vice president wanted to hear what we had for our first album on their label so we invited them to dinner at our house. Daryl told me to play "Do That To Me One More Time." When I finished singing it for him, Neil jumped up and said, "That's a smash!" I thought it was just a little song.

Daryl and I wanted to keep it as simple as possible when we recorded it. I'm the singer and he's the producer and has been since our first record. I can make suggestions but he makes the final decisions. This was Daryl's production idea. I played the keys on it and then Daryl put on the fancy stuff. We both studied classical piano for ten years, but I only play my own parts to accompany myself. He can sit down and start playing and really make it happen.

Neil was right. In February 1980 the song became our second #1 hit.

"Do That To Me One More Time"

Do that to me one more time
Once is never enough with a man like you.
Do that to me one more time
I can never get enough of a man like you.
Kiss me like you just did
Oh baby, do that to me once again.

Pass that by me one more time
Once just isn't enough for my heart to hear.
Oh, tell it to me one more time
I can never hear enough while I got you near.
Say those words again like you just did
Oh baby, tell it to me once again.

Do that to me one more time
Once is never enough with a man like you.
Do that to me one more time
I can never get enough of a man like you.
Kiss me like you just did
Oh baby, do that to me once again,
Oh baby, do that to me once again,
Oh baby, Do that to me one more time.
Do it again
One more time
Do it again
One more time
Do it again

One more time
Do it again
One more time

Billy Bob Thornton

"The Poor House"

Written by Billy Bob Thornton
Recorded by The Boxmasters

When I was a kid, no matter what anything cost, my parents and grandparents would always say, "You're gonna put us in the poor house." And that was an understatement even though it was only $.35 to get into the movies then! We were very poor. In the old days, there were literally poor houses; they were like jails.

I always try to write songs that have a story, although they are often dark. Most of the characters in the Boxmasters' songs, you might see on "Cops." This song is about a guy who's not that bright and his decision making ability is not always the best. He was on drugs and alcohol most of the time. He has a wife and kids, works at a menial job and probably gets fired a lot.

This guy is like Ralph Kramden on "The Honeymooners." His quick fix solution to his financial problems is to take the little bit of money they have, go to Reno and gamble it to win his fortune.

It's actually a sweet song at the end of the day because when it's all said and done, he calls his wife, tells her he didn't win money but he's bringing back the only thing he has, which is love for her and the kids. He's really trying, he just doesn't know how.

My mom loved this song when I played it for her. She's in her seventies now but pretty hip. She gave me my interest in music. Every night she would play a record on her record player in her bedroom, which was right next to mine. That's where I got my musical influences, mostly from the artists of Sun Records. Also, artists like Jim Reeves and Ray Price. My first album was given to me by my mom—it was King Creole. She still listens to music all the time.

I played drums in her brother's country band as a teenager. Her brother was kind of like the guy in "The Poor House." For example, a drinking buddy of his had just bought a new pickup truck even though he couldn't afford it. They were going out drinking one night and his buddy ran out of money for liquor so he took the passenger door off his new truck and sold it to a parts place. My uncle had to sit next to the open door hoping he wouldn't fall out. The apple doesn't fall far from the tree in this song.

This was The Boxmasters' first single so it is sentimental to the band.

"The Poor House"

Reno is sparkling ahead honey.
I thought I'd give you a call
Lookin' for tomorrow to be sunny
In the midst of this snowfall.

I let you and the kids down
For way too long now
Hopin' to turn our life around
If I can just figure out how.

I'm workin' on a plan
To save our home,
Keep us out of the poor house
Pay off those loans.
I'm workin' on a plan
To save our home,
Keep us out of the poor house
And I won't do it stoned.

I'll sit with the granny's at the nickel machines
And pull handles till my hands are blue
I'll do just about anything
To bring a future home to you.

I put down the pills and liquor
You know I tried to keep a job.
I just think this'll be quicker
If I can win a little off the mob.

I'm workin' on a plan
To save our home,
Keep us out of the poor house
Pay off those loans.
I'm workin' on a plan
To save our home,
Keep us out of the poor house
Now that I'm not stoned.

Well, my plan didn't work exactly honey
But I do have a little good news.
I'm not bringin home any money
But I didn't turn back to booze.
I guess it's back to the drawin' board
Ideas are starting to brew
I'm bringing back all I can afford

And that's love to the kids and you.

I'm workin' on a plan
To save our home,
Keep us out of the poor house
Pay off those loans.
I'm workin' on a plan
To save our home,
Keep us out of the poor house
And build a house of stone.

Photo credit Sandrine Lee

Pam Tillis

"Cleopatra, Queen Of Denial"

Written by Pam Tillis, Bob DiPiero, Jan Buckingham
Recorded by Pam Tillis

It was the early 90's and the "12 step" vernacular was very much in the mainstream so the term "in denial" was a frequently referenced mantra. A friend of mine left a dumb joke on my phone machine about Cleopatra and Mark Antony that got me thinking and gave me the impetus to write this song. The song was written for fun, very tongue in cheek, but the lyrics have come to mean more to me as time goes by. Sometimes the truth can be so simple it can sneak right up on you. Writers write from experience, from their imagination or for therapy. This song was a little bit of all three.

Bob DiPiero and Jan Buckingham and I went to the Bluebird Café in Nashville one evening and were inspired by the great songs we heard there. We came back to my house and started writing. We finished one song right away. I actually recorded that one too. Usually you're spent (in a good way) after finishing a song but I still felt energized and like there was something else I really needed to express. I threw out my ideas for "Cleopatra;" Bob and Jan got into the idea right away. From there, the song kind of wrote itself. It was almost like a conversation, we started jamming and laughing and the lines just came out.

There are three quotes that I thought of when writing this. I read an article somewhere that Cher said, "Women have a bad tendency to make a big deal over nothing—and then marrying him." My best friend, who wrote *Thelma and Louise*, says, "You get what you settle for," and *The Sweet Potato Queens' Book Of Love* says of men, "Be particular. They make them things every day." The woman in "Cleopatra" makes all kinds of excuses for her man's bad behavior and in her heart she knows it. She's just not able or ready yet to take off those rose colored glasses and face the two steppin' music!

A few weeks later, I went down to Billy Bob's in Texas to play. I had been toying around with the song some more because it had almost seemed too easy. I thought surely it can't be finished. There was no resolution or happy ending for "Cleo," although she's heading in the right direction by admitting she's in "de Nile!" I needed a new up tempo number in my show so I worked that song up with the band, regardless of my reservations, and premiered it that night at Billy Bob's.

I went into the ladies' room, the one closest to the autograph table, after I performed the set and a woman stopped me to say how much she loved the new song. As I was washing my hands, I asked if she was disappointed that the third verse didn't have a happy ending. She replied, "Oh no, honey, that's real life. Don't change a thing!" If she reads this, I thank her for not letting me screw it up. I recorded it shortly thereafter and it went on to be a hit and is still one of my most requested songs.

Some people thought it was just something cute and campy, but it has endured because of the underlying truth of it. After all, the flip side of comedy is tragedy. You put that to a dance beat and you just might have something! Seriously though, by poking fun at the situation, you make it easier to look at. That's the reason I can still sing it with a straight face. I know it might be just what somebody out there in the audience needs to help deal with their situation. Being honest in your relationships is a no brainer, but it can be a little too easy to be a little less than honest with yourself and to rationalize or accept situations we know we should change.

I guess I've been the Queen of Denial from time to time in my life, I confess. In fact, I was at my mom's the other day talking to her and my sister and we started discussing old boyfriends. My mom has a habit of making up words; she's like the Norm Crosby of moms. She called one of my old boyfriends "cavey." I knew she meant Neanderthal. We all had a good laugh, but I couldn't argue with her. That guy was a little less than evolved! I went through one abusive relationship and several others that were dead ends for one reason or another. I'm just glad I can sing "Cleopatra" these days knowing that I've been there, done that, and have the proverbial T-shirt and that I've sworn off what I call "fixer-uppers"… Girls save yourself a lot of heartache and reserve those emotional power tools for fixing up that person in the mirror!

"Cleopatra, Queen Of Denial"

Well, I said he had a lot of potential,
He was only misunderstood.
You know he {really didn't mean} to treat me so bad
He wanted to be good.
And I swore one day I would tame him
Even though he loved to run hog wild.

Just call me Cleopatra everybody, 'cause I'm the Queen of
    Denial.
I knew he didn't have any money
Yeah that's why he couldn't buy me a ring.

Oh and just because he bought himself a brand new pickup
    truck
Really didn't prove anything.
And he never had to say he loved me,
I could see it every time he smiled.

Just call me Cleopatra everybody, 'cause I'm the Queen of
    Denial.
Oh Queen of Denial, buyin' all his alibis,
Queen of Denial, floatin' down a river of lies.
{Yeah}
{Now} I'm not gonna jump to conclusions
Or throw away this perfect romance
Even though I {saw} him dancin' last night
With a girl in a leopard skin pants.
Yeah, he's probably stuck in traffic
And he'll be here in a little while.

Just call me Cleopatra everybody, 'cause I'm the Queen of
    Denial.
Oh Queen of Denial, buyin' all his alibis
Queen of Denial, just floatin' down a river of lies.

Written by Pam Tillis, Bob DiPiero, Jan Buckingham. © BEN'S FUTURE MUSIC; DUCK HOUSE
MUSIC; SONY/ATV SONGS D/B/A TREE PUBG CO.

Aaron Tippin

"Kiss This"

Written by Aaron Tippin, Philip Douglas and Thea Tippin
Recorded by Aaron Tippin

My wife, Thea, and I were in the kitchen at home with our son. She was cooking and she calls me the backseat cook. I always wonder why she doesn't just open a cookbook. I realized that I didn't want to argue and said, "Honey, let's just stop. What do you say we start all over, kiss and make up?" She said, "Kiss this!" and pointed to the appropriate place. She's from Montana and not afraid to open her mouth. She immediately followed with, "You know, that sounds like a song."

Over the next two weeks, as we wrote the song, it got funnier and funnier. It got to be a good story. The record company had a funny reaction—they were afraid that radio wouldn't play it. We recorded it anyway. Fortunately, they loved it when it was finished.

Thea had been writing with me a long time. She got the first country cut, the first cut of mine, the first chart record, our first

#1 record, and the first ACM nomination—all in one song. Phil (Douglas) is great with melodies, although he is a lyricist too.

It's a lot of fun writing with Thea. It's something else we can do together. We're partners in business, lovers, and have children together. We're kind of joined at the hip. I'm proud of her. In fact, I produced a jazz album on her. It's out of this world. I do a duet with her on "Hit the Road Jack." We have a new indie label so we get a chance to do what we want to.

"Kiss This"

She was a woman on a mission
Here to drown him and forget him
So I set her up again to wash him down.
She had just about succeeded
When that low-down no good cheatin'
Good for nothin' came struttin' through the crowd.

Ah, he was layin' it on so thick
He never missed a lick,
Professing his never ending love.
Oh, but I never will forget
When she stood up and said,
"So I guess you think we're just gonna kiss and make up
    doncha?"
That's when she said…

"Why don't you kiss, kiss this
And I don't mean on my rosy red lips
Me and you, we're through
And there's only one thing left for you to do
You just come on over here one last time
Pucker up and close yours eyes
And kiss this goodbye."

Well, the next thing I recall
She had him back against the wall,
Chewin' him like a bulldog on a bone.
She was puttin' him in his place
And I mean right up in his face
Draggin' him down a list of done me wrongs.
Well it was just about now
That the crowd gathered 'round,
They've come to watch him pay for his every sin.
She called him everything under the sun
And when we thought that she was done
She reared back and she let him have it again, man.
She said, she said...

"Why don't you kiss, kiss this
And I don't mean on my rosy red lips
Me and you, we're through
And there's only one thing left for you to do
You just come on over here one last time
Pucker up and close yours eyes
And kiss this..."

Kiss this
And I don't mean on my rosy red lips
Me and you, we're through
And there's only one thing left for you to do
You just come on over here one last time
Pucker up and close yours eyes
And kiss this goodbye
Kiss this goodbye...
(See ya)

Phil Vassar

"Just Another Day In Paradise"

Written by Phil Vassar and Craig Wiseman
Recorded by Phil Vassar

I wrote this with my buddy Craig Wiseman. It's a pretty simple song. I was trying to get out of my house one day. Everything was going wrong. As I was having coffee, with the kids screaming in the background, I started thinking about my life.

Craig and I were talking about our kids, our lives and I said what a good life we had, "Just another day in paradise," which registered with both of us. The song is about the everyday things in real life—how kids change our lives, how difficult it is for couples to get some privacy to sustain their relationships. You have to enjoy the moment and not worry about the little things so much.

I came out of a hectic moment, griping and talking about how busy we are, but when you're away from the craziness you have to step back and know how lucky you are.

I wouldn't change a thing in my life. This is as good as it gets.

"Just Another Day In Paradise"

The kids screaming, phone ringing
Dog barking at the mailman bringing
That stack of bills—overdue.
Good morning baby, how are you?
Got a half hour, quick shower
Take a drink of milk but the milk's gone sour,
My funny face makes you laugh.
Twist the top on and I put it back
There goes the washing machine
Baby, don't kick it.
I promise I'll fix it
Long about a million other things.

Well, it's ok. It's so nice.
It's just another day in paradise.
Well, there's no place that
I'd rather be
Well, it's two hearts
And one dream.
I wouldn't trade it for anything
And I ask the Lord every night
For just another day in paradise.

Friday, you're late
Guess we'll never make our dinner date.
At the restaurant you start to cry.
Baby, we'll just improvise.
Well, plan B looks like
Dominoes' pizza in the candle light
Then we'll tippy toe to our room

Make a little love that's overdue.
But somebody had a bad dream
Mama and daddy
Can me and my teddy
Come in to sleep in between?

Yeah, it's ok. It's so nice.
It's just another day in paradise.
Well, there's no place that
I'd rather be
Well, it's two hearts
And one dream.
I wouldn't trade it for anything
And I ask the Lord every night
For just another day in paradise.

Well, it's ok. It's so nice.
It's just another day in paradise.
Well, there's no place that
I'd rather be
Two hearts
And one dream.
I wouldn't trade it for anything
And I ask the Lord every night
For just another day in paradise,

For just another day in paradise.
Well, it's the kids screaming, the phone ringing,
Just another day.
Well, it's Friday. You're late.
Oh, yeah, it's just another day in paradise.

Diane Warren

"Because You Loved Me"

Written by Diane Warren
Recorded by Celine Dion for Up Close & Personal

I wrote "Because You Loved Me" for the movie *Up Close & Personal* (1996). I saw the film with the director, Jon Avnet, on a Friday. I thought, "What would I want to hear at the end of the movie?" Jon played me a tape of a gospel singer to give me a sense of what he was looking for—something really soulful.

I went into my office on Saturday, the following day, and the chorus came quickly. Michelle Pfeiffer's character is thanking Robert Redford's character for believing in her. The song became personal at the same time that it was telling the story of the film. Once I began, it became a way of thanking my dad for everything he did for me and the support he has always given me. He believed in me and my music from the time I was a little girl. When I was 15, he took me around to music publishers. Not only did he support my goals, he supported me financially while I was struggling in the beginning.

I had to wait for months to see if my song would be chosen to use in the film or if they would select one of the other four submissions. Thank goodness I had just started therapy! It got me through it.

This was the song that brought me to another level. The song was better than I was at the time.

This was the one time I thought I would get the Oscar, but I didn't. There have been so many versions from gospel to dance, Spanish versions and recordings all over the world. I am super proud of that song.

"Because You Loved Me"

For all those times you stood by me
For all the truth that you made me see
For all the joy that you brought to my life
For all the wrong that you made right
For every dream you made come true
For all the love I found in you
I'll be forever thankful baby.
You're the one who held me up
Never let me fall
You're the one who saw me through
Through it all.

You were my strength when I was weak
You were my voice when I couldn't speak
You were my eyes when I couldn't see
You saw the best there was in me
Lifted me up when I couldn't reach
You gave me faith cause you believed
I'm everything I am
Because you loved me.

You gave me wings and made me fly
You touched my hand I could touch the sky

I lost my faith, you gave it back to me
You said no star was out of reach
You stood by me and I stood tall
I had your love I had it all.
I'm grateful for each day you gave me
Maybe I don't know that much
But I know this much is true
I was blessed because I was loved by you.

You were my strength when I was weak
You were my voice when I couldn't speak
You were my eyes when I couldn't see
You saw the best there was in me
Lifted me up when I couldn't reach
You gave me faith cause you believed
I'm everything I am
Because you loved me.

You were always there for me
The tender wing that carried me
A light in the dark shining your love into my life
You've been my inspiration
Through the lies you were the truth
My world is a better place because of you.

You were my strength when I was weak
You were my voice when I couldn't speak
You were my eyes when I couldn't see
You saw the best there was in me
Lifted me up when I couldn't reach
You gave me faith cause you believed
I'm everything I am
Because you loved me.

Lyrics and Music by Diane Warren. © 1996 Realsongs, Inc.

Diane Warren

"I Don't Want To Miss A Thing"

Written by Diane Warren
Recorded by Aerosmith for Armageddon

I got the title for this song from a story I heard about an interview that James Brolin did. Talking about his relationship with Barbra Streisand, he said that he missed her when he went to sleep at night. The idea stayed with me. This is what every woman wants to hear from a man. I've never felt that way (except about my songwriting), but I could still write about it.

I sometimes do "method writing." I am able to become the person I'm writing about. And for Steven Tyler and Aerosmith to sing it—wow!! It was also a #1 country hit for Mark Chesnutt. People take songs like this into their hearts—it's very cool.

I have a great life and I can touch lives. I'm blessed to be able to do that. I can still sit in a room and write the same way I did when I was 13. I knew when I was little that this is what I wanted to do. Writing songs is the reason for me to be here.

"I Don't Want To Miss A Thing"

I could stay awake just to hear you breathin'
Watch you smile while you are sleepin'
While you're far away and dreamin'
I could spend my life in this sweet surrender
I could stay lost in this moment — forever
Every moment spent with you is a moment I treasure.

I don't wanna close my eyes
I don't wanna fall asleep
'Cause I'd miss you baby
And I don't wanna miss a thing
'Cause even when I dream of you
The sweetest dream would never do
I'd still miss you baby
And I don't wanna miss a thing.

Lyin' close to you
Feelin' your heart beatin'
And I'm wondering what your dreamin'
Wonderin' if it's me you're seein'.
Then I kiss your eyes
And thank God we're together
I just wanna stay with you in this moment forever, forever and
      ever.

I don't wanna close my eyes
I don't wanna fall asleep
'Cause I'd miss you baby
And I don't wanna miss a thing
'Cause even when I dream of you
The sweetest dream would never do
I'd still miss you baby

And I don't wanna miss a thing.

I don't wanna miss one smile
I don't wanna miss one kiss
I just wanna be with you right here with you
Just like this.
I just wanna hold you close
A feel your heart so close to mine
And just stay here in this moment, for all the rest of time
Yeah (yeah) Yeah (yeah) yyyeeeaaahhh.....

Don't wanna close my eyes
Don't wanna fall asleep
'Cause I'd miss you baby
And I don't wanna miss a thing
'Cause even when I dream of you
The sweetest dream would never do
I'll still miss you baby
And I don't wanna miss a thing.

I don't wanna close my eyes
I don't wanna fall asleep
'Cause I'd miss you baby
And I don't wanna miss a thing
'Cause even when I dream of you
The sweetest dream would never do
I'll still miss you baby
And I don't wanna miss a thing
Don't wanna close my eyes
I don't wanna fall asleep yeah
And I don't wanna miss a thing.

Lyrics and Music by Diane Warren. © 1998 Realsongs, Inc.

Kanye West

"Welcome To Heartbreak"

Written and Recorded by Kanye West

One day we were shooting in a hotel and I was talking to Dave Sirulnick, a producer from MTV, discussing ideas for a performance of mine. He had a small photo album of him and his wife and kids on the beach and doing different things together. It struck me that I really want to be married and have a family, but that hasn't worked out for me.

> *My friend showed me pictures of his kids*
> *And all I could show him was pictures of my cribs.*

I felt like I was in high school and jealous of what another guy had. I knew that was what I really wanted.

You have to put time and effort into a relationship with the right person and you have to be with the right person to have a family. Being number one is great and I want that but I also want to chase other dreams in my life.

He said his daughter got a brand new report card
And all I got was a brand new sports car.

It was the first time a rap artist spoke condescendingly about property, possessions like a sports car. People are so concerned with what they have or what other people have instead of what's really important—other people. Things like cars are usually used to show how people make it, but there is nothing more important than home and family.

Dad cracked a joke, all the kids laughed
But I couldn't hear him all the way in first class
Chased the good life my whole life long
Look back on my life and my life gone
Where did I go wrong?

We need to take the time to look past their possessions to the people themselves. I was so busy chasing my dreams and everything is always moving so fast that I didn't take the time to be part of everyday life and simple things like a walk to the store.

I became a prisoner of my own fans. I'm not complaining, and I know that I put myself there but, at the end of the day, I had to break out of prison, accept that I will never have a "normal" life, that it is part of the territory, and look beyond it. But I'm trying to live a more normal life—I'm in Hawaii now, where things are slow. I went to a Virgin MegaStore, which I love—I'm like a kid in a candy store there—and nobody was looking at me. It was one of those lost moments that I thank God for.

I expressed a lot of these same feelings in "Pinocchio Story." I don't have to be what a celebrity is supposed to be. I don't want to be a superstar shell of myself. I need to know "Who's the real person?" I don't want to simply be a caricature of myself.

Real life, what does it feel like?
I ask you tonight, I ask you tonight
What does it feel like, I ask you tonight

To live a real life
I just want to be a real boy.

The verse in "Welcome To Heartbreak" about missing my sister's wedding is absolutely true. I had to leave to catch a plane to London. These are real accounts of my life.

Oh my God, sister getting married by the lake
But I couldn't figure out who I'd wanna take
Bad enough that I showed up late
I had to leave before they even cut the cake
Welcome to heartbreak

It was a tough year after the breakup with my fiancée and losing my mom. This whole album was a poignant reality. I opened myself up to new ideas. I was heartbroken and deflated, lauded and idolized all at the same time. It was a time of the highest highs and the lowest lows.

Kanye West has become a global brand. What I have had to learn is how to separate myself from that and be Kanye, the person who can have a real life and be able to go to soccer games with my kids.

"Welcome To Heartbreak"

My friend showed me pictures of his kids
And all I could show him was pictures of my cribs.
He said his daughter got a brand new report card
And all I got was a brand new sports car, oh

And my head keeps spinning
Can't stop having these visions, I gotta get with it.
And my head keeps spinning
I can't stop having these visions, I gotta get with it.

Dad cracked a joke, all the kids laughed

But I couldn't hear him all the way in first class.
Chased the good life my whole life long
Look back on my life and my life gone.
Where did I go wrong?

And my head keeps spinning
Can't stop having these visions, I gotta get with it
And my head keeps spinning
I can't stop having these visions, I gotta get with it.

I've seen it, I've seen it before
I've seen it, I've seen it before
I've seen it, I've seen it before
I've seen it, I've seen it before

Oh my God, sister getting married by the lake
But I couldn't figure out who I'd wanna take.
Bad enough that I showed up late
I had to leave before they even cut the cake.
Welcome to heartbreak.

And my head keeps spinning
Can't stop having these visions, I gotta get with it.
And my head keeps spinning
I can't stop having these visions, I gotta get with it.

And I and I can't stop
No, no, I can't stop
No, no, no, no, I can't stop
No, no, no, no, I can't stop.

Can't stop, I can't stop, I can't stop
No, no, no, no, no, no, no, no
No, no, no, no
No, no, I can't stop.

I can't stop having these visions
I gotta get with it.

Ann Wilson

"Dog & Butterfly"

Written by Ann Wilson
Recorded by Heart

This, like a lot of songs, came from something literal and changed to something more poetic. I was upstairs in my music room waiting for my muse. It doesn't always happen on cue but, in hindsight, it did this time. I looked out of my window and saw the dog chasing a butterfly. He wouldn't give up; he just kept chasing that butterfly. I thought it was impossible, yet he kept on going. The chase took on another meaning for me. Like so much in life, the spirit is undaunted, you keep going after it.

Many people have said that it is that thought in this song that has helped them through rough times. When they're up against the wall in life, they could refer back to it and keep going.

Nancy (Wilson) and I, as Heart, were new at the time in 1978 or so, and this became our personal theme song as well. Now if we don't play it in our set, people are disappointed.

"Dog & Butterfly"

There I was with the old man
Stranded again so off I'd ran
A young world crashing around me
No possibilities of getting what I need.
He looked at me and smiled
Said, "No, no, no, no, no child

See the dog and butterfly. Up in the
Air he like to fly." Dog and butterfly
Below she had to try. She roll back down
To the warm soft ground laughing
She don't know why, she don't know why
Dog and butterfly.

Well, I stumbled upon your secret place
Safe in the trees you had tears on your face
Wrestling with your desires, frozen strangers
Stealing your fires. The message hit my mind
Only words that I could find

See the dog and butterfly
Up in the air he like to fly
Dog and butterfly below she had to try.
She roll back down to the warm soft ground
Laughing to the sky, up to the sky
Dog and butterfly.

We're getting older, the world's getting colder
For the life of me I don't know the reason why.
Maybe it's livin' making us give in
Hearts rolling in taken back on the tide,
We're balanced together ocean upon the sky.

Another night in this strange town
Moonlight holding me light as down,
Voice of confusion inside of me
Just begging to go back where I'm free
Feels like I'm through
Then the old man's words are true.

See the dog and butterfly
Up in the air he like to fly
Dog and butterfly, below she had to try
She roll back down to the warm soft
Ground with a little tear in her eye
She had to try, she had to try
Dog and butterfly

Up in the air, he liked to fly
The dog and butterfly, below she had to try.
She rolled back down to the warm soft ground
Laughing she don't know why
But she had to try, she had to try
Dog and butterfly.

Index

Bleeding Love... Ryan Tedder
Blink 182... Mark Hoppus
Blurry... Wes Scantlin
Bogart, Neil... Joan Jett, Toni Tennille
Bohemian Rhapsody... Roy Thomas Baker
Bon Jovi, Jon... Richie Sambora
Bon Jovi... Richie Sambora
Bono... Ed Robertson
Bowie, David... Iggy Pop
Boy George... Roy Hay
Boyz II Men... Nathan Morris
Break the Cycle... Aaron Lewis
Breaking Up Is Hard To Do... Neil Sedaka
Brick House... Walter Orange
Brill Building... Hal David
Broken Lady... Larry Gatlin
Brolin, James... Diane Warren
Browne, Jackson... Jack Tempchin
Brune, Ane... Billy Steinberg
Buckingham, Jan... Pam Tillis
Buckingham, Lindsey... Mick Fleetwood
Bug A Boo... Rodney Jerkins
Bunton, Emily... Mel B
Burn... Sean Garrett
Burroughs, William S.... Iggy Pop
Burton, Richard... Paul Anka
Bushy, Ron... Doug Ingle
C, Melanie... Mel B
Caldwell, Toy... Clint Black
Calendar Girl... Neil Sedaka
Campbell, Glen... Jeff Barry
Capitol Records... Tony Asher
Captain & Tennille... Toni Tennille
Careless... Stephen Bishop
Carey, Mariah... Carol Connors, Nathan Morris

Francis, Connie... Neil Sedaka

François, Claude... Paul Anka

Frankie... Neil Sedaka

Franklin, Aretha... Chynna Phillips, Joss Stone

Freaks and Geeks... Joan Jett

Frederiksen, Martin H.... Gavin Rossdale

Frey, Glenn... Jack Tempchin

From Here To Eternity... Toni Tennille

Fugees... Joss Stone

Garden Party... Rick Nelson

Gatlin Brothers... Larry Gatlin

Gaye, Marvin... Melvin and Mervin Steals, Walter Orange

Get Here... Brenda Russell

Gettin' It... Walter Orange

Gilbert & Sullivan... Roy Thomas Baker

Girls Just Wanna Have Fun... Billy Steinberg

Glaser, Brian... Carole Bayer Sager

God Only Knows... Tony Asher

Golde, Franne... Walter Orange

Golden Globes... Carly Simon

Gordy, Berry... Carol Connors

Gordy, Jr., Berry... Lamont Dozier

Gorley, Ashley... Darius Rucker

Gov't Mule... Warren Haynes

Gramm, Lou... Mick Jones

Grammy... Carole Bayer Sager, Chynna Phillips, Clint Black, Lisa
   Loeb, Mick Fleetwood, Rodney Jerkins, Siedah Garrett, Tom
   Higgenson, Walter Orange, Carly Simon

Grateful Dead... Warren Haynes

Greenfield, Howard... Neil Sedaka

Griffith, Melanie... Carly Simon

Groovin'... Smokey Robinson

Guice, Lenny... Ronald LaPread

Hall & Oates... Lisa Loeb

Hall, Daryl... John Oates, Lisa Loeb

Mama... Mel B
Man In The Mirror... Siedah Garrett
Manchester, Melissa... Brenda Russell
Mann, Barry... Neil Sedaka
Mardin, Arif... John Oates
Marshall Tucker Band... Clint Black
Martha and the Vandellas... Lamont Dozier
Martin, Dean... Richie Sambora
Martin, George... Tony Asher, Billy Steinberg
Marvelettes... Lamont Dozier
Mathis, Johnny... Carol Connors
May, Brian... Roy Thomas Baker
Mazza, Jim... Larry Gatlin
McBride, Martina... Clint Black
McCartney, Jesse... Ryan Tedder
McCartney, Paul... Tony Asher
McCary, Michael... Nathan Morris
McClary, Tommy... Walter Orange
McEntire, Reba... Roy Hay
McPhatter, Clyde... Neil Sedaka
Mellencamp, John... John Sebastian
Mercury, Freddie... Roy Thomas Baker
Messina, Jimmy... Kenny Loggins
Michel, Samuel... Joss Stone
Midler, Bette... Amanda McBroom
Midnight Blue... Melissa Manchester
Midnight Madness... Kelly Keagy
Monument Records... Larry Gatlin
Moore, Chanté... Clint Black
Moose 'n Me... Kenny Loggins
Morris, Wanya... Nathan Morris
Morrison, Barbara... Carol Connors
Moss, Jerry... David Cassidy
Moss, Jon... Roy Hay
Mother Earth... Toni Tennille

Rio Bravo... Rick Nelson
Robbins, Ayn... Carol Connors
Roberson, LaTavia M.... Rodney Jerkins
Robinson, Smokey... Roy Hay
Rock and Roll Hall of Fame... Rick Nelson
Rocky III... Jim Peterik
Rocky... Carol Connors
Rogers, Frank... Darius Rucker
Rogers, Kenny... Kim Carnes
Rolling Stones... Rick Nelson
Rollings, Matt... Clint Black
Rooster... Jerry Cantrell
Ross, Diana... Lamont Dozier, Smokey Robinson
Rothchild, Paul... Amanda McBroom
Rowland, Kelendria... Rodney Jerkins
Runaways... Joan Jett
Russell, Leon... Clint Black
Sager, Carole Bayer... Melissa Manchester
Sands, Tommy... Paul Anka
Sara Smile... Daryl Hall
Satisfied... Richard Marx
Saturday in the Park... Robert Lamm
Save A Rainy Day... Stephen Bishop
Save the Last Dance... Billy Steinberg
Sawyer, Diane... Carly Simon
Say Amen... Howard Hewett
Say My Name... Rodney Jerkins
Sayer, Leo... Amanda McBroom
SBK... Chynna Phillips
Schreyer, Mathieu... Shelby Lynne
Scotti Bros.... David Cassidy
Seward, Monty... Howard Hewett
Shaw, Arnold... Jeff Barry
She's Gone... John Oates
She's So Unusual... Billy Steinberg

U2... Ed Robertson
UNICEF... Angélique Kidjo
United Artists... Larry Gatlin
Up Close & Personal... Diane Warren
USC Marching Band... Mick Fleetwood
Usher... Sean Garrett
Van Gogh, Vincent... Iggy Pop
Vandross, Luther... Carole Bayer Sager
Venuti, Joe... Jim Croce
Virgin Records... Roy Hay
Waiting For A Girl Like You... Mick Jones
Walkin' in the Sun... Jeff Barry
Waller, Fats... Jim Croce
Wariner, Steve... Clint Black
Warner Bros.... Larry Gatlin, Carole Bayer Sager
Warner Chappell... Carole Bayer Sager
Warwick, Dionne... Hal David, Carole Bayer Sager
Wasserman, Harriet... Melissa Manchester
Way of the World... Philip Bailey
Wayne, John... Paul Anka
Weis, Danny... Doug Ingle
Welcome To Heartbreak... Kanye West
Wells, Greg... Ryan Tedder
West, Dottie... Larry Gatlin
West, Kanye... John Legend
What Makes You Different (Makes You Beautiful)...
       Howie Dorough
What The World Needs Now Is Love... Hal David
When I Said I Do... Clint Black
Where Did Our Love Go... Lamont Dozier, John Sebastian
Where the Boys Are... Neil Sedaka
Whip-Smart... Liz Phair
White, Maurice... Philip Bailey
Whitman, Walt... Carly Simon
will.i.am... John Legend

Meet Our Authors

Jack Canfield is the co-creator of the *Chicken Soup for the Soul* series, which *Time* magazine has called "the publishing phenomenon of the decade." Jack is also the co-author of many other bestselling books.

Jack is the CEO of the Canfield Training Group in Santa Barbara, California, and founder of the Foundation for Self-Esteem in Culver City, California. He has conducted intensive personal and professional development seminars on the principles of success for more than a million people in twenty-three countries.

Jack has received many awards and honors, including three honorary doctorates and a Guinness World Records Certificate for having seven books from the Chicken Soup for the Soul series appearing on the New York Times bestseller list on May 24, 1998.

You can reach Jack at www.jackcanfield.com.

Mark Victor Hansen is the co-founder of Chicken Soup for the Soul, along with Jack Canfield. He is a sought-after keynote speaker, best-selling author, and marketing maven. Mark's powerful messages of possibility, opportunity, and action have created powerful change in thousands of organizations and millions of individuals worldwide.

Mark is a prolific writer with many bestselling books in addition to the *Chicken Soup for the Soul* series. He is also the founder of the MEGA Seminar Series.

Mark has received numerous awards that honor his entrepreneurial spirit, philanthropic heart, and business acumen. He is a lifetime member of the Horatio Alger Association of Distinguished Americans.

You can reach Mark at www.markvictorhansen.com.

Jo-Ann Geffen is an entertainment industry executive who has represented many, many music acts throughout her publicity and celebrity booking career that has spanned over thirty-five years. She continues to preside over JAG Entertainment.

She moved to Los Angeles from New York in 1978 to open an office at Motown Records for the Commodores at the peak of their superstardom and traveled the country and the world on tour with them. She has worked in every genre of music and is very active with non-profits.

Some of the clients she has represented in music include Smokey Robinson, David Cassidy, Lamont Dozier, the Temptations, BJ Thomas, Ray Stevens, NAMM (International Music Products Association), the John Lennon Educational Tour Bus, Robin Gibb, Trackboyz, to name a few. Others on her roster, past and present. include Barbara Walters, Nancy Cartwright, South African Broadcasting Corporation, Sugar Ray Leonard, Body by Jake, Sinbad, Jackie Mason, FiT TV, the People's Choice Awards and many, many more. She has booked talent for the television academy, Children's Miracle Network telethons, Miss World, the Black Achievement Awards, and for concerts and events throughout the U.S. and the world. Some of those she has booked include Larry King, George Benson, Vanessa Williams, Christie Brinkley, Fran Drescher, Joe Cocker, Diahann Carroll, Pierce Brosnan, and a host of others.

Author is a new label she is happy to wear, accidental though it was. Called to a meeting in Las Vegas for a new PR client, she was in a conference room with the one of the creators and the publisher of the Chicken Soup for the Soul franchise listening to their success story and ideas before her own meeting was to take place. By some miracle, this idea popped into her head and she had to stifle blurting it out for over an hour until the meeting let out. Over lunch, sitting next to Bob Jacobs, the President of the publishing company, she presented her idea. Without hesitation, he replied, "I love it. Let's do it." The rest will hopefully be history.

Through her relationships and simply because songwriters are not often given the due they deserve (most of the time they're not even credited with their songs online) she has been able to speak with the writers of 101 of the greatest songs of all time, covering virtually every genre of music from Paul Anka's "My Way" to Kanye West's "Welcome To Heartbreak," Melissa Etheridge's "Come To My Window," and Richie Sambora and Jon Bon Jovi's "Livin' On A Prayer" and everything in between including legendary Motown hits, country classics, rock 'n roll and hard rock chart toppers.

Thank You

*W*here does one begin when so many people are involved? Without Joelle Jarvis I wouldn't have met Bob Jacobs, so a big thanks to Joelle. Bob, President of Chicken Soup for the Soul Publishing, loves these stories as much as I do and made a verbal deal with me the moment I mentioned the idea to him—for that I am very grateful. Thanks to the entire staff at Chicken Soup for the Soul.

Those who helped me along the way are many. They include my son, Jeremy, to whom I dedicated this book personally and who, professionally, has proven to be one of the most connected and knowledgeable people in the music business; Danny Hayes, not only a great lawyer, but also an amazing friend and supporter along with his entire firm, Davis Shapiro Lewit & Hayes; Eileen Bradley, one of my oldest friends and an amazing talent coordinator; publishing executive Brad Rains; Mark Young; and the many publicists, managers, record company and publishing executives, agents and personal assistants who helped to carve out some time from these talented and very busy songwriters' schedules. Some of you are old friends and associates, and I'm fortunate to have made some new friends along the way. You know who you are and, hopefully, how much I appreciate you.

I want to thank my clients, many of whom I am lucky enough to also call my friends, for their patience and support—David Cassidy, Lamont Dozier, Stefanie Schaeffer, Nancy Cartwright and Peter Kjenaas, NAMM (International Music Products Association), to name a few. Thanks to my JAG PR associates, Laura Johnson and Jane Covner, and my amazing assistant Lyna Avanessian.

I must thank Benny Ashburn and the Commodores. We grew up together in this business from the day they had their first audition at Lloyd Price's club in New York City in 1970. They gave me a graduate course in the music business in the streets of New York, on tour across the country and the world, and then moved me to Los Angeles where I've lived ever since. It's been an interesting journey—but that's another story.

My friends and family are always there for me. I'm lucky enough to say that the list is too long for this page, but you know who you are and how much I love you. I fear leaving someone out and suffering the ramifications!

Mostly, thanks to all of the amazingly talented songwriters without whom there would not be a book nor songs to reflect our moods, bring us up, soothe our pain, make us laugh and cry and play a lifetime role in our memory bank. What seems fairly unanimous is that songwriters believe they are fortunate to have their gift and largely feel like the mediums between their source and the pen. We thank them for heeding the call and for the great contributions they've made to our lives—and, of course, to this book.

~Jo-Ann Geffen

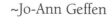

Improving Your Life Every Day

*R*eal people sharing real stories—for fifteen years. Now, Chicken Soup for the Soul has gone beyond the bookstore to become a world leader in life improvement. Through books, movies, DVDs, online resources and other partnerships, we bring hope, courage, inspiration and love to hundreds of millions of people around the world. Chicken Soup for the Soul's writers and readers belong to a one-of-a-kind global community, sharing advice, support, guidance, comfort, and knowledge.

Chicken Soup for the Soul stories have been translated into more than forty languages and can be found in more than one hundred countries. Every day, millions of people experience a Chicken Soup for the Soul story in a book, magazine, newspaper or online. As we share our life experiences through these stories, we offer hope, comfort and inspiration to one another. The stories travel from person to person, and from country to country, helping to improve lives everywhere.

Chicken Soup for the Soul

Share with Us

We all have had Chicken Soup for the Soul moments in our lives. If you would like to share your story or poem with millions of people around the world, go to chickensoup.com and click on "Submit Your Story." You may be able to help another reader, and become a published author at the same time. Some of our past contributors have launched writing and speaking careers from the publication of their stories in our books!

Our submission volume has been increasing steadily—the quality and quantity of your submissions has been fabulous. Starting in 2010, we will only accept story submissions via our website. They will no longer be accepted via mail or fax.

To contact us regarding other matters, please send us an e-mail through webmaster@chickensoupforthesoul.com, or fax or write us at:

Chicken Soup for the Soul
P.O. Box 700
Cos Cob, CT 06807-0700
Fax: 203-861-7194

One more note from your friends at Chicken Soup for the Soul: Occasionally, we receive an unsolicited book manuscript from one of our readers, and we would like to respectfully inform you that we do not accept unsolicited manuscripts and we must discard the ones that appear.

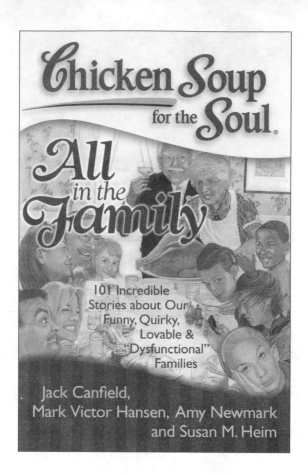

Almost everyone thinks their own family is "dysfunctional" or at least has a dysfunctional member or two. These stories of wacky yet lovable relatives, holiday meltdowns, and funny foibles, along with more serious stories about abuse, controlling family members, and flare-ups, show readers that they aren't alone. All in the Family is a quirky and fun holiday book, and a great bridal shower or wedding gift! Norman Rockwell's famous "Freedom from Want" Thanksgiving family painting appears on the back cover and is lovingly parodied on the front, driving home the point that all our families, no matter how much we love them, are just a little dysfunctional!

978-1-935096-39-9

Classic Inspiration...

Chicken Soup for the Soul
for the Soul
Count Your Blessings

101 Stories of Gratitude, Fortitude, and Silver Linings

Jack Canfield,
Mark Victor Hansen, Amy Newmark,
Laura Robinson & Elizabeth Bryan

This follow-on book to *Tough Times, Tough People* continues Chicken Soup for the Soul's focus on inspiration and hope in these difficult times. These inspirational stories remind us that each day holds something to be thankful for—whether it is having the sun shine or having food on the table. Power outages and storms, health scares and illnesses, job woes and financial insecurities, housing challenges and family worries test us all. But there is always a silver lining. The simple pleasures of family, home, health, and inexpensive good times are described. These stories of optimism, faith, and strength will make a great start to 2010.

978-1-935096-42-9

Stories you can call your own...

An old dog might not be able to learn new tricks, but he might teach his owner a thing or two. This new collection of stories is all about the little and lifelong lessons these loyal companions impart. Dog lovers will recognize themselves, or their dogs, in these 101 tales from the owners of these lovable canines. The lessons learned range in shape and size, just as their dogs do. Stories of learning to have a sense of humor, gain perspective, be kinder, overcome adversity, say goodbye, love unconditionally, stay strong, and about loyalty, listening, and family will delight and inspire readers, and also cause some tears and some laughter.

978-1-935096-38-2

Classic Inspiration...

Chicken Soup for the Soul.

What I Learned from the Cat

101 Stories about Life, Love, and Lessons

Jack Canfield,
Mark Victor Hansen & Amy Newmark
With a foreword by Wendy Diamond,
pet lifestyle expert as seen on *Today* and *Greatest American Dog*

Lessons come in all shapes and sizes—like our feline friends. Cats have always been wonderful companions and playmates that brighten and enrich the lives of their "staff," but they are also amazing teachers, often leading by example! Cat lovers, both lifelong and reluctant, share their stories of feline-inspired lessons about determination and perseverance, self-confidence and self-acceptance, and unconditional love and loyalty. Any cat lover will nod, laugh, and tear up along with these tales of who is really in charge, taking delight in simple pleasures, becoming a better person, putting things in perspective, healing and forgiveness, and saying goodbye.

978-1-935096-37-5

Stories you can call your own...

Chicken Soup for the Soul

www.chickensoup.com